Privatized infrastructure:

the Build Operate Transfer approach

Privatized infrastructure:

the Build Operate Transfer approach

Edited by
C Walker and A J Smith

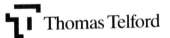

Published by Thomas Telford Publications, Thomas Telford Services Ltd, 1 Heron Quay, London E14 4JD.

First published 1995

Distributors for Thomas Telford books are
USA: American Society of Civil Engineers, Publications Sales Department, 345 East 47th Street, New York, NY 10017-2398
Japan: Maruzen Co. Ltd, Book Department, 3–10 Nihonbashi 2-chome, Chuo-ku, Tokyo 103
Australia: DA Books and Journals, 648 Whitehorse Road, Mitcham 3132, Victoria

A catalogue record for this book is available from the British Library

ISBN: 0 7277 2053 8

Typeset by MHL Typesetting Ltd, Coventry
Printed in Great Britain by Redwood Books, Trowbridge, Wilts.

Cover photograph: the Skye Crossing, courtesy of Miller-Dywidag and George Young Photographers.

Foreword

When I first arrived in Hong Kong — and for many years afterwards — the only way to reach Hong Kong Island was by ferry or water-taxi, the so-called 'walla-wallah'. Now, thousands of cars and trucks pour onto the island every day through tunnels deep under Hong Kong's busy harbour. The tunnels are major transportation arteries for the city, linking Hong Kong Island with the rest of the territory. However, unlike in other territories, they were not built by government. They were built, and are operated, by private, profit-making companies.

Until a decade or two ago, this would have been unthinkable. The planning and construction of public works were everywhere regarded as one of government's principal responsibilities. Increasingly, however, this view has changed. We are returning to the model of a century ago when most of the world's major public works — canals, railroads, tollways, tramways, bridges, telephone systems — were financed and built by private enterprise.

There are good reasons for this change. Many governments are either unable, or unwilling, to raise the taxes or to issue the debt needed to finance large-scale, capital-intensive projects. They may also be ill-equipped to oversee the construction or subsequent management of such projects. In contrast, private investors are willing to take on the risk if there are sufficient rewards, and private companies, which must operate subject to the discipline of the marketplace, are often efficient at handling the specialized nature of infrastructural development.

Meanwhile, we see the number and scale of projects rising sharply. This is especially true in Asia where fast-growing economies have outstripped the infrastructure require to support them. Again, Hong Kong is a good example. The Western Harbour Tunnel and a number of the services for the territory's new airport project are being financed and built by private enterprise. And almost every week I read of another new construction project — a power plant or a new port or highway — being undertaken somewhere in the world by private enterprise.

So this book could not have come at a better time. It reflects the rebirth of an old and proven model for the private construction of 'public works', the increasing need to upgrade and expand such works, and the recent experience in Asia and elsewhere of how to put that model to work.

I congratulate the authors on their endeavours.

Sir William Purves, Chairman of HSBC Holdings plc
May 1995
London

Authors

Charles Walker has worked for a contractor, government and a consultant in Hong Kong and the UK. Much of his career was spent with the Maunsell Group overseeing infrastructure works in Hong Kong. He has lectured to undergraduates on risk analysis, privatization concepts and project management of major infrastructure. This is the second book he has edited and co-authored.

John Mulcahy is Director of Project Finance for HSBC Capital Limited. He has been based in Hong Kong working on project finance since 1987, and has also been involved in successful project financings in Singapore, Thailand, Malaysia, Indonesia and Taiwan.

Adrian Smith is presently an Associate Professor in the Department of Building and Construction, City University of Hong Kong, where he has responsibility for the Quantity Surveying degree programme.

Patrick T.I. Lam is an Assistant Professor in the Department of Building and Real Estate at the Hong Kong Polytechnic University. A Chartered Surveyor and Chartered Builder by profession, he was sponsored by the Jones Lang Wootton Travelling Scholarship to travel extensively in the Pacific Rim area.

Robert Cochrane is currently Managing Director of Coopers & Lybrand's management consultancy division in Hong Kong where he has regional responsibility for consultancy advice on utilities and infrastructure projects.

Preface

'Society gains when men compete to better their position', was the maxim advocated by Adam Smith (1727–1790), one of the fathers of economic philosophy. Adoption of this advice has been instrumental to the financial well-being of a number of countries over the years. When in power, supremos Ronald Reagan and Margaret Thatcher were latter-day advocates of this ethos through their championing of privatization concepts, the echoes of which are now dismantling government monopolies around the world. The belief that private initiative could do better than state bureaucracy has been accredited by such esteemed institutions as the World Bank and the United Nations.

With traditional roles undergoing such a radical review it is not surprising that innovative techniques evolve to address other fiscal environments in our now multipolar financial and construction communities. From Budapest to Bangkok, Mexico City to Manchester, these exciting ideas are addressing the demand for the new and refurbished infrastructure which governments are increasingly unable to build. A dynamic process is underway, with new alliances being formed and sovereign states taking a new approach to their previous role of identifying and funding the necessary infrastructure.

This book captures a significant consequence of this global phenomenon — the creation of the Build Operate Transfer arrangement for infrastructure procurement. Under the acronym BOT or BOOT, with the second 'O' adopted when ownership rights form part of the contractual formula, a concept has evolved which it is said, provides a 'win-win' for all involved; effectively a 'costless' scenario for these financially constricted governments. The crux of the formula is to address the relationship necessary to satisfy the political, financial and construction demands, and to ensure that the revenues generated by the completed entity satisfy all three. Since, in a sense, all construction is local, each BOT/BOOT arrangement put in place has a unique revenue stream to capture — a tolled bridge across the Thames has a different set of issues to that across the Mekong, a power station in the Turkish countryside is different to that in downtown New York. The basic criteria are, however, the same in that governments, funders and builders must have a transparent formula which ensures that the risks involved are placed with those best able to carry and, therefore, to price them. This is what each BOT/BOOT scheme ought to set out to achieve, and while the reader will appreciate that the contractual arrangements will be different, the book's objective is to explain how, where and why the concept evolved and the various ways in which the formula continues to evolve. This latter aspect applies particularly to BOT/BOOT's of the future and those currently in negotiation. Progressive refinements are a characteristic of the concept resulting from the public and private sectors' increasing awareness of and proficiency with the techniques at hand.

The pursuit of BOT/BOOT success is the book's central theme, as profiled case studies will persuasively evidence. However, the study is not simply a ringing endorsement. It highlights the pitfalls as well as the windfalls. You will read of an Asian expressway dogged by political interference, a Mexican toll road with mounting debts, the pedantic nature of Britain's public inquiry system, cancellation of a Canadian airport terminal agreement, and of much needed infrastructure which has progressed no further than a promoter's drawing board due to the inability of those involved to overcome the dinosaurs of the establishment.

The study sets out to document and explain the many issues associated with the often complex BOT/BOOT relationships, as well as ways to overcome these complexities. It will become apparent that, as the concept has more risk and control passed to the private sector, much of government's traditional contribution is capped. Lenders have to judge whether they will get their money back and equity investors must decide whether they could get a better return elsewhere. A series of disciplines often not previously applied to purely public investments is, therefore, brought to bear. BOT/BOOTs are also essentially recent innovations with a very small number having passed the half way point of their concession period let alone providing a viable rate of return to their equity holders. Commercial confidentiality, often a stumbling block to objective comment, is overcome by anonymity afforded to those sensitive parties who understandably are reluctant to broadcast the downfalls or bountiful rewards they have experienced.

Capturing the diverse and intricate make-up of BOT/BOOT applications dictated a co-authoring approach. Each of the five contributors has first hand experience in their respective areas, with additional input based on taped interviews with those directly involved in specific cases. The wider issues associated with the concept are drawn from academic and technical publications mainly from the UK, USA, Singapore and Hong Kong where a number of BOT/BOOTs have been well documented. Other sources are banking, legal, accounting and construction literature from companies of international standing such as Hongkong Bank, Morgan Grenfell/Deutsche, Bank of America, Clifford Chance, Coopers and Lybrand, Trafalgar House, Campenon Bernard SGE, Nishimatsu Construction, Italstat, Parsons Brinckerhoff, Bechtel, Kumagai Gumi, Philipp Holzmann and Maunsell International, all leading proponents in the field. The review is therefore global, mirroring the frequent cosmopolitan make-up of BOT/BOOT arrangements.

The book contains a considerable and often repeated number of organizational and institutional names together with financial and legal terms. In general the text will initially use the full description with initials in brackets and thereafter the shortened form.

The term 'promoter' applies to those who first identify the project — it can be a government department calling for interested parties to make submissions, a contractor who approaches government with the concept or alternatively a financial group, often instigated by a merchant bank. The private group/company formed to accept the franchise, to manage the BOT vehicle, is named the 'sponsor' or 'concessionaire'. Sometimes the 'promoter' becomes the 'sponsor' or a partner in the 'sponsor's' group. Both terms are often interchanged but reference to the specific BOT being discussed explains the separate roles involved.

Monetary values will be designated usually in the local currency with sterling pounds or US dollar values in brackets (with a billion being adopted as a thousand million). The text generally adopts BOT shorthand to include the modified BOOT concept. There will also be reference to a 'shadow toll' BOT road concept or Design Build Finance Operate (DBFO), the acronym increasingly adopted in UK literature.

Finally, as the logic and structure of the formula are better understood, it should become increasingly easy to pre-determine the elixir of success. This suggests a growing acceptance of the concept as an alternative way to provide answers to our increasingly clogged streets, jammed telephone lines, outdated railway systems, and polluted rivers. We, therefore, commend you to discover the remarkable story so far — we are confident it will stimulate your mind and excite your anticipation for a new tomorrow and the new century ahead.

Charles Walker (Edinburgh)
Adrian Smith (Hong Kong)

Contents

1. How the concept evolved   1

2. Granting authority's perspective   12

3. Funder's perspective   31

4. Concessionnaire's perspective   50

5. Financial engineering   71

6. Financing techniques   83

7. Estimating for major projects   101

8. Estimating techniques   114

9. Life cycle costing and financial modelling   131

10. Risks and their mitigation   143

11. Risk analysis   160

12. Legal framework   172

13. Procurement options for infrastructure projects   187

14. Case studies: 202
    Hong Kong Cross Harbour Tunnel
    Shajiao 'B' power station, China
    Toronto Airport
    North—South Highway, Malaysia
    The Dartford Bridge, UK

15. Infrastructure economics and the role of government   231

16. Key success factors for BOT projects   240

17. Future developments in the private financing of
    infrastructure   252

Chapter 1

How the concept evolved

History records that the Industrial Revolution began when Abraham Darby first smelted iron with coke in 1709. Urbanization and the need for associated infrastructure were to follow. Governments of the time had only rudimentary taxation arrangements primarily to service heads of state and any wars they might embark upon. Infrastructure was therefore left to individuals to finance and build. The canals, turnpikes and railroads of Europe and later the Americas, China and Japan were procured in this way.

From the late 1700s, however, tax revenues on the wealth generated from the ongoing phases of the Industrial Revolution meant that governments were increasingly able to directly fund their own infrastructure, but where large or specialist undertakings were suggested the concession or franchise arrangement was sometimes adopted. The mid-1800s saw a number of these being established in different parts of the world, the French being leading activists of the concept. According to Monod[1] the need for water distribution initiated the first concession being granted in 1782 to the Perier brothers in Paris. From a small start the network expanded rapidly but political events overtook the agreement and the City of Paris cancelled the franchise following the French Revolution. The most notable spread in the use of concessions occurred after about 1830 in France. Their use, however, was not confined to France, and concessions were let in Spain, Italy, Belgium and Germany. The use of concession contracts declined in industrialized countries as the initial infrastructure was completed but the wonder of the age, the 195 km Suez Canal which opened for international navigation on 17 November 1869, was a 99-year concession. Championed originally around 1840 by Englishman Thomas Waghorn and later by Frenchman Ferdinand de Lesseps, the Suez Canal Company was empowered by the Egyptian government to build and operate the canal. They could fix and levy transit dues at maximum defined rates of which government were to receive 15%. De Lesseps was to later promote the Panama Canal adopting a similar concession approach.

Industrialized countries generally funded new infrastructure between the late 1800s and the 1970s from their respective fiscal resources or sovereign borrowings. These governments also played a central role in identifying needs, setting strategic policy and procuring the construction either by direct ownership or a closely controlled franchise (e.g. Bell Telephone Co. of USA). This traditional approach has by and large been followed by less developed countries with public finance supported by bond instruments or direct sovereign loans by such organizations as the World Bank, Asian Development Bank and the International Monetary Fund.

A series of influences emerged, however, in the late 1970s, which placed pressures on this established system for both the developed and developing countries of the world. To understand the part played by the Build Operate Transfer (BOT) concept in this, one has to appreciate the fundamental influences at play.

There are various criteria for confirming the label 'developed country'. It is generally accepted that a country with established infrastructure prior to World War II and with a per capita gross domestic product (GDP) in excess of US$2000 (1990 prices) should be classified as 'developed'. The countries of Western Europe, North America, Japan and Australia comply with this definition. The infrastructures of these developed countries are under strain from two principal influences. The first is that the existing and limited additional infrastructure is unable to keep pace with growth. An article in *The Economist* on 6 March 1993 cited examples of this when it stated:

> Between 1970 and 1991 Britain built an extra 9% of main roads and motorways. Over the same period, passenger cars drove 116% more miles; vans and goods vehicles, 75% more. Crowded Britain is not unique. Between 1970 and 1990 America's vehicle miles almost doubled, while the amount of its urban roads rose by just 4%.

More recently in August 1994 the Confederation of British Industry estimated that congestion on British roads is currently costing UK firms £15 billion per year.

Demands made by higher standards of living coupled with inadequate and often poorly maintained infrastructure are therefore prime influences. Another principal influence is the importance placed on health and welfare demands. The increasing longevity of the populations in the developed world has resulted in ballooning health

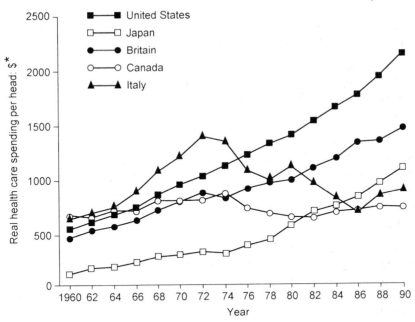

* Deflated by GDP deflators and adjusted by purchasing-power parities

Source: OECD

Figure 1.1   Trend of real spending costs per head

care costs for these societies to shoulder. Figure 1.1 profiles the trend of real spending costs in US$ per head of population of five typical examples.

A 1993 Organization for Economic Cooperation and Development (OECD) report cited France as Europe's highest-taxed country and also as having particular problems with a massive and growing 'social protection' debt to be paid by a shrinking working population. The report stated that:

> Between 1980 and 1990 health spending in France grew by an annual average of 5.1 per cent, while GDP grew by an average of just 2.9 per cent.

Since there is a limit to government taxation levels, it became evident to the developed countries of the world that they were facing a major fiscal conflict between social protection and infrastructure — a way to defuse this had to be found.

The criteria for 'newly industrialized countries' (NICs) are countries now establishing their infrastructure and with a per capita GDP moving through the US$2000 (1990 prices) dividing line. Malaysia, Thailand, Hong Kong, South Korea, Taiwan, Singapore, Mexico, South Africa and the oil-rich countries of the Middle East comply. These NICs all share a common, omnipotent demand on their limited infrastructure — urbanization. Balchin *et al.*[2] argue that:

> The enormous migration of people into cities and towns has produced a very distinct possibility of an uncontrollable urban explosion — unprecedented increase in population, greater demands on the urban infrastructure, higher rates of pollution etc.

This apt description of the effects of urbanization describes the situation facing most of the NICs of the world. A visit to grid-locked, smog-bound, central Bangkok, Taipei or Mexico City will provide the reader with the reality of the fallout from an uncontrolled urban explosion. An article in *The Economist* on 4 September 1993 quantified Bangkok's problems as:

> Only 8 per cent of the surface of Bangkok is covered by roads, compared with more than 20 per cent in London or New York. The price of land has risen so sharply that buying space for roads is prohibitively expensive. Meanwhile, the number of people trying to move around Bangkok is growing. The population of the city was 6 m in 1987, has grown to 9 m by 1991 and is likely to hit 11·5 m by 1998. Economic growth means more people are able to afford cars. Car sales are expected to increase by 23% this year (1993). Everyday 500 new vehicles take to the road.

The governments of these NICs are also very much aware that when economic growth outstrips infrastructure development, a choke is applied to that growth. In the case of Bangkok a recent *Asia Inc.*[3] article quantified the problem as:

> the current traffic congestion shaves 1 per cent from Thailand's gross national product and costs the average resident 40 days a year in commuting time.

Countries with limited infrastructure and low GDP per capita, such as in the African and Indian subcontinents and most countries in South America, are commonly classified as 'Third World Countries'. These indebted countries of the Third World miss out on growth prospects caused by their severe austerity in fiscal spending. It is also now accepted that lax lending criteria of the post-war (World War II) era caused the problem in the first place. A 1990 World Bank report by Augenblick and Custer[4] comments:

> the growing third world debt crisis has meant that developing countries have had less borrowing capacity and fewer budgetary resources of their own to finance the projects that are needed.

These countries, despite their need for new infrastructure financing, have a reduced capital pool because of the servicing of this debt. This long-term credit squeeze is a fundamental feature of the project-development landscape in Third World countries today. A way out for these debt-ridden countries has to be found.

In the 1970s it became clear that governments globally had major fiscal shortcomings in funding public works. How then to finance projects without Draconian tax regimes which themselves would smother the very growth the infrastructure provides for? Total privatization can and does provide an answer for certain projects or services in certain countries. The concept, however, lends itself to whole or complete sectors of a country's infrastructure — power or water supply and distribution, ports, railways, airports or motorways. This requires both massive investments and major regulatory changes for countries embarking on this path. Reservations with the potential strategic, long term effects of the concept have in turn led to the evolution of another approach to infrastructure funding.

Non-recourse financing is a form of project financing in which lenders look solely to the cash flows of a project to repay debt service, and where they have no recourse to other assets of the project participants should things go wrong. The non-recourse approach is only used in cases where the project is clearly capable of supporting that debt. Commercial banks, pension funds and investment trusts are in the business of lending to such projects. A standalone project such as a tolled tunnel, bridge, canal or motorway, with a quantified revenue stream is such an opportunity. What better way to save the public purse than when the

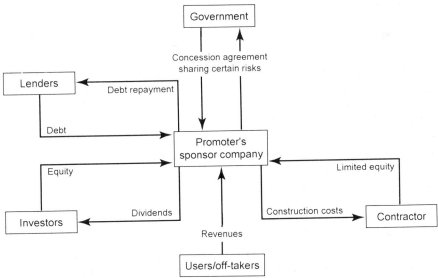

Figure 1.2 Schematic layout of the relationship of the principal parties to a BOT

private sector offers to build this infrastructure at no cost, and some time later, in a much shorter period than the long-term, 99-year, old-fashioned-type concessions and well within the economic life of that infrastructure, return it to public ownership? This innovation allows projects to be undertaken that might otherwise not have been possible because of fiscal restrictions. The community benefits by having use of the facility without being indirectly taxed to fund building that facility. The concept requires three constituents, a willing government, a viable project and funders willing to take the risk of bank-rolling the project. What then is the contractual vehicle that brings all three together?

The technique that characterizes a Build Operate Transfer (BOT) arrangement, is the granting of a concession which empowers the right to operate and profit from the entity created by that concession. On expiry of the concession, the entity, bridge, canal, etc. transfers at no cost to those who granted the concession — for infrastructure projects this is most often government. BOT concessions are typically 5 to 30 year terms. Figure 1.2 shows the schematic layout of the relationship of the principal parties to a BOT.

It is reported that the acronym 'BOT' was first coined in the early 1980s by Turkey's late Prime Minister Targut Ozal. Adoption of the concept can, however, be identified earlier when, in Hong Kong in the mid-1950s, a privatized cross harbour vehicular tunnel was first proposed. Literature adopts both 'BOT' and 'BOOT' shorthand with the second 'O' incorporated when property development rights form part of the concession. For example, when a private sector group has a concession to build and toll a motorway project for 20 years, this is a BOT. If, however, their concession also allowed them to own, build and rent warehouse space (for 20 years) at certain locations along the motorway then the contractual arrangement in place is described as a Build Own Operate Transfer (BOOT) agreement.

The development and execution of any major project can often be a difficult and uncertain process. The formalized risk relationships between government, lenders, investors and contractors are central to the project's success — they form the crux of all BOTs. They are for the promoter/developer to address, arrange, document and regulate. The more complex the undertaking, the more complex the BOT vehicle. The perceptions and aspirations of each party will be different. The promoter/developer must bring these into a workable formula with a certain transparency that gives all involved the confidence that no one party is taking unreasonable risk or benefiting from unentitled reward.

In any BOT arrangement the contracted parties must acknowledge the conventional wisdom that risk should be assumed by the party within

Table 1.1 Significant components of BOT projects

Construction phase	
Risks	Solutions
Completion delays	Experienced turnkey contractor
	Penalties, liquidated damages, performance bonus
	Completion/performance guarantees
	Proven technology
Cost overruns	Fixed-price/lump-sum contracts
	Standby credit
	Increased equity
Force majeure	Insurance
	Government indemnities
Political risk	Insurance
	Export credit agency cover
Infrastructure	Government assurances

Operation phase	
Risks	Solutions
Revenue stream	Market study/traffic growth, etc.
Performance/technical	Proven technology
	Performance guarantees
	Contractor's equity
	Deficiency agreement
Operation/maintenance	Contractor/licensor involvement
	Experienced operator
Foreign exchange	Flexible price formula
	Central bank assurances
	Swaps
	Escrow accounts
Other contingencies	Government support
	Covenants

whose control the risk most lies. A major function of the BOT arrangement is, therefore, to recognize and provide a mechanism for the assignment and management of those risks. The analysis and allocation of risk is, therefore, central to the structuring of the BOT. Putting these networks in place can be an extremely fraught and complex process. The

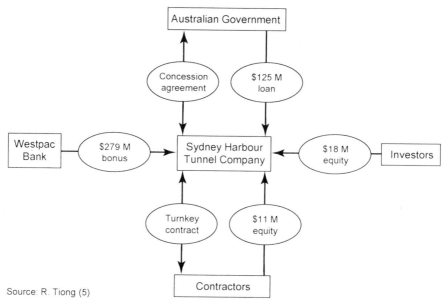

Source: R. Tiong (5)

Figure 1.3   Sydney Harbour Tunnel (1991 prices; US$ values)

experience and talents involved will make or break the outcome. In BOT infrastructure projects there is first construction risk and then operation

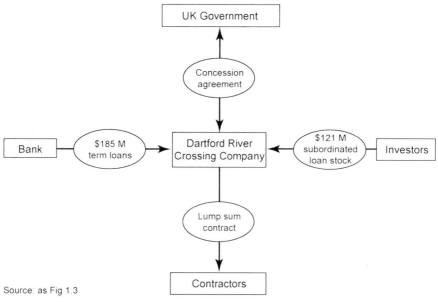

Source: as Fig 1.3

Figure 1.4   Dartford Bridge (1991 prices)

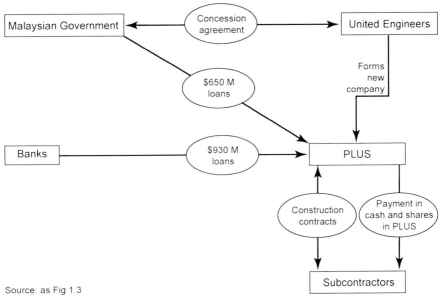

Source: as Fig 1.3

Figure 1.5   Malaysian North—South Highway (1991 prices; US$ values)

risk. The BOT vehicle must therefore address both. The significant components are briefly summarized in Table 1.1.

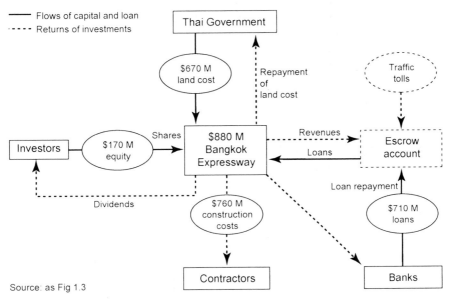

Source: as Fig 1.3

Figure 1.6   Bangkok Expressway (1991 prices; US$ values)

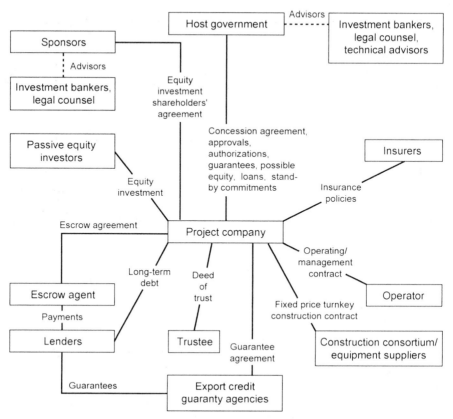

Figure 1.7 Contractual arrangements for a typical BOT

BOT operational structures

The BOT structure will vary to reflect the political and physical project environment. Figures 1.3–1.6 represent outline arrangements for projects in Australia, UK, Malaysia and Thailand, and are presented as examples. Figure 1.7 details the contractual arrangements required to be in place for a typical BOT.

BOT in practice

A number of examples of BOTs in practice are given in the case studies in Chapter 14, and the first of these, the Hong Kong Cross Harbour Tunnel opened in 1972, emplifies how a BOT evolves from conception to a viable entity satisfying the win-win aspirations of all parties involved. This project highlights many BOT characteristics — a recognizable revenue stream, a constricted government, a local champion, long gestation period, positive outcome and the concept's continuing evolution.

Two notable landmark-examples of concession agreements were mentioned earlier — the water distribution scheme built by the Perier brothers in France and Ferdinand de Lessep's Suez Canal. Both shared a common end brought about by political upheaval. With the Perier brothers it was the French Revolution, with the Canal it was the 1956 Suez war. Long franchise durations bring with them this inherent political risk which modern BOTs attempt to minimize. The next three chapters review how each of the principal partners, i.e. government, funders and concessionaires view and measure political and other major risks and costs, and how they formalize their relationships to ensure that the success they plan for will eventually come to fruition.

References

1. MONOD J. *The private sector and the management of public drinking water supply.* World Bank, 1982.
2. BALCHIN P., KIEVE J. and BULL G. *Urban land economics and public policy.* Macmillan Education, 1988, 4th edn.
3. *Asia Inc.*, 1994, **3**, No. 3, March 12.
4. AUGENBLICK M. and SCOTT-CUSTER B. *The BOT approach to infrastructure projects in development countries.* World Bank Working Paper, August 1990.
5. TIONG R. *The structuring of BOT construction projects.* Construction Management Monograph, Nanyang Technological University, Singapore, 1991.

Chapter 2

Granting authority's perspective

Introduction

As the party granting the infrastructure concession is most likely to be a government or government authority, the single term 'government' is now adopted to describe the entity with rights to grant the concession. There can, however, be others in the utility and private sectors granting BOT concessions. The Standard Chartered Bank of Hong Kong, for example, granted Nishimatsu Property (HK) Ltd, a subsidiary of the Japanese construction giant Nishimatsu, a 25-year concession to sub-let 30% of the Bank's new headquarters which Nishimatsu had agreed to construct at no cost to the Bank. For 25 years Nishimatsu has rental income which, they anticipate, will recoup their construction costs plus profit — a BOT approach in a private/private context. This concept is looked at in greater detail in Chapter 13.

During the 1970s, 1980s and 1990s governments worldwide have been selling state-owned assets, primarily as an additional source of revenue. In 1988–92 the UK government led the privatization league accruing some US$44 billion. But, if asset sales were expressed relative to GDP, then the governments of New Zealand, Mexico, Argentina, Malaysia and Portugal sold larger proportions of their economy (see Fig. 2.1).

In New Zealand, sales of state assets were equivalent to an average of 3.6% of GDP in the five-year period, compared with just under 1% in the UK. Another country set to join the league of sell-off activists is India with US$1.3 billion programmed to be hived off in the year 1994/95. This includes over 200 state-sector companies in mining, oil, tele-communications, steel, aviation, ports, shipbuilding, railways, bus transport and hotels. It was, however, the demise of Communism in the east European countries which triggered a tidal wave of mass privatization. The European Bank for Reconstruction and Development (EBRD), with Germany's 'Trenchant' privatization agency in

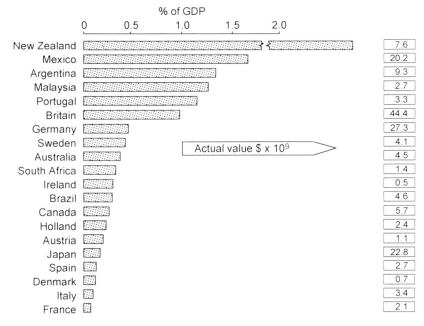

% of GDP

	Actual value $ x 10^9
New Zealand	7.6
Mexico	20.2
Argentina	9.3
Malaysia	2.7
Portugal	3.3
Britain	44.4
Germany	27.3
Sweden	4.1
Australia	4.5
South Africa	1.4
Ireland	0.5
Brazil	4.6
Canada	5.7
Holland	2.4
Austria	1.1
Japan	22.8
Spain	2.7
Denmark	0.7
Italy	3.4
France	2.1

Sources: *Privatisation International*, OECD, EIU

Figure 2.1   Privatization proceeds relative to GDP: 1988–92 average

partnership with the World Bank led the financing of this thrust. There are other countries around the globe with little or no state apparatus to sell. The USA is one example with much of its power, tele-communication and transport sectors already privately owned.

All countries have their own public/private mix which, allied to their political ethos, sets enthusiasm for or against the uptake of privatization concepts. It is not for this book to address the moral and social agenda each country should have, except to recognize that documented evidence suggests private sector enterprises are more efficient and productive than public ones. Real cost data from the USA acknowledges that publicly owned hydro-electric generating plants produce power which costs 21% more per kilowatt hour than private plants. Alternatively when comparing water schemes, the average operating costs per 1000 gallons of water produced is 25% less for private companies. With refuse collection, a nationwide study of 1400 communities concluded the private collectors were 30% less costly than the public systems. Similar conclusions have been reported from studies in Canada and Switzerland where again real costs were qualified and quantified.[1]

Aware of such statistics, governments obviously have to address their own political climate. Privatization might reverse previous nationalizations which could upset those who advocated that policy in the first place. In non-democratic regimes, where the military is often close to nationalist activists and supposed defenders of the poor and under-privileged, as in some Central African states, one generally finds private sector involvement is resisted. The military has also been against the concept in the more liberal Turkey, Brazil and Argentina, where it again originally initiated many of the state enterprises.[2]

In democratic countries opposition can be expressed by casting votes in favour of the opposing political party. State officials can therefore regularly gauge satisfaction with the process by following periodic election results. Political opposition to the private sector is often based on ideological grounds or driven by self-interest considerations, but also arises from government departments fearing that privatization will lessen their power. An editorial in *The Times* in 1994 exemplified this when criticizing a UK Treasury Department's attempt to block the privatization of certain sectors of London's underground rail system:

> The Northern Line is but one small example of sorely needed infrastructure investment. The ideas are there, the money is there, and the private sector needs merely to be given the nod. Yet, even after 14 years of Conservative rule, the Treasury still clings to the doctrine of public sector good, private sector bad. Officials are convinced that private companies can make profits on public sector projects only by taking the taxpayer for a ride. They still refuse to believe, despite all the evidence from privatization, that the private sector can often build something more cheaply than the public sector even when profits have been taken into account.[3]

Even in the UK, a hotbed of privatization, the concept continues to meet resistance. Reservations that privatization is not a panacea are also voiced by agencies such as the United Nations Development Programme (UNDP) which has monitored the overall consequences in 80 countries. Its 1993 report[4] states that '. . . markets are, after all, not an end in themselves, they are a means to human development'. To keep human development and the market in balance it warns of the 'seven deadly sins of privatization', as follows.

(a) The wrong reason, such as short-term revenue for the national treasury.
(b) The wrong environment; for instance, the government either continues to interfere with efficiency or provides no anti-trust regulation at all.
(c) Cronyism and corruption by disposing of assets in secrecy or without competitive bidding, thus inviting corruption and enrichment of government cronies.

(d) Financing budget deficits by selling public enterprises. Instead, a government must retire its national debt and face up to the painful choice of raising taxes or cutting public spending to balance its budget.

(e) A poor financial strategy. Government should take care to achieve widespread distribution of shares to nationals and foreigners alike in a way that maximizes revenue and protects the national interest.

(f) Poor labour strategies, such as buying labour co-operation with unrealistic hiring promises. Instead, they should invite pre-sale labour dialogue and participation in management, in retraining, and in lay-off policies and action.

(g) No political consensus. Privatization is a political as well as an economic act and should not be forced through by edict.

'The enumeration of these sins,' say the report's authors, 'is a caution not against privatization, but against privatizing within the wrong framework and without a human development purpose in mind.'

While government officials and politicians might remain suspicious of privatization they are increasingly aware of the documented inefficiencies of nationalized sectors of economies worldwide — the people of the former USSR can no doubt confirm this view. The emotive bloc for diehard socialists has subsequently weakened as we move through the 1990s. This accredited efficiency coupled with the ongoing demands of urbanization has pressured governments to seek a technique to balance their budgets and provide or upgrade their infrastructures without increases in taxation levels, while at the same time re-thinking the full implications of the radical step of privatization. A compromise, a middle way, a more widely acceptable concept that joins the public interest with efficiencies of the private sector is therefore being sought by many.

A new partnership is born

In order to claim that BOT is the answer, one has first to confirm that it satisfies the needs of those involved. What then are governments' needs or priorities with regard to the essential services that underpin any society, since adequate provision of electricity, gas, water, sewage disposal, telecommunications and transport infrastructure are pre-requisites of that society?

(a) Governments generally encourage efficiency and growth, as these in turn create wealth which, if equitably spread, benefits all in that society. Achieving efficiency and growth focuses policy decisions as sustaining this growth requires the appropriate infrastructure.

(b) Governments should continually balance their budgets to ensure that taxation levels do not rise to smother the very growth the infrastructure provides. Not to do so endangers the stability of society and the government.

(c) Governments must address and set long-term policy objectives for their people — a social and economic strategy vis-à-vis other objectives, infrastructure being one, is for committed government to address.

As these prerequisites are inherent in successful government how then does BOT bring together core issues to provide the answer?

The win-win solution

What could be better than to acquire expensive new infrastructure or upgraded facilities at little or no cost to the state? This is the fundamental attraction of BOT. It not only takes spending off the government's balance sheet but also brings in the commercial skills of the private sector both in identifying viable projects and in running them efficiently when they are built. The Channel Tunnel is one very striking example of private finance addressing a need which the public sector was unwilling or unable to fulfil. The finance has been raised by a mixture of corporate risk capital, public subscription and bank loans. In effect, the way the £12 billion project is financed means that all the commercial risks are borne by private organizations. As the project costs overrun, and the assumptions regarding future traffic and revenue vary from that expected, it is the promoters and their financial backers (bankers, bond-holders or other shareholders) who now bear the risk.

The transfer element of the Channel Tunnel and all other BOTs ensures that government retains strategic control of the state's assets. This mortgage facility answers the 'sell-off' implication that critics of privatization raise. Who can further fault the following benefits to the public/government?

(a) Relief of financial burden.
(b) Relief of administrative burden.
(c) Reduction in size of (inefficient) bureaucracy.
(d) Better service to the public.
(e) Encouragement of growth.

(f) Government can better focus and fund social issues such as health, education, pensions and the arts.

From government's point of view, if the first five of these six criteria are attained then a particular BOT will be deemed successful. However, the BOT concerned has also to operate successfully and profitably. The two go hand in hand. The remainder of this chapter will review areas which government alone must address, if the marriage of public and private sector interests is to work.

Adequate legal framework

BOT concepts depend largely upon the willingness of entrepreneurs to risk developing an enterprise hoping it will meet the needs of enough customers to ensure its viability. But the willingness of entrepreneurs, and those who lend them money to take these risks, depends very much on the legal environment in which they operate. If the law does not contain strong protection for sanctity of contracts, backed by an impartial, efficient judicial system, then entrepreneurship becomes restricted. Readers in countries with well-established, sophisticated and upheld legal practices can be excused for having little comprehension of what limited or abused laws entail. Widespread corruption, for instance, is often the beneficiary of an inadequate legal framework. The Philippines is a country whose institutions are riddled with high-level corruption. It is a tragedy that its people have fallen into poverty while the nations around have prospered. An adequate legal framework implies that the BOT developers can structure a contract vehicle that will co-exist with that country's laws. The internal BOT relationships are a separate issue and are the subject of Chapter 12.

Each BOT has a concession agreement which formalizes the understanding between government and concessionaire. This interface is unique. A BOT bridge in Britain is quite different from a similar project in Vietnam even if the physical bridge structures are exactly the same. How the UK BOT contractual vehicle addresses the complexities of UK laws will be totally different to that in Vietnam. Dispute resolution is an issue both concessions must address. As with all disputes, recourse to a neutral arbitrator is usually deemed to be the ultimate solution for settling conflicts. In most countries of the developed world, unbiased local judgement is usually available, albeit costly. In the less developed world recourse to a neutral arbitrator in another country is a means of allaying sponsor and funder fears. If these concessionaires and funders are foreigners as is often the case, then the government concerned might be unhappy about abdicating their adjudication rights. This is for governments to address — if they want a particular piece of infrastructure then sovereign rights or 'face' might well have to be compromised. President Nasser's acquisition of the Suez Canal 12 years before the contracted due date incurred a £28 million payment in compensation, a figure arrived at by an arbitration tribunal sitting in Paris. The Suez Canal Company eventually received the final and full amount in 1965. More recently a Thai court ordered the opening of a US$125 million expressway in Bangkok which had been kept closed by a toll dispute. The opening of the road in early 1993 was delayed when the government, trying to appease road-users, told the Bangkok Expressway Co. Ltd (BECL), who had a 30-year concession to build and operate the road, that it could only collect two-thirds of the toll agreed in the original contract. Foreign bankers were not amused and one is quoted as saying, 'the Thai people and the Interior Ministry will never know the damage that has been done'.[5] Legal agreements were not upheld and commitment to building the remainder of Bangkok's much needed infrastructure will suffer because the international funders and contractors now perceive Thailand to be a more difficult place to do business as a result of the government's action. Evidence of this manifested itself in 1994 when there was no funding support for a US$600 million Thai railway project. The concessionaire, Thai Kanjanapas, had to cancel their US$600 million Euro-convertible debenture issue due to lack of interest.[6] Breakdown of legal responsibilities come under the heading of Sovereign Risk. The extreme example of Sovereign Risk is when the entity is taken out of the operator's or owner's hands via expropriation by government or others. Fortunately this blight of the 1970s is something the world suffers less from, as Fig. 2.2 indicates.

While some countries lack adequate legal framework, some it can be claimed suffer from the reverse, over regulation. *The Economist*, in a 1992 article,[7] accused the UK of this when sympathizing with the private sector:

> On average, it takes 15 years to get a new (UK) trunk road from the time the government first thinks about it; actually building it takes only two or three years. Although private roads (BOT) legislation was intended to speed up the process, many companies are put off by the wearisome length of the planning and public inquiry process.

Most countries have public inquiry legislation. The position of a country on the continuum between totalitarianism and full democracy determines the importance placed on a public inquiry judgement. In the

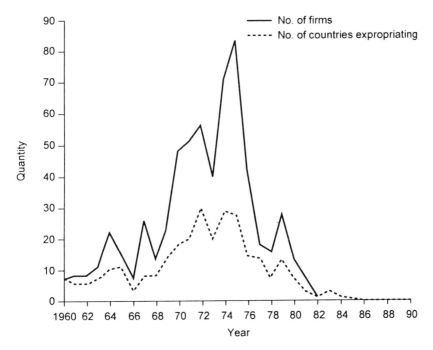

Figure 2.2   Expropriation during the seizing seventies

UK a project could wait 18 months just to get to the hearing stage — in Iraq it might be 18 minutes should the head of state wish a 'go ahead' decision. The UK authorities now realize that BOT schemes, if they are to be encouraged, need a modified or multi-stage approach to the public inquiry hurdle. The chronology of the Birmingham North Relief Road (BNRR) (Table 2.1) illustrates the problem.

This review highlights recent UK legislation changes to assist the early phases of BOT projects. There has been a streamlining of controls and inputs which reduces the amount of detailed submissions by the promoter/concessionaire in the initial phase, greater consultation prior to detail scheme design and a shorter more formal hearing immediately prior to construction to confirm the final implications of the project. The Channel Tunnel Act passed by the UK parliament on 23 July 1987 took only 15 months from its first reading, on 15 March 1986, in the House of Commons — such is the speed when political championing and government pull together with a project which involved relatively few land acquisitions and planning consents.

As the BOT concession has to marry with local laws it is important to ensure lawyers are brought on board from the beginning. Legal fees

Table 2.1 *Birmingham North Relief Road — chronology*

Date	Action
May 1989	UK Government's Green Paper *New Roads by New Means* invites private sector, via BOT arrangement, to pre-qualify to bid for BNRR concession
December 1989	Government announces three groups had been selected to bid (*a*) Joint venture between Trafalgar House of UK and Trouppo IRI (Italy) under Midland Expressway Ltd (MEL) name (*b*) Tarmac and Balfour Beatty joint venture (both UK) (*c*) Manufacturers Hanover (Germany) and Cofiroute (France) joint venture
June 1991	*New Roads and Street Works Bill* passed by Parliament for acceptance of BNRR bids
August 1991	Secretary of State of Transport announces MEL had won concession to design, build, finance and operate the BNRR
February 1992	Concession Agreement signed between Department of Transport and MEL
December 1993	Chancellor announces Government would adopt shadow tolling as payment method for privately financed roads
May 1994	Design Build Finance Operate (DBFO) concepts approved
June 1994	Public Inquiry finds Preferred Route acceptable

typically amount to $0 \cdot 1 - 0 \cdot 2\%$ of the project's final cost. Lawyers and the formalized documentation they prepare are an essential early requirement if the BOT vehicle is to establish the relationships required. Governments must understand exactly what they are consenting to; constructors as to what, where, and when they are to build and how they will be paid; funders as to who has first claim on the debt and what happens when the money is not forthcoming. It is for governments and their officials to realize that their country's legal fabric will have to be modified with legislation drafted to allow a particular BOT to be established and then to honour the concession period.

State credibility

No authority other than the government in office has the right to commit its sovereign state to a concession pledge. As the concession's duration might well exceed the term of office of the incumbent government then promoters, concessionaires, funders and builders must have confidence that future governments will not revoke the concession agreement, as with the Thai government in the Bangkok Expressway. Tables of 'Country Risk' are produced by various organizations (e.g. Dun and Bradstreet/ the Economist Intelligence Unit — *EIU/Business Risk International*) to measure a country's credibility. Afghanistan would be at the opposite end of the scale from Switzerland. Financial institutions, banks and investors who need to make informed judgements on the creditworthiness of the country in which the BOT is located will access such data. Foreign and domestic debt levels, economic policy and political risk outlook are given weightings in the overall assessment categories which are compiled in tabular form (see EIU example in Tables 2.2 and 2.3).

Ratings go from A to E in this case with 'A' described as:

A: contains countries with no foreign exchange constraints on their debt service ability, no problems financing their trade activities, whose economic policies are deemed to be effective and correct regarding the conditions they face (whether in a recession or a boom), and which have a working government (not always a multi-party democracy in the European mould *vis-à-vis* Singapore) capable of effective policy implementation. There are no significant constraints here on any international financial transaction.

whereas 'E' is described as:

E: these countries are likely to have a high and rising level of arrears. They are characterized by severe fiscal imbalance and hyper-inflation. Foreign exchange is scarce, and their relations with multilateral lenders severely strained. Often they are in or on the verge of civil war or undergoing violent political change. Political risk is usually extremely high: 'stay out'.

The significance and importance of a country's international standing is for the incumbent government and those who succeed them to recognize. For the net lender nations of Japan, and countries of Western Europe credibility is obviously high but for countries of the developing world where BOT opportunities frequently occur the reverse is sometimes the case. Take the position Vietnam now finds itself in. For two decades it was more or less ostracized by the international community. President Clinton's withdrawal of the USA embargo in 1993 changed this and now the Asian Development Bank (ADB) is

Table 2.2 Credit risk rating scores (Jan. – Mar. 1993) — E and D categories

	Total	Previous rating	Debt/ GDP	Debt/ service ratio	Interest payments ratio	Current account/ GDP	Savings/ investment	Arrears build-up	Resort to IMF	Single export rely	Economic policy	Politics	Short-term trade
E Category													
Yugoslav Republics	100	100	5	5	10	5	5	5	5	5	20	20	15
Iraq	95	95	0	5	10	5	5	5	5	5	20	20	15
Zaire	95	95	5	0	10	5	5	5	5	5	20	20	15
Sudan	90	90	5	5	5	5	5	5	5	5	15	20	15
Cameroon	90	85	5	5	10	0	5	5	5	5	15	20	15
Angola	90	80	5	5	5	5	5	5	0	5	20	20	15
Yemen	85	80	5	5	5	5	5	5	5	0	15	15	15
Bulgaria	80	80	5	5	10	5	5	0	5	5	20	15	10
Congo	80	80	5	5	5	5	5	0	0	5	15	15	15
Zambia	80	80	5	5	10	5	5	5	0	5	15	10	15
Cote d'Ivoire	80	80	5	5	10	5	5	5	0	0	15	10	15
Kenya	80	75	5	5	10	0	0	5	5	0	15	20	15
D Category													
Nicaragua	75	80	5	5	10	5	5	0	5	0	15	15	10
Algeria	75	75	5	5	5	0	5	0	5	5	10	20	15
Ecuador	75	70	5	5	10	0	5	0	5	5	15	15	10
Brazil	70	70	0	5	5	0	0	5	5	5	15	20	10
Gabon	70	70	5	5	5	5	5	5	5	0	15	10	15
Jordan	70	70	5	5	5	5	5	0	0	5	10	20	15
Malawi	70	70	5	5	5	5	5	0	5	0	15	20	10
Peru	70	70	0	5	5	5	5	0	0	5	15	20	15
Panama	70	70	5	5	5	5	5	0	5	0	10	20	15
Zimbabwe	70	70	5	5	0	5	5	0	0	5	15	10	15
Paraguay	65	65	0	0	5	5	5	0	5	0	15	15	10
Bolivia	65	65	5	0	5	0	5	0	5	5	10	15	15
Pakistan	65	65	5	5	5	0	5	0	0	0	15	15	15
Poland	65	60	5	5	5	0	5	0	5	0	15	15	15
Honduras	60	65	5	5	5	0	0	0	5	0	10	15	10
Jamaica	60	60	5	5	5	0	0	0	5	5	10	10	15

Source: EIU/Business Risk International.

Table 2.3 Credit risk rating scores (Jan. – Mar. 1993) — B and A categories

	Total	Previous rating	Debt/ GDP	Debt/ service ratio	Interest payments ratio	Current account/ GDP	Savings/ investment	Arrears build-up	Resort to IMF	Single export rely	Economic policy	Politics	Short-term trade
B Category													
Kuwait	40	50	0	0	0	0	5	0	0	5	10	10	10
Israel	40	50	0	5	5	0	0	0	0	0	10	15	5
Indonesia	40	40	5	0	5	0	5	0	0	0	5	10	10
Colombia	40	40	0	5	5	0	0	0	0	0	10	15	5
Hungary	40	40	5	0	5	5	0	0	0	0	15	15	0
Thailand	35	35	0	0	5	5	5	0	0	0	5	10	5
Australia	35	35	0	5	10	0	5	0	0	0	5	5	10
Malaysia	35	30	0	0	0	5	5	0	0	0	5	10	10
Czech Republic	30	45	0	0	0	0	0	0	5	0	0	10	0
Cyprus	30	30	0	0	5	5	5	0	0	5	15	15	0
UAE	30	30	0	0	0	0	0	0	0	0	5	10	5
New Zealand	30	25	5	5	5	0	5	0	0	5	5	0	0
Chile	25	25	5	0	5	0	5	0	0	5	5	5	5
China	25	25	0	0	0	0	0	0	0	0	10	10	5
A Category													
South Korea	20	20	0	0	0	0	0	0	0	0	5	10	5
Hong Kong	15	15	0	0	0	0	0	0	0	0	5	10	0
Portugal	15	15	0	0	5	0	0	0	0	0	5	5	0
Taiwan	10	15	0	0	0	0	0	0	0	0	5	5	0
Spain	10	10	0	0	0	0	5	0	0	0	5	0	0
Singapore	5	10	0	0	0	0	0	0	0	0	0	5	0
CCRS Average	55·1	55·2	2·6	2·6	4·6	1·7	3·2	0·8	2·4	2·4	11·3	13·7	9·9

Source: *EIU/Business Risk International*

willing to stand as guarantor for the US$40 billion of infrastructure requirements forecast in the next ten years. Vietnam is now perceived as less risky, with an increasing number of BOT entrepreneurs looking for opportunities to put in place infrastructure where none before existed.

State concessions

As each separate BOT development is unique and a function of a number of interrelated influences, there is no standard BOT agreement. The fiscal, legal, social and physical pond the promoter swims in is different from day to day, country to country, project to project. The criteria for success are therefore complex but trends or distinguishable characteristics are discernible. Fiscally constricted countries tend to have BOTs with high debt and low equity levels, the reverse being the case in more affluent societies. If confidence in the legal and fiscal structure is low, inducements are often put in place by government such as tax breaks, relaxation of import controls on equipment, fixed currency transaction rates, guaranteed toll revenue and intellectual property protection. These are examined in greater detail in the following chapters. Concessions are for the promoter to champion by convincing the government that they are needed to ensure success of the project. The level of response depends on the bureaucracy they are dealing with. As mentioned earlier the UK Treasury Department has for the past 30 years perceived no need to upgrade the Northern Line yet that same department was happy to sanction £151 million of public money to build the little used Humber Bridge in 1971. Although the motives of British officialdom or any other are not for discussion here, it none the less will be recognized that as the world gets smaller, more and more governments are aware of the groundswell of private sector involvement. A UK based journal, *Privatisation International* monitors privatization matters, and valued some US$54 billion worth of concessions in 1994 compared with US$23 billion in 1990. Although these were a mix of BOTs and total privatization, government officials must recognize the move away from traditional procurement methods. The officials must enter negotiations with an awareness that properly structured, the BOT in question will benefit their society. These officials are in touch with the political considerations which invariably dominate policy decisions. If the BOT sponsor is required to lobby his own legislation bill through a national parliament, the chances of ultimate success are very slim. As knowledge of the concept is more widely appreciated, confidence in the formula will increase. Acceptance for example of rates of return on investment of 10% in North America, 16% in South-East Asia, 25% in China, 35% in the Philippines are not necessarily to be looked upon as excessive, but as what any business in that particular sector of that particular country's economy is likely to achieve. A BOT agreement is a marriage between public and private, and it is for state officials to recognize their areas of legal and fiscal credibility together with a mix of incentives that have to be in place for the concept to flourish.

Where do BOTs flourish? The simple answer is almost everywhere. The appendix at the end of Chapter 2 shows an overview taken in early 1995 and reflects the stages of those reported at that time. The reader will be excused for forgetting how recent most BOTs are but nevertheless should realize that uptake of the concept is on an exponential curve and those listed are an attempt to capture the phenomenon.

One final comparison to convince any remaining sceptic of the success of private sector involvement may be drawn from a comparison of two tolled river crossings. Tolled river or esturial crossings, in an over-trafficked and congested island, present the ideal opportunity for financial success. Two such UK bridges within 700 km of each other, the (public) Humber Bridge and the (BOT) Dartford Crossing (Queen Elizabeth II Bridge) highlight the financial success of one and failure of the other.

In 1986 the British government issued bid documents for the third Thames crossing at Dartford. The UK contractor Trafalgar House decided to respond on a basis of a BOT package and, with the Bank of America, established Dartford River Crossing Ltd (DRC). The eventual formula included the revenue from two existing tunnel crossings which assisted in reducing the debt period during the construction and early operational phase of the new bridge. DRC won the concession and the bridge was opened ahead of schedule and within budget in October 1991, with the agreement that the concession would terminate and the crossing would revert to government on payment of outstanding debts or before the year 2008, whichever came sooner. Original projections were that traffic flows would increase by 10% in the first year and 2·5% in the second. Actual flows increased by 18% in the first year and 7·5% in the second year, with 37 million crossings from October 1992 to October 1993. On this basis the bridge will be transferred by 2002 at the latest. Clearly then a success — why? There are five significant factors:

(*a*) an early champion, Trafalgar House
(*b*) a willing government which then consented to including the

existing tunnels in the package
(c)   early completion
(d)   realistic revenue predictions
(e)   lower than expected interest rates.

How then does the Humber Bridge, built a decade earlier, compare? A Conservative government voted money to build the bridge in 1971 when the estimated cost was £28 million. However, bad weather, technical problems and industrial disputes in the late 1970s resulted in a nine-year construction period instead of the planned five years. Built under traditional procurement arrangements, using public money with a tendered contractor, the interest charges increased the debt to £151 million before the first paying customer drove across. The tolls, fixed low to encourage cross-estuary traffic and aid Humberside's economy, could only be raised after lengthy and expensive public inquiries. They have been held at £1·60 for cars and £10·90 for six-wheeled lorries since 1989. The Labour-controlled Hull City Council, which has a majority on the management board insists on this freeze to encourage growth. The traffic figures for 1994 are around 15 000 vehicle crossings per day, which pay only enough to service 25% of the interest charges on the debt. In mid-1994 the outstanding debt was £440 million, rising by £1·42 every second. A white elephant — why? There are six primary reasons:

(a)   protracted construction
(b)   indecisive risk allocation
(c)   no champion to control the project
(d)   high interest rates
(e)   low revenues
(f)   unrealistic traffic projections.

Ironically, for the Humber Bridge, the private sector might come to the rescue. A £1 billion east coast motorway connecting the industrial northeast with outer London is being considered, but government plans for the existing A1 road are crucial to the viability of this private scheme. This particular issue is considered in more detail in Chapter 4.

References

1.   BOUSTANY S.A. *Privatisation and its role in the reconstruction of Lebanon.* Massachusetts Institute of Technology, MSc thesis, 1992.
2.   BERG E. The role of divestiture in economic growth. *Sloan Management Review*, **47**, 1990.

3. THE TIMES. Private Functions. *The Times*, 7 March 1994.
4. UNDP Human Development Report, Oxford University Press, 1993.
5. SOUTH CHINA MORNING POST. 'Business News'. *South China Morning Post*, 2 September 1993.
6. SOUTH CHINA MORNING POST. 'Business News'. *South China Morning Post*, 25 May 1994.
7. THE ECONOMIST. 'Privatisation Problems'. *The Economist*, 31 October 1992.

Appendix

Overview of known BOT projects, early 1995

Country	Project	Status
Argentina	3 Buenos Aires highways	Under construction
	River Plate Estuary Bridge	In negotiation
Australia	Sydney Harbour Tunnel	Operating
	M5 Motorway	Operating
	M4 Motorway	Operating
	M2 Motorway	Out to tender
	City Link, Melbourne	Proposed
	Eastern Corridor, Brisbane	Proposed
	Loy Yang 'B' Power Station	Under construction
	Collie Power Station (300 MW)	Under construction
	Yan Yen Water Treatment Plant	Under construction
	Prospect Water Treatment Plant	Under construction
	MacArthur Water Treatment Plant	Under construction
Brazil	Rio-Niteroi Bridge	Under construction
	Via Dutra Road Link	In negotiation
	South American Superhighway	Under construction
Canada	Terminal 3 of Toronto International Airport	Operational
	Northumberland Straits Crossing	Proposed
China	Shajiao 'B' power station	Operational (debt repaid March 1994)
	Shajiao 'C' power station	Under construction
	Shenzen/Guangzhou Highway	Operational

Country	Project	Status
China (Continued)	Jiangmen/Zongshan Highway	Under construction
	Taiping/Macau Superhighway	Proposed
	Pearl River Crossing at Qiao Island	Proposed
	Huaneng Power Project	Unknown
	Shenzen Airport/Yantian toll road	Under construction
Costa Rica	San Jose toll road	Unknown
Cote d'Ivoire	Water distribution	Operating
Denmark	Fermer Belt Bridge	In negotiation
Eire	Ringsend Highway, Dublin	Proposed
France	Toll roads (various)	Operating
	Water treatment (various)	Operating
	TGV Est	Under construction
Greece	Rion–Antiron Bridge	Under construction
	Attica Highway	Under construction
Hong Kong	'Central' Cross Harbour Tunnel	Operating (debt repaid 1977)
	Western Rail Corridor	Proposed
	Eastern Cross Harbour Tunnel	Operating
	Western Cross Harbour Tunnel	Under construction
	Tate's Cairn Tunnel	Operating
	Route 3 (Country Park Section)	Under construction
Hungary	M1, M5 and M15 Motorways	Under construction
India	Worli Bandra Link Bridge	Proposed
	27 Ports	In negotiation
	Nada River Bridge	Proposed
Indonesia	Cikampek/Cerebon toll road	Under construction
	Coal and nuclear power plants	Proposed
	Paiton Swasta I/Coal	Under construction
	Umbulan Water	Under construction
Israel	Mount Carmel Tunnel	In negotiation
Italy	Toll roads (various)	Operating
Laos	Champasac Hydro Dam	Under construction

Country	Project	Status
Malaysia	North Kelang Straits Bypass	Operating
	Kepong Interchange (toll road)	Operating
	Labuan Water Supply Pipeline and Treatment Plant	Operating
	Kuala Lumpur Light Rail System	Proposed
	Ipoh sewerage	Operating
	New Kuala Lumpur International Airport	In negotiation
	North-South Highway (42 separate contracts)	Operating
Mexico	28 toll highways (4000 km)	9 Operating (2400 km)
	4 toll bridges	2 Operating
	Mexico City Light Rail	Operating
Oman	Manah gas turbine power plant	Proposed
Pakistan	Hab River power plant	Contracts signed
	Fauji foundation power plant	Letter of intent
	Habibullah-Siemens Consortium power plant	Letter of intent
Philippines	Various Metro-Manila power plants	Operating and under construction
	International container terminal	Proposed
	Several large coal fired power plants	Proposed
Poland	Walbrzyeh power plant	Under construction
Portugal	Tagus Bridge (£550 million)	Under construction
Spain	Toll roads (various)	Operating and proposed
Thailand	Bangkok Second Stage Expressway	Operating but concession re-entered by government
	Bangkok Metro	Under construction
	Various toll roads	Proposed
	Second Bangkok International Airport	Proposed
Turkey	Akkuyu nuclear power plant	Abandoned
	1000 MW coal fired power plant	Contracts signed

Country	Project	Status
Turkey (Continued)	Additional coal fired power plants	Proposed
	Hydro power plants	Under construction
	Bosphorus Third Bridge	Abandoned
	Bosphorus Tunnel	Proposed
	Istanbul Airport	In negotiation
	High-speed rail link between Istanbul and Ankara	Proposed
	Water plant (Izmir)	Abandoned
	Ankara Metro	Proposed
	Toll roads	Proposed
	Port facilities and free trade zones	Proposed
UK	Eurotunnel (UK/France)	Operating
	Birmingham Northern Relief Road	Construction about to begin
	Manchester Metro-link	In negotiation
	Second Severn Bridge	Under Construction
	East Coast Motorway (600 km)	Proposed
	Bristol Light Rail	Withdrawn
	Dartford Bridge	Operating (debt paid off early)
	New Mersey Crossing	Proposed
	Skye Bridge	Under Construction
	New Tamar River Crossing	Proposed
	Third Forth Crossing	In negotiation
	Edinburgh – Carlisle Toll Road	Proposed
	Croydon Tramlink	Proposed
USA	Lax – Palmdale Rail Transit	Proposed
	Dulles Toll Road Extension	Under construction
	Denver Toll Ring Road	Under construction
	Florida High Speed Rail	Under construction
	Interstate SR91	Under construction
	Boston Artery Tunnel	Proposed
Vietnam	Highway 1	Under construction
	Power distribution	Under construction
	Power plants (10 by year 2000)	In negotiation
	Hanoi Airport	Proposed

Chapter 3

Funder's perspective

Introduction

There are many ways in which project finance can be obtained. This chapter provides an overview of aspects influencing BOT finance; specific financial issues are considered in depth in later chapters. This chapter also attempts to predict the future global direction of BOT project finance which will be brought about when these techniques are used more widely. The mechanics of project finance are considered in more depth in Chapters 5 and 6.

Project finance

It is appropriate to first address the meaning of BOT project finance and in particular to understand that it varies from project to project, and country to country. The variability manifests itself primarily because each project has its unique mix of debt and equity with the lenders' perception of viability generally being different from that of the investors. Lenders tend to focus on the downside risks while investors tend to look at the upside opportunity. It is frequently the case that the banker views a project, and the country in which it will perform, as having a particular set of credit risks, while simultaneously investors perceive different criteria. One example highlighting this would be a business venture in Korea in the early 1980s, when South Korea had the highest sovereign debt of any Asian country. All of its debt service ratios and other key indicators were very negative. Most bankers were extremely unwilling to make fresh loans to South Korean businesses. Political stability had remained questionable ever since the assassination of President Park in 1979. The rise in oil prices and the world recession in 1981 had hit South Korea badly. There were domestic political tensions and strong pressures from the labour unions. Inflation had averaged 20% during the previous five years. Nevertheless South Korea came out of this crisis in the early 1980s with a renewed vigour which only those who had studied the history and character of the Korean people could have foreseen. The strong work ethic which had enabled the Koreans to build up their industries (steel, shipbuilding, cars and the massive construction industry which had undertaken vast projects in the Middle East during the previous decade) all testified to the almost military discipline and commitment to work, to savings and to nation building which characterized the Koreans more than any other Asian nationality. Meanwhile, the tiny Seoul stock market was capitalized at US$3 billion compared to the nation's GNP of US$75 billion.[1] A perceptive observer might well have compared this situation with that of Japan 20 years earlier. So, despite the obvious risks, Korea proved to be an outstanding investment opportunity in 1984. In fact, the stock market capitalization grew by a factor of 25 between 1984 and 1990.

Both potential lenders and investors raise different questions which none the less overlap when analysing the commercial viability of the revenue stream assessment. The financial engineering subsequently arranged reflects this, juggling the debt/equity mix to optimize and respond to the confines in which the BOT vehicle will operate. This environment, as Chapter 2 highlights, is a function of the country — the BOT finance vehicles of western Europe for example, are very different from those in other areas in the world. However they all share three conception characteristics. These are:

(a) government unwilling or unable to provide refurbished or new infrastructure
(b) identification of an omnipotent need
(c) funding bodies comprehensively convinced of the potential for commercial success.

With (a) and (b) in place, (c) will follow. Unfortunately the global demand for infrastructure monies outstrips the available funding, which goes some way towards explaining why BOTs flourish in some countries and not in others. The fiscal surpluses of Switzerland, Germany, Norway, Singapore, Japan, South Korea, Taiwan, Brunei and the oil-rich states of the Middle East preclude BOT concepts, simply because direct government borrowings are cheaper to put in place. Conversely cash-strapped UK, USA, Turkey, Malaysia, Philippines, Thailand, Vietnam, Mexico, China and Hong Kong are countries where the three crucial conception characteristics are particularly heightened and therefore private project funding can generally find a role. The project finance landscape is changing rapidly to address this role with increasingly sophisticated techniques being evolved. The innovations are brought about by the competitive nature of tendered bid submissions. In the UK for example, the Dartford Crossing, conceptualized in 1986, is financially engineered in a different way to that of the Second Severn Crossing, which was developed only three years later.

It is for the developer or the sponsoring group to package the financial formula. The group and their financial advisers know that their stand-alone project has a large hole of early development and construction debt. Early injection of equity reduces this debt without incurring interest payments but comes with the trade-off that investors will push for high tolls to maximize their dividends. This pressure may be seen by the lenders as adding risk to the viability of the revenue stream predictions. A balance, unique to the particular project, has therefore to be attained. Typically the proportion of equity is much smaller than the loans, and the lenders will seek to impose guarantees against cost overruns and construction completion dates.

Lender's perspective

Lenders comprise agencies such as banks, insurance companies and pension funds. The primary concern of the lenders will be the concessionaire's predicted annualized balance sheet, as evidenced by the financial model, together with any necessary security guarantees. Lenders seek to arrive at a realistic and full understanding of the BOT vehicle in question. Achieving credibility is complex and time consuming. Funders' confidence in the concessionaires' proposed arrangements is essential as capitalized interest payments form a large early part of the projects critical outgoings — reducing this liability to a minimum is therefore of major significance. Below, areas are reviewed where the lenders are likely to require assurance that their liabilities and risks are being meaningfully addressed and mitigated against.

Revenue stream guarantees

BOT projects can be sub-divided into two principal groupings. The first group includes roads, bridges or tunnels with many tolled customers, whereas the second group includes projects with one major customer and will include power, sewage or water treatment plants where the customer is often a government utility who in turn charges the consumers. The latter generally have less risky revenue streams and enjoy construction and maintenance costs which are relatively simple to quantify. In addition the first group has a further handicap in that they are built for long-term needs and may not reach full user thoughputs for decades, and this will generally be reflected in their longer concession periods. Schemes which are dependent on vehicle traffic typically have some form of government support to make them attractive to the private sector. In Malaysia's North–South Highway project, which has a substantial amount of foreign currency borrowing, the government via the central bank provided a 17-year external risk undertaking to make up the shortfall if exchange rates dropped by more than 15% against the initial borrowing rates. The UK approach for the Dartford and Severn Bridges is to have variable concession durations, dependent on the performance of the project. For the Skye Bridge, tolls increase via an indexed formula based on 1990 ferry figures. This allows for increases up to a set maximum should poor revenue conditions prevail.[2] Hong Kong, with its transfer to China in 1997, has a number of extra variables for BOT projects to address. Concern over the viability of the 1993 Western Harbour tunnel project may have been one of the major reasons why the government received only one bid. Faced with this, the government agreed, after negotiation, to allow increased tolls in the event that cash flows fell below a minimum threshold due to poorer traffic volume, or if inflation or interest rates rose higher than originally calculated. The concession allowed for investor equity returns to be within a predetermined range throughout the franchise period. For the first three years of operation this range is set at 15 to 16·5%. Thereafter the range is 15 to 18·5%. The Hong Kong government, keen to bolster funding confidence, accepted this deal to ensure the £84 million tunnel link to the new airport would be built.[3]

Development property rights

As the construction phase relies on draw-down payments from the committed lenders, granting early development ownership rights helps to minimize the extent and duration of the debt. The financial rationale of the BO(O)T vehicle is improved by lease returns throughout the concession period, especially if early rentals and pre-sales payments can be achieved. The Hanoi–Haipong road project in Vietnam is currently underway with this facility being adopted. Similarly Hopewell Holdings have secured 8000 hectares of land for a £170 million motorway project in China which they can utilize for warehouse and retail space at the intersection locations along the highway. Although property development was an important element in the financing of Britain's railway construction in the last century, the British government now argues against it as a means of assisting road funding viability. Reasons given include the following.

(a) A dense road network with widespread development opportunities limits the value of new road associated developments.

(b) Land-use patterns should be determined objectively via formalized planning processes and not on the basis of deals.

(c) Planners are anxious to avoid generated traffic.

Export credits

Infrastructure projects almost always include components of construction plant, operating plant, vehicles and mechanical and electrical engineering equipment. The manufacturers of these often have access to government agencies who use export credits as a form of export promotion. If a BOT project has contractors who can benefit from this support, then the number of cost centres is able to be reduced. Agencies such as the UK's Export Credits Guarantee Department (ECGD) or the USA's Overseas Private Investment Corporation, Japan's Export Insurance Division and Germany's Hermes organization guarantee against certain political and commercial risks in the project's host country with respect to the financing of the construction and operating equipment procured. An example of the range of support given by Britain's ECGD is detailed in the following, which is extracted from ECGD promotional literature:

INSURING CAPITAL GOODS
When exports are high value or project related they are handled by the Project Group.

The most straightforward cover provided by the Project Group is basic insurance against non-payment. Because of the nature of the business supported, this insurance is tailored for each contract and is known as a Specific Guarantee. Under this cover, exporters are paid 90% of any loss caused by buyer default, insolvency or any political loss. Within the policy, additional cover is available to protect against losses incurred during the manufacturing period.

CREDIT TERMS
Non-payment is not the only worry for exporters involved in project business. Overseas buyers often seek long credit terms which can cause cashflow problems. The Project Group has a range of facilities to help. Although a bank will often be willing to accept a Specific Guarantee as security, better terms can be obtained by using one of the guarantees issued to banks.

FINANCE

Complementary to the basic insurance is the Specific Bank Guarantee. Under this, the Project Group guarantees the bank repayment of finance extended in relation to the insured contract. The security offered by a Bank Guarantee means that banks can lend at very favourable rates. Furthermore, for most markets, finance is provided at concessionary fixed interest rates.

BUYER CREDITS

There is an alternative to the exporter providing credit to his buyer. A UK bank can lend to the buyer so that the exporter can be paid on cash terms from the loan. Under this arrangement, called a Buyer Credit, ECGD guarantees full repayment of the loan which is usually for 80−85% of the contract value. The balance is paid direct from the buyer as a down-payment.

LINES OF CREDIT

Buyer credits are only available when the contract value is at least £1 million, but for smaller contracts the Project Group guarantees Lines of Credit. These are simply credits extended to an overseas borrower by a bank in the UK to enable purchases to be made by any approved buyer in that country from any UK supplier. The minimum contract value under Lines of Credit can be as low as £20,000. Lists of current lines are published regularly and are available from any of ECGD's Regional Offices or from the Publicity Branch in London.

Under both Buyer Credits and Lines of Credit, again for most markets, concessionary fixed interest rates are available which can help to make an export package much more attractive to a potential buyer.

PROJECT FINANCING

ECGD was the first export credit insurer to announce its policy towards supporting Project Financing ventures, often referred to as Build-Own-Operate-Transfer schemes.

Three cover options are offered to banks willing to finance UK capital supplies to such ventures: standard political risk cover; additional political risk cover, against breaches of specific undertakings by the host government; and commercial viability cover against a shortfall in earnings that prevent repayment of bank loans. The minimum eligible loan value is £20 million. Details of the scheme and pre-conditions for consideration of projects by ECGD are available from Project Group underwriters in London or from the major banks active in this field.

EXCHANGE RATE MOVEMENTS

The Project Group can also provide a measure of cover against exchange rate movements during the period between date of tender and award of contract.

70 YEARS EXPERIENCE

Overall, ECGD aims to provide exporters of all kinds and sizes — large and small, goods or services — with a comprehensive range of facilities and support. It offers exporters 70 years experience and expertise.

These export credit agencies have historically been reluctant to provide a guarantee where a host country guarantee is unavailable. This situation is changing, however, and the agencies are, on a case by case basis, beginning to look at projects where the repayment depends upon the financial and economical viability of the projects such as BOTs.

Uninsurable risk

Some risks, such as 'force majeure', are either not insurable or not insurable at a reasonable cost. Banks and export credit agencies will normally be reluctant to assume these uninsurable risks and will seek to have support provided by one or more of the other parties. Equity investors may assume the force majeure risk themselves but normally will not be willing to protect the lender's banks against force majeure. The banks will therefore normally insist that the host country's government address certain of the force majeure risks.

In-place escrow accounts

To help convince potential funders they will be repaid, a hierarchy of credit service arrangements is frequently put in place, via an escrow account, to ensure that the 'senior' debtors are first in line. The role of those who manage the escrow account is to ensure the flow of capital and revenues to the parties during the concession period as directed by the formulated agreement of seniority. The account is usually established offshore if foreign lenders or investors are involved.

Intellectual property/exclusivity protection

If a promoter or sponsoring group identifies and formulates a concept, which on being brought to government is subsequently made public by open tender, that promoter is likely to be less inclined to repeat the effort with another scheme. There is evidence that some governments are becoming aware of the deterrent effect this has. In Malaysia, for example, the promoter is given a pre-determined exclusivity period during which he must satisfy the government that he has a competitive or particularly advantageous bid in order to stop the project being opened to competition. In Australia, the Sydney Harbour Tunnel was awarded to its original proposers on the justification that they had been involved in the formative stage. If lenders know a country's government acknowledges such protection, and as a result is perceived to be generally sympathetic to BOT concepts, they in turn are going to be more amenable in supporting sponsoring groups operating in that country. There is also the ripple effect of the ongoing commercial development with beneficial spin-offs to the bank's other clients. These issues combine to heighten lenders' confidence and, as BOT formulas become more widely recognized, should see borrowing rates reduce.

Financing BOT projects represents a profitable lending opportunity for banks since the margins they earn are normally well above those for a similar-sized corporate loan. Banks are, therefore, increasingly keen to add BOT loans to their portfolios. In so doing they are faced with the paradoxical situation of insisting that cashflows are sufficient to ensure rapid repayment of the loan whilst at the same time hoping the loan will remain outstanding for as long as possible. This influence has seen loan durations lengthen and in some instances stretching as far as twelve years. 'Mezzanine debt' is a concept which has developed to address the need for finance that takes a higher risk than conventional debt, and in exchange receives a lower risk than equity with an appropriately lower reward. Its attraction is that it can be tailor-made via a formalized agreement to suit the particular preferences of the different parties involved. This is considered in more detail in the later chapters dealing with financial issues. Insurance companies and pension funds are increasingly attracted to this concept.

Measures of project viability

Accepting that there is no single criteria by which a banker or investor expects to judge the financial viability of a project, there are, however, recognized measuring tools which can be used. Aware of these, the sponsoring group will make available figures, generated from the financial model, which indicate the project's likely financial characteristics for both lenders and investors to review, verify or amend. The important measures are identified as the following.

(a) Return on investment (ROI): The internal rate of return for the unleveraged projected cashflows to be generated by the project. The project is usually deemed feasible, and therefore fundable, if ROI is sufficiently high, ideally eight to ten points above prime borrowing rate.

(b) Return on equity (ROE): The internal rate of return for the leveraged cash flows projected to be generated by a project. The project is usually considered to be attractive if ROE is a least ten points above the prime rate.

(c)   Net present value (after taxes) (NPV): The difference between the present value of annual residual cashflows after debt amortization, interest and income taxes, and the present value of equity investment at a specified discount rate. The project is only considered feasible if the NPV is positive and yields an acceptable return on investment compared with other alternatives.

(d)   Payback period (PP): The amount of time required to recover initial investment. This may be measured as unleveraged returns against total cost (excluding construction, interest and fees), or on dividends against equity disbursements. This measure is very much a function of the project's size but it is obviously desirable for the payback period to be as short as possible, particularly if the country and sovereign risks are high.

(e)   Debt service coverage (DSC): Expressed as a percentage ratio of the project's net cashflow from operation to its debt service due in any period as shown below:

$$\frac{\text{revenue} - \text{operating costs} - \text{taxes} - \text{increase in working capital}}{\text{principal} + \text{interest}}$$

The project will only normally be considered viable if the minimum DSC is in excess of 125%.

Because of commercial sensitivities, published historical statistics on the above five headings are not commonly available. The World Bank's (Augenblick and Scott-Custer) 1990 paper,[4] however, cited the ROE shown in Table 3.1.

As has already been discussed, it is for the promoter/developer to establish the optimum debt/equity mix for the particular BOT being considered. The World Bank paper[4] has equity investments which are typically 10 to 30% of the total project cost, with the debt balance (90 – 70%) being raised from commercial sources backed in developing countries by export credits together with bilateral and multilateral lenders. Some reported equity/debt mixes are shown in Table 3.2.

Investors' perspective

Typically the construction contracting team will agree to invest early equity in the concession company to fund initial outgoings prior to actioning loan draw downs. This commitment encourages government and lending confidence at the pre-concession stage. Formalized agreement usually allows all or part of this initial equity to be released at

Table 3.1   *Reported equity returns in BOT projects*

Project	Information Source	Projected return on equity: %
Pakistani Power Projects	Presentation of Mohammad Akram Khan, Advisor, Ministry of Water and Power, Government of Pakistan, London BOT Conference, June 1989	18
Gazi Power Plant, Turkey	Stevenson. *The Turkish BOT power project experience*. May 1989	16
Labuan Water Supply Project Malaysia	Remarks of Mohamad Hanafiah Omar, London, BOT Conference, June 1989	18−20
Bangkok Second Stage Expressway	BECL, Presentation to Investors, September 1988	3−21*

* These are figures for the base case assumptions. The 3% return is for the first 10 years; it becomes 21% over the 31-year life of the concession.

some point in the operational phase, usually after senior debt has been repaid. Concession policy will determine when these contractors can sell their interest in the scheme, but obviously this will not be until the investment becomes attractive to institutional investors, usually after the construction is complete. These contractors might wish to retain equity as long-term income to be set against the peaks and troughs that bedevil the construction industry worldwide. Alternatively and most commonly however, contractors see themselves first and foremost as contractors, and not part of a company operating a tunnel or bridge. They argue against the 'loss of opportunity' which such long-term investment incurs preferring to maximize their contracting expertise instead. It will also be appreciated that a BOT project, once constructed, offers pristine infrastructure with relatively low operating costs when compared to a process industry. With completion risk no longer an issue a BOT project has utility-type appeal with the reward range that such equity provides.

Appreciating that a 15% return doubles the initial principal every five years, it is interesting to note Hong Kong's Cross Harbour Tunnel Company, termed by some a 'cash cow' has, between 1987 and 1992, reported between 60 and 80% earnings paid out in cash dividends. Another way of qualifying the 'cash cow' description is to imagine that

Table 3.2 Equity/debt mixes

Developed countries	Project	Equity/debt
Australia	Sydney Harbour Crossing	5:95
UK	Channel Tunnel	20:80
	Dartford Bridge Crossing	0:100
	Second Severn Bridge	0:100
	Midlands Expressway	25:75*
	Skye Bridge	0:100
Hong Kong	Original Cross Harbour Tunnel	0:100
	Eastern Harbour Crossing	25:75
	Tate's Cairn Tunnel	28:72
	Western Harbour Crossing	30:70
Developing countries		
People's Republic of China	Shajiao 'B' power plant	3:97
	Guangzhou-Shenzhen-Zuhai Highway	20:80*
Malaysia	North–South Highway	10:90
Thailand	2nd Stage Expressway	20:80
	Bangkok Elevated Transport System	7:93*

* Estimates

the reader bought a board lot of 1000 shares when first offered on 30 July 1974 at HK$5·25 per share. The accrued dividends 'milked out' in the intervening years until 31 December 1993 (prior to rights issue) would be HK$20 640, with a top share price for 1993 of HK$18·50 (i.e. total return of HK$39 000).[5] The Cross Harbour Tunnel Company is thought of as a utility-type share with unspectacular growth but sizeable and reliable dividends each year; increasing noticeably in the latter years as Table 3.3 indicates.

Ironically, the original financial group led by Wheelock Marden was reputed to have offered Costain shares in lieu of outstanding construction claims — Costain apparently declined, as did the design consultants who were made a similar offer. Another surprising aspect was the government permitting the Cross Harbour Tunnel Co. (and its phoenix, the 1993 Western Harbour Tunnel Consortium) taxation offsets against expenses. This is known as an accountant's dream.

Table 3.3 Cross Harbour Tunnel Company dividends

Year	Dividend (cents)	Year	Dividend (cents)
1975	44.0	1985	114.0
1976	50.0	1986	116.0
1977	58.0	1987	130.0
1978	64.0	1988	138.5
1979	90.0	1989	143.5
1980	95.0	1990	146.5
1981	105.0	1991	146.5
1982	107.5	1992	146.5
1983	114.0	1993	140.0
1984	115.5		
		Total since 1975: 2064.5	

(100 cents = HK$1)
1994 P/E ratio — 12.25% with a yield of 5.98%
Source: The Stock Exchange of Hong Kong Ltd.

British BOT landscape

In the UK, although the wish list for BOT funding is extensive, at the time of writing (end 1994) only the Channel Tunnel, Dartford River Crossing, Manchester Metrolink, Second Severn Crossing, Skye Bridge and Birmingham North Relief Road have progressed beyond Concession Agreement stage (Fig. 3.1). These six major projects, albeit with inordinately long lead times and costly bids, point to increasing private-sector involvement. Comparing two, the Dartford and Severn River Crossings, the financing engineering formulas involved reflect the recipe changes that have taken place in just a few years. Both share typical BOT funding scenarios and problems:

(a) The problem of keeping the tolls at a level which would satisfy government and would be competitive with other consortia bidding for the contract, while simultaneously generating sufficient revenue to adequately repay lenders.

(b) The problem of having to attract potential lenders to a new type of project where they would be required to accept substantial risks of construction, traffic and revenue forecasts.

For the Dartford project, the promoter/concessionaire, Dartford River Crossing Ltd (DRC), had to address these issues and prepare a bid,

Figure 3.1 The Skye Crossing

taking on board the government's stance that nominal or no equity return should be generated by the project. DRC's solution was to become the borrower of the total debt package which included two types of long-term fixed-rate loan stock (with different returns and maturities) and a medium-term floating-rate bank loan. The rationale behind the two types of loan stock was that one would accept the 'equity' risk while the other would not.[2] If the total loan stock had absorbed this risk the balance between fixed and floating rate debt would have been destroyed and the pricing of the 'equity' based loan stock would have been affected. Pricing was, as always, an important consideration because of perceived competitive pressures.

Lenders were provided with added security bearing in mind the inadequate capitalization of the borrower by the provision of performance guarantees from the contractors. Also, all surplus funds would be held by DRC and the use of these funds would be closely controlled by covenants within the loan documentation. Should surplus funds at any time equal or exceed the outstanding debt, then the debt would be immediately prepaid, the concession terminated and the crossing would revert to the government. Should revenues fail to reach projected levels, the crossing would still revert debt free to the government at the end of the agreed concession period.

The lessons of Dartford had indicated that to produce competitively low and politically acceptable tolls levels, the developer's/promoters' financial structure could not include large amounts of equity, as the required returns, except in the case of high traffic growth, would require unacceptably high tolls. With this in mind, and aware that further innovation would be required for the Severn Crossing bids, John Laing plc and France's GTM Entrepose jointly began developing their ideas. Basically the challenge was to transfer risk, which previously had been taken by the developer group, to other parties. It was therefore necessary to develop a BOT vehicle that allowed the developer, with only nominal equity, to obtain the concession, design and construct the new bridge, maintain and operate this in conjunction with the existing bridge and arrange funding to reflect this scenario. To increase the attractiveness of the Laing/GTM bid, a concept was developed that effectively reduced the concession length by nine years based on an unchanged traffic projection and toll structure that gave lenders the security they required. The concept was that instead of a fixed-concession length it would be variable, dependent on experienced performance. The type of project finance which matches this is index-linked debt via index-linked bonds.[2] How these are structured is examined in a later chapter. The conceptual financial structure was deemed attractive by government and the Laing/GTM consortium expect to open the new bridge in 1996. Traffic over the existing Severn bridge, although down following the toll increases, is still around 19–20 million movements per annum.

In the UK at the time of writing the government, although advocates of the privatization concept, are criticized for lacking a cohesive approach in pushing ahead more effectively. A key obstacle to the use of private finance in public projects is that private finance is always more expensive than direct accredited government borrowing. Consequently the Treasury insists that privately financed projects must bring gains in operational efficiency to more than offset the extra cost of private funding. They are only prepared to allow privately funded public projects after comparison with a similar project in the public sector, whether or not there is any prospect of that public sector scheme ever being built. Using non existent or unavailable Treasury funds as a comparator is seen as an excuse for refusal and a further form of

Treasury control. The private sector claim that the real comparisons should be between the cost of finance and the economic and social cost of not undertaking the project at all. Interestingly the opposition Labour party share this view.

Under the Maastricht Treaty, all European Community partners will have common debt/deficit definitions. The treaty has two fiscal elements with which all members will have to comply:

(*a*) whether the government deficit exceeds 3% of the GDP
(*b*) whether government debt is above 60% of the GDP.

The UK national accounts treat the public sector as an integrated whole. Money raised on capital markets by state owned industries is consolidated with borrowing by central and local government to produce the public sector borrowing requirement (PSBR). In UK terms, this currently adds the activities of public corporations and government trading bodies (such as the Royal Mint) together with those activities of government which involve taxation to fund public services. The Maastricht convergence criteria for government borrowing are defined purely in terms of the latter. The common sense of this is that, for analytical purposes, it is better to treat activities which earn a market return as different from those which do not. The Maastricht Treaty therefore offers the UK Government the opportunity to present Britain's public sector accounts in a way which is consistent with its European partners and which better reflects the underlying reality. Altering the accounting rules will lower Britain's PSBR which in turn will allow the private sector less expensive rates of borrowing.

Another area of hoped for change is UK legislation to allow, again as in EC countries, the creation of companies whose sole business is the identification, implementation and operation of infrastructure projects. These companies are profit-making and multi-purpose. They can and do use profits acquired on one project to finance and execute others. The UK Government to date has discouraged and legislated against this concept by insisting that the Dartford Bridge, Second Severn Bridge, Skye Bridge and Birmingham North Relief Road operating toll companies are each set up as single purpose non-profit-making organizations, with fixed maximum concession periods based on net present values calculated on actual toll income determining the reversion point. Again the UK Government/Treasury approach is seen as hindering the Private Finance Institution (PFI). Currently PFI projects have to comply with set Treasury criteria to ensure that they:

(*a*) involve significant risk transfer to the private sector (*b*)   provide good value for money having regard to the extent and nature of the risk transferred.

Maximizing the risks transferred to the private sector will not necessarily achieve these two objectives. While almost any risk can be transferred, the cost of doing so may be disproportionate in the case where the concessionaire is less able to understand and control these risks. Applying these principles to water, sewerage and vehicular road/bridge/tunnel projects it is normal to transfer:

(*a*)   design risk
(*b*)   construction risk
(*c*)   operation risk
(*d*)   interest rate risk.

Government is expected to retain:

(*a*)   land procurement and planning permission risk
(*b*)   general inflation risk
(*c*)   resale or residual value risks
(*d*)   regulatory risk.

The demand risk is shared by a formula which envelopes the low and high income streams. At the time of writing only the four projects mentioned previously have been able to comply with the Treasury's exacting and arbitrary demands. Minimum or zero equity requirements also frustrate the financiers who have suggested tax-efficient debenture bonds as one of many means of reducing the early hole of debt characteristic of BOT projects. Until the Treasury's cautious view of the private sector is relaxed somewhat the UK road construction scene appears directed along with the shadow tolling, design build finance operate (DBFO) method of procurement presently favoured by Whitehall. DBFOs and highway BOTs share the same fundamentals. Each requires a sponsor to arrange funding, undertake the design, construction and operational phases and return the infrastructure to government in good condition. They differ, however, in that the DBFO sponsor recoups his outlay via shadow tolls paid by government at predetermined values and indices agreed in the concession document. The concession also determines direct toll values should government wish to implement these at a later date. Shadow tolling has a number of attractions for established and compact road networks found in the UK. These are reviewed in Chapters 4 and 13. By adopting DBFO concepts, government continues to face pressing funding issues — how long can

Table 3.4 *Sources of infrastructure funds*

Fund	Size: $billion	Investors	Description
Global power investments	2.5	GE Capital Corp., Soros Fund Management International Finance Corp.	Invests in power projects
AIG Asian infrastructure fund	1.2	American International Group Inc., Singapore's Temasek Holdings Ltd, Government of Singapore Investment Corp.	Invests in all types of infrastructure
Asian infrastructure fund	1	Peregrine Investments Holdings, George Soros, Frank Russell Co., International Finance Corp., Asian Development Bank	Invests in all infrastructure sectors throughout Asia
Inter-privatization fund	6	Lehman Brothers, KPMG and Russian partners	Infrastructure in the Soviet Bloc
Cons. Electric Power Asia Ltd	1.8	Public Listed Company in Hong Kong	Power stations in Asia

the present levels of licence fee, petrol tax and other income sustain fiscal demands?

It is difficult then at this time to envisage whether the BOT 'leap of faith' will meaningfully take place in the foreseeable future. The terminology adopted by the Department of Transport in the 19th August 1994 call for DBFO pre-qualification submissions quoted below does not give grounds for optimism:

Item 1.7

The Department recognises the novelty of the DBFO arrangements and the many different views the Tenderers may have as to the scope of obligations and allocation of risk under the DBFO contract. The Department does not have a settled view of these obligations nor on the final allocation of risk. Nor can it, in this wholly new market, prejudge what potential Tenderers may be prepared to offer.

When the UK Government overcomes the novelty, has a settled view and has an understanding of what the private sector has to offer then perhaps the British construction industry can begin to be allowed to provide the answers society so urgently needs. Meanwhile unemployment will remain high, road and rail infrastructure will fail to cope with increased demands and Britain's rivers and coasts will be the dirtiest in Europe.

In concluding this chapter the reader will be aware of the crucial importance project finance plays. Refinements such as those exemplified in the Second Severn Bridge and the toll increase formula of Hong Kong's recent Western Harbour Crossing suggest that the world's contracting, lending and investing sectors are willing to adapt and participate in the exciting new world of private-sector infrastructure. However, as more projects emerge, getting them financed will continue to require a balance between equity and debt to be set, which as explained is a function of the project and the financial/political climate in each country. International banks generally want host countries to provide certain guarantees or concessionaires to add an extra layer of equity before they will lend. Additional equity, as we know, increases project costs and in turn only tends to erode returns. Investors understandably also prefer well-structured deals with everything in place and the risks understood. But even then, if the rate of return is deemed unreasonable, money will not be invested. One way to spread equity risk however, is for infrastructure investment funds to invest across a number of projects in different countries. Table 3.4 shows some funds known to the author.

With infrastructure stocks and bonds being traded in markets around the world and financier George Soros involved, the traditionalists face change. A country on the crest of this change is India. Unlike many developing countries India has the established judicial framework of trust laws, company laws and contract laws necessary for BOT concepts to flourish. Britain, if the Treasury reverses its acceptance criteria, also has the potential for much more private-sector involvement.

By the end of the century, bourse markets around the world could see trading of Second Severn Bonds for M25 stock and perhaps some Bombay Ring Road futures!

References

1. LLOYD GEORGE R. *The East-West pendulum*. Woodhead-Faulkner, Cambridge, England, 1992.

2. HODGSON P.J. BOT schemes and the lessons learned for Eastern Europe. *Proc. EBRD Conf., Budapest.* April 1992.

3. LUK, Dr. J.W.K. Route 3 privatisation. *Asian Construction Management Association Conf,* Hong Kong, 1994.

4. AUGENBLICK, M. and SCOTT-CUSTER B. *The build, operate and transfer (BOT) approach to infrastructure projects in developing countries.* Working Papers, World Bank, August 1990.

5. Published data from Hong Kong Stock Exchange daily press releases, June 1994.

Chapter 4

Concessionaire's perspective

Introduction

A fuller definition of a BOT infrastructure concessionaire is that private group/firm which has formed to receive a concession to build own/ operate and later transfer back to government a limited or non-recourse funded project. This group has a number of commercial partners whose relationships with one another are formally structured to reflect the different phases of the project's evolution. Typically, in the past, the consortium has been led by a civil engineering contractor with financial and legal advisers, together with planning, design and quality assurance consultants.

Development phase

The beginning of the development phase has been compared to an Indian rope trick — sustainable, but without visible means of support. Events usually commence with governments inviting 'expressions of interest'. The following text is for a Pakistani port project:

> Government of Pakistan plans to develop a deep sea port at Gwadar through the private sector on build own and operate (BOO) or build, operate and transfer (BOT) or mixed funding basis. Gwadar is located in the vicinity of Straits of Hormuz. A road network is being developed to service the hinterland for import/export from Pakistan, Central Asian States (CAS) and Afghanistan. It can also develop into transhipment station capable of serving Gulf and East African ports with fast feeder services. Development land adjacent to port is also available for setting up of Export Processing Zones, Industrial Parks, Transhipment yards and Warehousing. Government of Pakistan recently commissioned an expert feasibility study of this port through

a firm of international repute. Copies of the report as well as related documents are available to interested firms, on request.

Concrete and final proposals on BOO or BOT or mixed financing basis for developing the proposed port may be delivered by 28 February 1993 at the given address.

The lead contractor/promoter, on deciding to prepare a preliminary submission, must identify a viable team. He begins by promoting his particular concept to potential partners. There is a need to understand the aspirations of these various participants as well as their interaction with one another. Aware of these, the lead promoter will identify the common objective and bring together a unified package to achieve this goal. The process can be both time consuming and expensive for all parties. The first rule is that David and Goliath rarely mix well. Large and small organizations have different attitudes to risk, and different abilities to absorb the likely cost overruns during the development period. The legal, technical and financial parties have different management cultures which the promoter and later sponsor must also reflect.

Often the first aspect to be addressed by the newly formed team is to recruit political and governmental support for the project — without this combined commitment BOT evolution is stunted. With only one of the two, the proposed BOT becomes a football which will suffer long development periods or even abandonment. There is also an inherent tension in the relationship between the public and the private sector universally, and even more so if foreigners are perceived to be making 'super profits'; sound political and bureaucratic support, therefore, must be established early.

The prospective concessionaire has to be patient, when addressing these issues with government officials, particularly those with little or no BOT experience. Montague[1] argues thus:

Without active goodwill towards the project on the part of the government, it is almost certain to be entombed in the impenetrable layers of bureaucracy that distinguish any government, in the developed or developing world. It is not uncommon for a BOT project to require the active concurrence of half a dozen government departments whose officials may be, to a greater or lesser extent, impervious to the charms of the promoters of the project. If the project sponsors are compelled to treat individually with each government department, the sense of urgency which contributes to the momentum of any project is likely to be lost and there is always a danger of constant renegotiation as the demands of one department succeed those of its predecessor.

· Government reactions to BOT projects are the cause of much anguish for project sponsors. But patience is the order of the day.

Handling the subtle complexities of political clout and bureaucratic ability are essential ingredients the promoter must resolve. The end objective of this phase of the evolving BOT is to be sure a concession will in fact be granted and champions and mentors are in place to lobby for this legislation to be passed. One major problem, requiring considerable tact and diplomacy, which the successful sponsors have to overcome is to convince governments to accept that their role is primarily an enabling one while the concessionaire must be left to manage.

The duration of the pre-concession phase varies from project to project, and from country to country, but the global trend is a general shortening of time involved. While many early Turkish BOT proposals never got to the concession stage even after eight to ten years, the trend in Western Europe is between four and six years with the dynamic governments of south-east Asia now letting concessions in less than two years from conception.

Included in the sponsor's team will be design consultants who, at the promotional stage, will have undertaken a concept design. The design will reflect the contractor's expertise and construction equipment available so as to optimize the bid value. Given reasonable confidence that the scheme will go ahead, the preliminary design work can begin with the designers keen to 'lock in' the contractor to a committed approach. This is crucial to minimize the number of design iterations. To prevent this, close cooperation between the design team and the contractor team is essential, with their hierarchical relationships being clearly defined. This is necessary to ensure that the designers' extra costs are reimbursable due to the cost advantages of subsequent design modifications in construction. Failure to formalize these relationships will cause friction later.

In the final months before awarding the concession, government will approach each of the bidders to better assess the strengths and weaknesses of their respective proposals — innovative financial and construction engineering will be analysed to verify credibility and checked to ensure specific criteria are addressed. Winning bid characteristics are a stable toll regime, early completion/earlier handover, capped construction cost, an improved environment and long design life.

The following case study itemizes the early stages of the Tate's Cairn Tunnel, a recent vehicular tunnel BOT in Hong Kong.

(*a*) From the late 1970s, traffic volume between two urban areas grew by around 12% per annum.

(b)   There were only two road links through the hills which separate the two areas. Both were operating at full capacity for several hours a day, and heavy traffic congestion was becoming a common occurrence.

(c)   By the early 1980s a second tunnel was part of the government's plans as a vital artery for both private and commercial traffic.

(d)   Two international contractors, Nishimatsu and Gammon (part of the Trafalgar House Group), felt the project would be an ideal job to utilize their in-house skills. Nishimatsu is a leading tunnelling contractor, while Gammon has wide experience in building major roadworks. As the proposal was being developed, the joint venture in 1985, appointed Standard Chartered Asia as financial advisers, Maunsell Consultants Asia as engineering consultants, and the MVA Consultancy as transport planners.

(e)   A pre-emptive BOT bid was made to the government in November 1986. The proposal contained outline drawings and information covering the tunnel's beneficial effects on the existing transport infrastructure, engineering and construction methods, financing, operations, toll structures and suggested hand-over date to the government. Construction was planned to commence in mid-1987 with completion within 42 months.

(f)   The proposal was well received. The government had initially estimated a 54-month construction schedule and there was also the added bonus that the BOT format would take a considerable amount of pressure off the capital-works budget.

(g)   The government, however, was bound by its own policy to invite competitive tenders for the project. Tender documents containing a project brief and outlining a 'conforming schedule' were issued in May 1987. Six consortia submitted bids, including the Gammon–Nishimatsu joint venture.

(h)   During the drawing-up of their proposals, the Gammon–Nishimatsu joint venture had made certain amendments to their plans. These included a streamlining of the design and construction methods for both the tunnel and the roads and a restructuring of the toll system which allowed the tolls to be fixed for a set period after opening. (The cost of preparing the bid was approximately £2 million).

(i)   Financial engineering was as follows:

      (i)   Equity: £50 million provided by shareholders.
      (ii)   Debt: Equity Ratio <3:1.

      (iii) Borrowing:Pproject cost £180 million; 15.5 year floating rate term loan £130 million.

      (iv) Assumed interest rates: 8.5% p.a. during construction; 10.0% p.a. during repayment period.

Tolls are anticipated to rise at around 10% p.a. in three-year steps which will lead to a final rate of return of just under 13% p.a.

(j)   The Gammon – Nishimatsu tender won the project on the basis of stable tolls and a short construction programme. Instead of the initial proposal of 42 months, a reduced schedule of 37 months was proposed. This was in part due to the innovative design and construction method for the tunnel.

(k)   For this project it was the contractor who had set up its own tunnel operating company in order to receive the franchise from the government. For a time, in effect, the contractors were their own client (see Fig. 4.1 for formalized relationships).

(l)   The Tunnel Company is the corporate body responsible for the financing, design, construction and operation of the tunnel and its approaches.

(m)   In February 1988, the government offered the joint venture, acting on behalf of the proposed Tunnel Company, a 30-year franchise to build and operate the project. During the final stage of negotiations with the government, further equity partners were introduced and the shareholdings redistributed. The franchise was later formalized by the concession being awarded to the Tunnel Company in July 1988.

(n)   When the tunnel and its approach roads opened in July 1991, it was 20 months since the Tunnel Company secured its £130 million term loan facility to fund much of the construction and the early years of operation.

(o)   Despite high inflation towards the end of the project, it was completed within its original budget of £180 million.

Before moving to the construction phase, the crucial role played by the revenue stream is a subject the promoters must examine in the development phase.

Revenue stream

The promotion team, if the BOT is to have the potential to succeed, must apply a vigorous and starkly realistic economic assessment of the

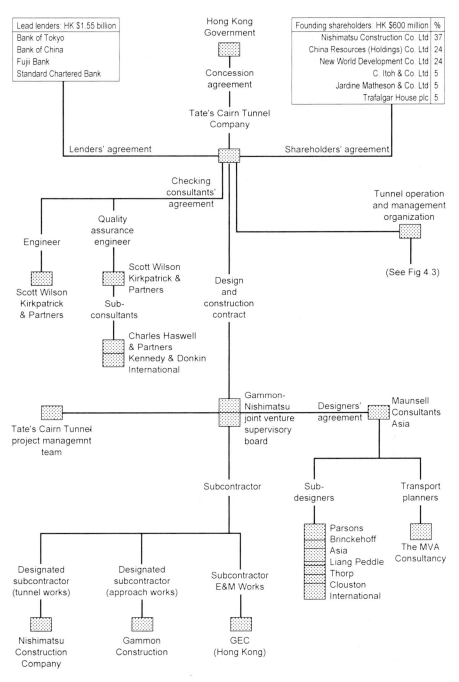

Joint source: J.W.Downer, Maunsell International / J.Porter, Nishimatsu Construction

Figure 4.1 Formalized relationships during Tate's Cairn Tunnel construction

commercial viability of the overall undertaking. It is after all a business venture with all the financial disciplines that must be addressed. These the promoters will examine with their financial advisors, usually a merchant bank, who in turn review with potential funders. The crux, understandably, is the qualification and quantification of income over the period of the concession. Such issues warrant a book in themselves and while certain of these are addressed in other chapters we will now look at some of the fundamentals.

The first of these is that the potential partners must be convinced of a need. For telecommunication systems, sewage disposal, water or power supply, for example, it is assessing what in fact exists and the potential for more. In the latter of these four, power, a simple review of global statistics such as those in Table 4.1, will inform and convince the entrepreneur, the promoter, the government, the sponsors and their funders, that there is a tremendous shortfall and therefore potential for new generation capacity in China and India.

Quantifying revenues for a tolled highway project is, on the other hand, a much more obtuse problem. In less developed countries where few or no roads previously existed, one must identify the need, establish a feasible toll, and estimate construction, financial and operational costs to evaluate the likely returns on investment. If confident that no other road will be built in the concession period and that the predicted returns are reasonable then the project appears worthy of detailed examination. In more developed countries it is much more difficult because the users can move to other, non-tolled, routes. Aware of this stumbling block, the UK's Department of Transport (DoT), via the concept of shadow tolling, have a formula which breaks this impasse; Design Build Finance Operate (DBFO) concessions will be offered to the private sector. Instead of direct tolls being paid by the user, certain DBFOs (see Table 4.2) will be funded by shadow tolls paid by the DoT in proportion to traffic levels using the road. How the DOT recoups its funding is another issue.

The *New Civil Engineer* (NCE)[2] suggested that the DoT hopes DBFOs will bring forward around £350 million of road spending each year which otherwise would not go ahead, with 1998 being given as the target date for electronic tolling of all UK motorways and trunk roads. Accepting that DBFOs and BOTs are in fact similar concepts, coupled with the further formula variation of refurbish operate transfer (ROT) for upgrading existing road networks, the reader has some idea of where future UK road-funding strategy is moving. Interestingly, if ROT and BOT combined, the £1.42 per second compounding debt of the Humber Bridge, highlighted in Chapter 2, might be less crippling. Figure 4.2

Table 4.1   Global statistics on power supply

Country	Population in millions	Electricity generated (million kWh)	Per capita consumption (kWh)
USA	241·60	2 488 861	10 320
Australia	15·97	126 972	7951
East Germany	16·64	116 245	6984
West Germany	61·05	409 292	6810
France	55·39	339 617	6138
USSR	278·61	1 599 000	5739
UK	56·76	301 319	5308
Japan	121·49	576 339	4751
Singapore	2·59	10 467	4041
Italy	57·22	194 880	3407
Hong Kong	5·53	18 400	3327
Yugoslavia	23·27	76 763	3299
Taiwan	19·11	56 974	2981
Poland	37·46	104 292	2784
Hungary	10·63	27 986	2633
South Korea	41·57	62 560	1505
Malaysia	16·11	13 700	850
Thailand	52·55	23 040	438
China	1053·20	445 500	423
Philippines	55·58	20 700	372
Pakistan	99·16	26 968	272
India	750·90	178 000	237
Indonesia	166·94	21 330	128
Bangladesh	100·62	4 720	47

Source: Compiled from mid-1980's World Bank/Asian Development Bank Statistics

indicates the proposed route of the ambitious £1 billion East Coast motorway, seen as a viable BOT project by its promoters, chief of which is Humberside County Council. The problem, however, is that an upgraded non-tolled A1 to the west would undoubtedly attract traffic. What better answer than to give both routes to a single private sector concessionaire with an ROT shadow tolled A1 partially funding the construction of the BOT east coast motorway which, in turn, would revitalize not only the viability of the Humber Bridge but also the economic well-being of Sunderland, Middlesbrough, Hull, Lincoln, Boston, King's Lynn and Cambridge. But is this a win-win scenario,

Table 4.2   DBFOs funded by the DOT

	Estimated construction cost: £million (1992)	Length: km
First Tranche DBFOs (autumn 1994)		
M1−A2 Link road	200	30
A1(M) Alconbury−Peterborough	144	21
A419/A417 Swindon−Gloucester	39	55
A69 Carlisle−Newcastle	9.4	84
Second Tranche DBFOs (May 1995)		
M40 junctions 1−15	40	122
A19/A168	30	123
A30/A35	50	104
A50/A564	20	56

the cynics will ask? There are of course many and varied arguments but the acceptance of shadow tolling is a radical move by UK authorities to have the end user begin to accept financial liability for the country's much needed new and refurbished infrastructure. Coupling this with concession agreements secures society's retention of state apparatus while at the same time bringing private sector efficiencies. Where all this might lead is looked at in greater detail in the concluding chapter.

Since a quantifiable economic assessment is the crux of any business proposal, the promoters will prepare their financial model reflecting revenue stream and other sensitivities involved. This is done with a number of computer runs based on permutations of pegged assumptions of the project's cost centres and revenue stream vis-à-vis the core factors of interest and inflation rates. Each run identifies the particular 'S' curve of financial viability detailing predicted payback durations, rate of returns, etc. Tables 4.3 and 4.4 are computer printouts for a 1992 Malaysian highway project which identified the maximum deficit criticality of year five.

Before leaving the revenue stream issue, the promoter, early in the development phase, will give some thought as to how the tolls will be collected. Capturing the tariffs via a comprehensive 'fare-box' for sewage, water and power is relatively easy to arrange and audit by a metering system. Direct tolling of vehicular traffic is time consuming and expensive, adding 3 to 10% to the overall cost of the project.[3] It

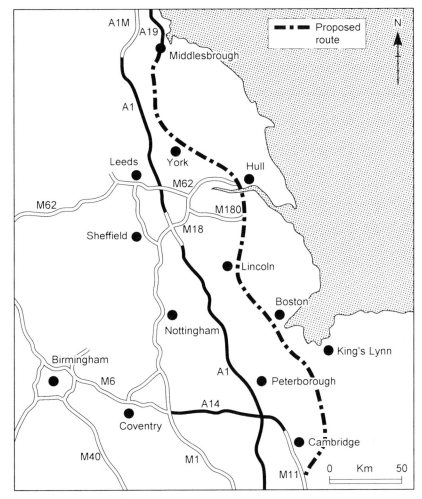

Figure 4.2 Proposed route of the £1 billion East Coast motorway

could be further argued that in the case of the Humber and pre-privatized Severn Bridges, for example, their artificially low tolls were not worth collecting if real costs were taken into account. The adoption of vehicle Toll Tags able to be monitored by electronic readers which debit the users account is a technical innovation that can reduce the fare box costs but these, like shadow tolling, can only be imposed in developed societies where comprehensive arrangements can be imposed. In the less developed Third World countries, stopping to pay remains the only feasible option.

Table 4.3 Project cashflow statement for Malaysian highway project (M$)

		Year				
		1	2	3	4	5
	Total	1992	1993	1994	1995	1996
Toll revenue	1 670 057	18 091	19 357	20 712	31 635	33 849
Ancilliary revenue	2944	50	52	54	55	57
Total inflow	1 673 002	18 141	19 409	20 765	31 690	33 907
Contract billings	304 813	12 288	66 077	87 758	69 819	58 684
Less: net retention	0	1027	5290	1879	−2891	−1430
Contract disbursements	304 813	11 261	60 787	85 879		72 710
Design fees	10 942	5823	1156	1536	1222	1027
Site costs	67 292	4601	4777	4959	5149	5346
Construction costs	383 047	21 685	66 720	92 375	79 081	66 487
Highway maintenance	83 426	5500	5693	5892	6098	6311
Toll operation	96 263	2500	2625	2756	2894	3039
Management expenses	26 342	1190	4967	6497	5253	4847
Administration expenses	57 758	1500	1575	1654	1736	1823
Performance bonds	1769	270	271	273	274	276
Insurance	13 518	1541	1547	1554	1595	1605
Concession fees	10	10				
Land acquisition costs	5000	5000				
Survey and site investigation	6096	6096				
Other preliminary expenses	3500	3500				
Total outflow	676 730	48 792	83 398	111 000	96 932	84 028
Net project cashflow	996 272	−30 651	−63 990	−90 234	−65 242	−50 121
Cummulative cashflow		−30 651	−94 641	−184 875	−250 117	−300 239
Cumulative toll revenue		18 091	37 447	58 159	89 794	123 643
Maximum deficit in year	5	Contract payback years			11	
Project internal rate	13·13%	Project payback years			13	

Construction phase

The maxim that risk is best allocated to those best able to cope is particularly applicable to the construction phase. Bankers perceive this to be the period with the greatest risk, but constructors point out there is no more risk with a BOT project than with any other construction — the same influences of weather, unforeseen ground conditions, force majeure, labour disputes and so on apply. Contract conditions with strict cost and time penalties coupled with appropriate insurance cover are put in place as with any multi-disciplinary project. The importance of comprehensive risk analysis and lump-sum, fixed price contracts, are looked at in more detail in Chapters 10, 11 and 13.

Table 4.3 (continued)

				Year					
6	7	8	9	10	11	12	13	14	15
1997	1998	1999	2000	2001	2002	2003	2004	2005	2006
36 219	46 134	49 363	52 819	61 694	66 012	70 633	82 077	87 822	93 970
119	123	127	132	136	141	146	151	156	162
36 338	46 257	49 490	52 950	61 830	66 153	70 779	82 228	87 979	94 132
10 187									
−3269	−606								
60 113	13 456	6060							
178									
1697	1775	1857	1943	2033	2127	2225	2328	2436	2549
15 331	2382	1857	1943	2033	2127	2225	2328	2436	2549
2375	2459	2545	2634	2726	2821	2920	3022	3128	3237
3191	3350	3518	3694	3878	4072	4276	4490	4714	4950
856	148	153	158	164	169	175	181	188	194
1914	2010	2111	2216	2327	2443	2566	2694	2828	2970
18	18	19	20	20	21	22	23	23	24
135	171	183	195	228	243	260	302	322	345
23 821	10 537	10 385	10 860	11 375	11 897	12 444	13 039	13 640	14 269
12 517	35 719	39 106	42 091	50 455	54 256	58 335	69 189	74 339	79 862
−287 722	−252 002	−212 897	−170 806	−120 352	−66 096	−7760	61 429	135 767	215 630
159 862	205 996	255 359	308 178	369 871	435 884	506 517	588 594	676 416	770 386

The transfer element in the BOT formula allows the receiving authority to spell out exactly what is expected at the end of the concession period but it is a low maintenance regime during the concession period that is uppermost in the concessionaire's mind. These factors combine at the design stage when durability coefficients form a key part of the input. A global characteristic of BOT projects is they are designed and built to higher standards than their traditional neighbours. With the contractors involved usually taking early equity in the venture, they are less likely to skimp on materials or to produce shoddy workmanship. This coupled with adoption of quality assurance programmes and the interacting roles of BOT projects, encourages greater cooperation and a less adversarial approach to

Table 4.4 Project cashflow statement for Malaysian highway project (M$)

		Year			
		16	17	18	19
	Total	2007	2008	2009	2010
Toll revenue	1 670 057	108 789	116 404	120 166	132 766
Ancilliary revenue	2944	168	173	179	186
Total inflow	1 673 002	108 956	116 577	120 345	132 952
Contract billings	304 813				
Less: net retention	0				
Contract disbursements	304 813				
Design fees	10 942				
Site costs	67 292	2667	2791	2921	3057
Construction costs	383 047	2667	2791	2921	3057
Highway maintenance	83 426	3351	3468	3589	3715
Toll operation	96 263	5197	5457	5730	6017
Management expenses	26 342	201	208	215	223
Administration expenses	57 758	3118	3274	3438	3610
Performance bonds	1769	25	26	27	28
Insurance	13 518	398	426	440	485
Concession fees	10				
Land acquisition costs	5000				
Survey and site investigation	6096				
Other preliminary expenses	3500				
Total outflow	676 730	14 958	15 651	16 360	17 135
Net project cashflow	996 272	93 998	100 926	103 985	115 818
Cumulative cashflow		309 627	410 554	514 539	630 356
Cumulative toll revenue		879 174	995 578	1 115 744	1 248 510
Maximum deficit in year	5				
Project internal rate	13·13%				

problem-solving. This attractive feature is not fully appreciated yet.
Early completion with the subsequent early toll revenue is another
obvious carrot for cooperation but insisting on and ensuring durable
construction is seen as paramount. Midland Expressway (BNRR)
director, Riccardo Starace, states from autostradas experience:

> Spending 2–5% more on the materials for the subgrade and pavement can
> prolong the life 50%.[4]

Fast-tracked, quality-assured construction with direct response and
responsibility by the designer are all aspects of value engineering
making demands on the consultant and construction scene around the

Table 4.4 (continued)

	Year				
20	21	22	23	24	25
2011	2012	2013	2014	2015	2016
134 520	136 396	150 631			
192	192	192			
134 712	136 589	150 823			
3199	3348	3505			
3199	3348	3505			
3845	3980	4119			
6317	6633	6965			
239	247				
3790	3980	4179			
29	30	31			
492	499	551			
17 904	18 709	19 596			
116 809	117 880	131 227			
747 165	865 045	996 272	996 272	996 272	996 272
1 383 030	1 519 427	1 670 057	1 670 057	1 670 057	1 670 057

world. The technology and information transfer that this entails is particularly attractive when promoting BOTs in the developing world.

The operational phase

This constitutes the longest period of time in the life of the venture. Promotion and marketing have convinced backers and government to launch the 'business', the constructors have taken their three to five years to create the 'business' apparatus, now all that remains is for that apparatus to perform commercially. The operation phase, in effect, is a *fait accompli* with a 'cast in place' (no pun intended) recipe for success (or failure). This is the theory, what typically are the realities?

As with all human endeavour the early conception period of development has an element of 'wish-wish' success. It is highly likely that promotion calculations will have adopted optimistic user throughputs coupled with 'lowish' operation costs reflected in maintenance and salary outlays. This legacy has elements that in part survive the scrutiny of the financial engineers and ultimately manifest themselves some way along the operational phase. It is for the operating team to recognize the 'business' fabric they have inherited. Recognition begins by identifying development phase decisions that determine operation phase criteria, as exemplified by the earlier quotation from Riccardo Starace. Minimum maintenance with minimum staff collecting 100% of the toll income are the ideals, but how can the BOT concessionaire achieve this? A crucial ingredient is to ensure experienced operational input/feedback early in the development phase to encourage realism. The concessionaires should take on board these concepts to reinforce the need for the durable construction, low maintenance equipment, efficient self-monitoring/self-auditing/toll collection and others that characterize the particular venture. In the case of a road or vehicular tunnel or bridge, for example, durable construction will have predominately concrete — not asphaltic — road pavements, composite-plastic above-ground furniture in lieu of (rusting) painted metal arrangements, non-staining and cleanable wall surfaces, self-cleansing drainage systems, limited vegetation liabilities, solid state electronics, etc. Ensuring realism during the development phase is achieved by appointing an experienced general manager after receipt of the concession. His role initially will be to comment and monitor developments so that towards the latter end of the construction phase he can recruit his operational team reflecting the strengths and weaknesses of the apparatus they will adopt. In the year before opening they will be trained and equipped to be 'up and running' from day one. Figure 4.3 outlines the arrangements typically put in place for a tolled vehicular entity.

The traffic, engineering and administrative managers roles are as follows.

(a) The traffic manager's department will include traffic control and surveillance and toll collection (except for shadow tolled projects). Operations will be handled from a central control room which monitors flows, collections, accidents, breakdowns and other emergency situations. Mimic display boards, CCTVs, vehicle loop detectors, fire and smoke sensors, computer toll monitoring and relevant back-ups are systems the traffic manager's team will utilize. His team must be trained and equipped to handle any situation at any time. Heavy recovery vehicles, fire tenders, road sweepers and washer units are examples of his vehicle fleet.

(b) The engineering manager's role is defined by preventative maintenance procedures. These ensure that at no time are traffic/revenue interrupted. Scheduled maintenance for cleaning, lighting, accident/fire alarms, emergency telephones, electrical and mechanical equipment are all undertaken on a daily basis.

(c) The administrative manager's department usually consists of three sub-sections: accounts and general office, stores and canteen. The first deals with accounting and general administration which includes toll revenue reconciliation, prepaid toll sales, personnel and salaries. The second deals with spare parts for maintenance and emergency repair of plant and equipment. The canteen will be required on a 24-hour basis, 365 days per year.

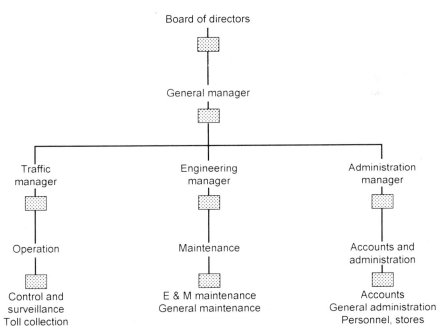

Figure 4.3 The typical arrangements for a tolled vehicular entity

Table 4.5 Proportional cost breakdown for first two years of tunnel operation

	1992/93: %	1991/92: %
Operations cost	9·6	9·6
Maintenance	5·5	3·6
Rates, wayleave, crown rent and royalties	2·4	2·2
Services (utilities, professional, insurance)	3·8	4·0
Depreciation	32·2	33·3
Financial charges (interest repayments)	46·5	47·3
Total	100·0	100·0

Table 4.5 quantifies the proportional cost breakdown for the first and second year of operating the tunnel project profiled earlier.

This twin-tubed tunnel had a throughput of 25 048 000 vehicles in year 1992/93 and is operated with 260 staff.

Before leaving the operational phase it is worth noting that as tolled projects involve cash transactions a 'reinforced honesty' regime has to be in place if abuses are to be restricted. Human nature the world over likes the challenge of circumventing supposedly theft-proof systems and procedures. It is, therefore, not surprising if a lonely toll collector on the midnight shift gives some thought to fiddling these controls. Proactive human resource management will motivate most of the team most of the time but if a weakness exists inevitably a frustrated individual will challenge the system. As a basic procedure, employees must

(a) wear a uniform and agree to body searches at any time
(b) carry no cash when in uniform
(c) not know booth allocation beforehand
(d) have vehicle classifications separately monitored and permanently recorded
(e) make end of shift pay-ins not knowing cash totals
(f) have toll income separately monitored and permanently recorded.

Operational management of a directly tolled entity has, as with any business, a number of issues to address. Many existing BOT companies now offer consultancy and training services to those who wish to learn from their experience. With the upsurge of new projects this in itself is another source of income for the operational BOT company.

The overall package

The process from conception to transfer will extend over a number of years, with the concessionaire being called upon to overcome a series of issues. The goal posts will undoubtedly be moved, especially in the development phase. The team's role is to coordinate the packaging along the way. The pitfalls are many. W.E. Stevenson[5] of the EBRD cites the following as the most likely

- inappropriate sponsor/government motivations/expectations
- mis-managed development process
- weak sponsors (corporate, individuals), government disunity
- contractor performance/financial failure
- completion delays
- cost overruns
- technical failure or obsolescence
- anaemic (weak) project economics
- uncompetitive cost structure
- contractual breakdown
- tax increases, permitting reversals
- force majeure event (physical, political, commercial, economic).

The complexity of BOT packaging as Figure 4.4 outlines, is often criticized.

Overcoming and accommodating this complexity is for the successful concessionaire to achieve. This is both an art and a science with different emphasis at different stages within each phase. The team composition will reflect the input required. One experienced team leader, J.W. Ferrigno,[6] now with Bechtel, explains:

One of the most difficult problems to deal with in the packaging of these projects is the very long development periods — up to four and five years is not unusual. This leads to the operation of the Rule of the Two Nineties: The first 90% of the task takes 10% of the time and the last 10% takes the other 90%.

In addition, the high complexities and long development periods lead to quite high development and negotiation costs and a scarcity of appropriate sources of cash equity. Indeed, finding the right project developers and investors who combine the relevant knowledge, skill and political complexion, together with the ability and willingness to commit cash equity for development and implementation is not easy. Although investment funds for sound projects are available, development capital is more scarce.

The long process from conception to completion and the inevitable setbacks can severely impact morale and sap the staff's energy and create periods of the Project Blues.

He further comments on financial engineering 'fickleties':

While representatives of financial institutions are generally highly professional and competent, project creditors, as institutions, naturally tend to vacillate, sometimes without warning, from keen interest to apathy

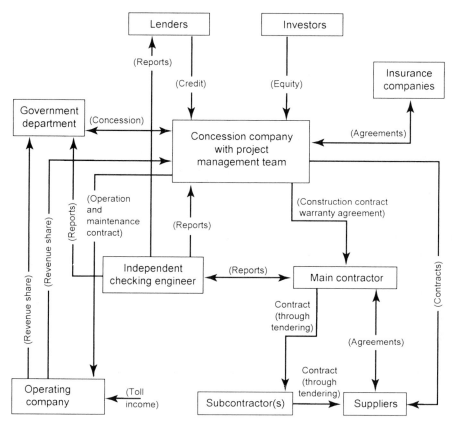

Figure 4.4 Basic organizational chart and contractual outline structure for a typical BOT

during the long development periods of BOT projects. And once internal approvals have been obtained and a commitment letter has been issued, they also have a tendency to become somewhat rigid in their thinking about the terms and conditions of the credits they have agreed to extend and of the BOT project documents. This lack of flexibility can not only prevent the successful packaging of a basically sound project, it can make a particular contender for a project uncompetitive.

In essence this packaging exercise is project management in its purest form. In the beginning the sponsor's team are promoting the concept and therefore must exude all the enthusiasm and vision of good salesmen with a background of commercial insight and market awareness. Moving into the development phase necessitates a talent for detail with a presence of innovative leadership to ensure the right element is in the right place at the right time. This development phase is the most crucial because this is where the project can become bogged down under the inertia of multidimensional negotiations restrained by sceptical funders and the pedantry of the legal profession. This requires an experienced team manager with high organizational capacity together with administrative and communication skills to overcome the many hurdles. Moving through to the construction and operational phases requires primarily planning, scheduling and analytical skills to ensure that the goose will lay golden eggs at the end of the day.

While team numbers will never be static and the number of projects in the pipeline will vary, as will the stage of development of each separate project, there is a growing trend for international contractors, design consultants, legal firms and merchants banks to retain their inhouse BOT specialists. These individuals are seconded to more than one project and are, therefore, contributing and accessing input at a number of stages on any number of jobs. Growing acceptance of BOT techniques heightens the need for BOT project managers per se which will in time evolve via academia to institutional status.

References

1. MONTAGUE A.A. Structuring BOT projects — resolving the jigsaw. *Proc. 2nd Int. Conf. on Const. Projects.* June 1989.
2. NEW CIVIL ENGINEER. Private road schemes up for grabs. *New Civil Engineer,* 21 April, 1994.
3. FARRELL S. *Private finance for new roads — measures that would make it easier to obtain.* (Private communication), January 1993.

4. NEW CIVIL ENGINEER. Costs stretch toll road team. *New Civil Engineer,* 17 June 1993.
5. STEVENSON W.E. The Turkish BOT power project experience. *Proc. EBRD Conf., Budapest.* April 1992.
6. FERRIGNO J.W. The successful packaging of BOT projects — some lessons learned, *Proc. Instn. Int. Res. Conf., Taipei.* September 1992.

Chapter 5

Financial engineering

The role of the financial adviser

Most companies undertaking BOT projects will employ a financial adviser, normally a merchant or investment bank, to assist them in the financial packaging of their proposal. It is not unusual that the financial adviser will also be assigned the task of actually raising the necessary debt and equity for the project. The financial adviser is normally appointed by the project promoters or the project company to determine the financial feasibility of the project under the limitations and constraints of the financial markets; a project that requires 20-year debt to meet some internal equity return criterion when only 10-year debt is available is probably not a viable project. Making that project viable under the constraints of financial reality requires financial engineering. Financial engineering is the purview of the financial adviser.

One critical faculty that a financial adviser brings to a project is the ability to compare the proposed BOT project to other similar projects. Most financial advisers in reputable firms will have a wealth of experience to draw on in terms of comparing the project return of a proposed toll road project to other road projects in a particular country. A financial adviser might be working on two or more BOT projects at once. Often developers and contractors are working on their first BOT project (or their first in that particular country). It may be no use to expect a 30% internal rate of return on equity for a project when other similar types of projects have accepted 20%. Likewise, if the proposed project produces a 15% return when others have produced 20% returns, is it really prudent to invest so much time, effort and capital in undertaking such a project? While that is ultimately the decision of the project promoters, the experience and counsel of the financial adviser will play a major role in that process.

The determination of whether to employ a financial adviser or not really depends on the experience and backgrounds of the project promoters. For example, most major oil companies, embarking on major oil and gas projects that will require limited recourse financing, will not employ an independent financial adviser. Their reasoning is that they generally know their business better than a banker does, and over time they have built up sufficient in-house capability to put together the financial package in a form acceptable to project lenders. Their relationships with major project lenders are also sufficiently strong to obtain valuable financial advice while arranging the debt.

Such has not been the case in most infrastructure BOT cases. Perhaps it is because developers and contractors undertake relatively few BOT projects in relation to their other lines of business that establishing the required in-house expertise is not cost-effective. Another reason may be that most BOT projects are undertaken on a consortium approach and, therefore, an independent financial adviser's view is useful in separating and smoothing over the possibly different objectives of the project partners. Yet another reason (related to the first two) is that oil companies often have the luxury of comparing the cost of limited recourse financing versus utilizing their balance sheet to raise funds. A consortium undertaking a BOT project would not entertain such a choice. It is a fact that most BOT projects around the world employ independent financial advisers to help in making those projects a reality. It is quite possible as the trend towards more BOT projects continues and develops, and as contractors develop more in-house expertise, that the need for independent financial advisers will decline. What will always be needed is the ability to find innovative financial solutions to the challenge of packaging BOT projects to raise finance.

The financial adviser is normally brought into the project at an early stage of development, certainly before the major project documents are signed. The experienced financial adviser will provide considerable value in drafting and negotiating the project documentation. His insights will focus on the financial viability of the project documents. There have been some potentially good BOT projects scuttled because the project partners were too eager to sign before checking whether the agreement would be acceptable to financial institutions. Examples of this are a power purchase agreement for a power plant that is not firm enough in its off-take arrangement, or a construction contract that allows for a high degree of remeasurement. An independent financial adviser, for whom the bulk of his remuneration is tied to the success of the project, can help project sponsors avoid such pitfalls. It is the prerogative of the project promoters whether to heed such advice.

An advantage of using an independent financial adviser is the ability to identify and source the most cost-effective financing available for the project. The financial adviser provides a valuable function in knowing the relative cost of various financing sources. He should normally not be locked into a particular source of funding and should present various options to the project promoters explaining the advantages and disadvantages of each particular funding source. In developing countries those sources may be very limited and they are often linked to sources of imported foreign equipment. A financial adviser should know of most sources of advantageous funding for the country and industry in question. Increasingly, a financial adviser for BOT projects must possess not only in-depth country and industry knowledge about financing conditions, he must also have global reach for funding sources.

BOT projects provide a virtually infinite scope for financial engineering. This stems from the variety and complexity of such endeavours. What financial engineering cannot do is to allow projects to defy gravity. Just as there are limitations to the amount of stress a steel beam can withstand, so there are constraints on the terms and conditions of financing acceptable to project investors and lenders. There is often an attempt by project promoters to pass on so much of the risk to project lenders that the lenders would be taking equity risk. No one willingly takes on equity-type risk for a banker-like return. As Peter Nevitt states:

> Lenders advance funds only where they are at least 99% sure that they will be repaid with interest. Lenders advancing funds on any other basis are flirting with bankruptcy because of the high leverage of lending institutions. Investment companies which are leveraged two to one can take equity risks. Lenders which are leveraged twenty and thirty to one are not in a position to take equity risks.[1]

Not to mislead readers, it should be stated that the laws of financial engineering are not as immutable as the laws of physics and engineering. It is more precise to say that each country and each project has its own specific gravity. This is what makes financial engineering as much art as science. For example, in Kumagai Gumi's BOT for the Sydney Harbour Tunnel, Westpac (the financial adviser) was able to place 40-year bonds with Australian institutional investors, while in one of Vietnam's first Build Own Operate (BOO) projects, the renovation of the Thong Nhat Metropole Hotel in Hanoi, a US$5 million loan for five years had to be shared among three banks and offshore support still had to be offered.

Another important function of the financial adviser in a BOT project (which we have already noted most often involves a consortium approach) is the identification and allocation of risks. The author has been adviser to a few consortia where screaming matches between promoters occurred over the allocation and pricing of risks. Occasionally, the financial adviser is invited to join in the match to scream or be screamed at; most often, the adviser should play the role of referee rather than participant. It is the job of the financial adviser to obtain the lowest cost, most effective financing for his client. This can only be achieved by correctly identifying the project risks and allocating those risks to the parties that are best able to undertake them. The principle is that those parties best able to take the risk will be best able to price it. Part of the financial adviser's role is to ensure that those covered risks are adequately priced. Financial engineering comes into play when a particular risk (e.g. completion risk) is divided among several parties (e.g. the contractor, the project company and the shareholders). It may also be necessary to bring other parties to the table if none of the existing project sponsors is able or willing to effectively price a particular risk.

Finally, a financial adviser should be able to assist the project promoters in the extensive negotiations that will take place in a BOT project. These will entail negotiations with the relevant governmental authorities, with the contractor, with suppliers of equipment, with funding institutions and passive investors. It is frequently useful to have independent advisers on board who can provide dispassionate advice in the midst of often tense and sometimes tedious negotiations. The financial adviser should be able to provide valuable financial engineering every step of the project development stage until the successful conclusion of negotiations.

Financial modelling

This subject is discussed in Chapter 9, but in the context of financial engineering, the computerized financial model plays a critical part. Just as the engineer's blueprint should reflect how a power plant should be built, so the financial model should reflect the financial condition intended for the project. In most BOT projects, the financial adviser has the responsibility of developing the computerized financial model. Constant reworking of the model utilizing various sensitivities is often how ideas for creative financial engineering are born.

Financial engineering objectives and methods

Financial engineering for BOT projects essentially comes in two forms.

(*a*) Structuring the various agreements related to a BOT so as to enhance the creditworthiness of the borrower. The credit enhancement reduces the risk to lenders and lowers the cost of borrowing to the concession company.

(*b*) The development of innovative financial instruments that improve the viability of the project. This serves to improve the attractiveness of the project to other equity investors and potential project lenders.

Enhancement of credit structure

Because of the complex nature of most BOT projects, most financial engineering comes under the category of credit enhancement. Clearly, there is a growing trend particularly in the more developed financial markets to apply increasingly sophisticated financial instruments to limited recourse project financing. However, most BOT projects continue to be financed primarily by commercial bank loans. Unless and until institutional investors are willing and able to analyse and accept limited or non-recourse project risk, most financial engineering will centre on the manipulation of the project structure.

Enhancement of the credit structure not only has implications for the borrowing cost to the concession company but also can have a significant commercial impact as well. An example of this was the troubled Second Stage Expressway project in Bangkok.

The First Stage Expressway (FSE) was built and owned by ETA, the Expressway Authority of Thailand. The Second Stage Expressway (SSE), while linked to the FSE, was undertaken by a consortium led by Kumagai Gumi on a BOT basis. The traffic on the SSE alone was not sufficient to service the debt required nor to provide an adequate return. The revenue of the FSE was considerably greater and, more importantly, proven. A proposal was made by the SSE consortium to request a revenue-sharing scheme between the FSE and the SSE over the 27-year operating period of the concession. To its credit, ETA saw the necessity of such a compromise and accepted it in principle. As it was finally negotiated, the SSE project company (called BECL) would receive 60% of the combined revenues of the FSE and the SSE during the first 9 years of the operating period. ETA and BECL would split evenly the revenues of the two expressways for the second 9-year period. For the remaining 9-year period, BECL would receive 40% of the revenues while ETA received 60%.

What would have been a non-viable project was made feasible by financial engineering. Another example of where financial engineering can enhance the viability of the project was the Bristol Light Rail Project in the UK.[2] The need for new intraurban rail transportation to relieve road congestion is recognized the world over. While there is significant scope and interest for private sector involvement, no rail projects are financially viable on a standalone basis. It was clear to the sponsors of the project, Advanced Transport for Avon Ltd (ATA), that some government funding would be necessary but a critical objective was to minimize the use of public funds for the project. A scheme was developed that sought contributions from property developers, landowners and shopkeepers who would make contributions to the Bristol Light Rail in recognition of the enhancement of land values along the railway's route. The intent was to give ATA a guaranteed level of contribution over time in return for ATA building and operating a railway. Since the contributions were to be made over time, the funding in the interim period was to be provided by commercial banks. A more recent example of a successful rail project being financed on a BOT basis, in fact, the first in Asia, is the Kuala Lumpur Light Rail Project for which the Hong Kong & Shanghai Banking Corporation (HSBC) acted as the financial adviser. In that project, the issue of the insufficiency of the farebox revenue was resolved after considerable negotiation with the granting of some property development rights by the municipal government of Kuala Lumpur at concessionary pricing in order to make the entire project viable.

In the examples above, while the financial advisers may have helped engineer the solutions to the projects' feasibility, none of those projects could have been successfully financed without the recognition by the host government that some form of compromise was necessary in order to attract private sector investment on a BOT basis. Based on these and other BOT experiences, one could draw the conclusion that the best way to achieve government financial support for a project is to request indirect funding from the government through subsidized property development rights or deferral of the host government's share of the revenue for a period of time. The latter could be done through revenue sharing as in the SSE case, or for example through tax holidays, or as in the United States, marketed through the granting of tax-exempt mutual bonds.

Governments tend to shy away from requests for direct funding to enhance the viability of a BOT scheme. An example where this did occur was in the North – South Highway in Malaysia where the government of Malaysia provided the project company with a subordinated loan which could be drawn if project revenues fell below a projected target level. These funds ultimately have to be repaid by the concession company, but the support by the government of a certain level of revenues provided sufficient comfort to Malaysian banks for them to lend to the project.

Another aspect of credit enhancement that requires financial engineering skills is the allocation of risks. It has been said that 'project finance is a shifty business'. It often boils down to who takes the risks and how much risk is taken. The various parties to a BOT project are continually vying to shift certain risks away from themselves and on to other parties. In quite a number of BOT projects, the success of the project hinges on the correct allocation of the risks to the various parties. The financial adviser and project sponsors can use the 'empty chair theory of financial engineering' which can be attributed to Glenn Van Schalkwyk of Toronto Dominion Bank.[3] During negotiations, if there is a deadlock among the various parties to the project as to who takes a particular risk, value added financial engineering can be achieved by asking if there is some other party that can fill 'the empty chair', i.e. take the risk and adequately price it. An example of this technique was evident in the first privatized power project in Asia, Hopewell Holdings Shajiao B Power Plant in the People's Republic of China. The off-taker of the power from the 750 MW plant was the Guangdong General Power Company (GGPC). The difficulty was that the GGPC was an unknown entity to international bank lenders and not licensed to deal in foreign exchange. Furthermore, its entire revenues were based in renmenbi (the PRC currency) which at that time foreigners were not allowed to hold. Thus the natural offtaker of the power, GGPC, was an unknown credit risk. Lenders did not know how to price that risk and the project sponsors were unwilling or unable to take that risk. A solution was found by inviting Guangzhou International Trust and Investment Company (GITIC) to fill the empty chair. GITIC, which is a trading and investment company with significant holdings in Hong Kong as well as in China had borrowed internationally and was an acceptable credit risk to international lenders. Furthermore it had considerable revenue in foreign currency and was authorized to deal in foreign exchange. GITIC guaranteed GGPC's power purchase payments to the international lenders. The lenders were still taking a risk on Hopewell's ability to produce the power, but the payment risk of GGPC had been taken by GITIC and reasonably priced.

Allocation of risk and the scope for financial engineering

The allocation of risk begins with the identification of two broad categories of risk in a BOT project: investors' risks and lenders' risks. Emerson[4] states:

> Investors are at risk when they decide to support a project with their participation in the equity and their legally binding agreement to provide any additional finance necessary to satisfy the lenders to the project. The degree to which investors can minimise these risks depends on the degree to which they can reduce their equity participation to the project by introducing other equity and loan finance to the project or transfer the identified risks to third parties.

He further identifies lenders as being concerned about the adequate allocation and provision for certain categories of risk. He states:

> . . . lenders are usually prepared to accept only those (risks) which apply once production has begun leaving pre-completion risks with the investors in the project.

While in a broad sense that is true, the general experience of BOT projects is that the project promoters and contractor try to place as much of the pre-completion risk onto the lenders as possible. No issue in a BOT project engenders more lively debate than the issue of completion risk and its allocation to the various parties. Equally large amounts of value-added financial engineering and diplomacy are required to resolve this thorny issue. As Emerson notes, the standard structure for completion risk in a BOT project is a fixed-price, fixed-time construction contract with a reputable contractor with adequate penalties for delays and cost overruns. This contractor's obligation is often accompanied by a completion guarantee from the shareholders to cover any cost overruns and delays that are not the responsibility of the contractor under the construction contract. These latter may be due to variation orders requested either by the concession company or the host government. By structuring a tight construction contract, the shareholders' risk is minimized and the party that is best able to assess and price the risk (the contractor) takes most of the risk. The shareholders' obligation may be on a joint and several (or possibly only several) basis depending on the relative strength of the shareholders. The lenders are not taking direct technical completion risk, the area of project risk they are least able to assess or accept.

From a lender's perspective that is perhaps the ideal structure for covering completion risk in BOT projects. In reality, lenders are not always so well covered in terms of the exposure to cost overruns and delays, as lenders to Eurotunnel and the North–South Highway in

Malaysia can attest. In Eurotunnel, a combination of variation orders on the fixed portion of the construction contract, and significant remeasurement on the rail car supply contract coupled with the lack of shareholder completion guarantees led to massive refinancing requirements from lenders which were clearly not anticipated at the outset of the project. The lack of shareholder support for completion risk placed that risk on the lenders (as well as shareholders).

The Eurotunnel example shows how financial engineering can sometimes backfire. Because of the massive scope of the undertaking, a considerable amount of equity would need to be raised from sources outside the Anglo-French contracting consortium. The joint companies were allowed to issue shares first in private placements with institutional investors and then to the public in a massive initial public offering (IPO), even though the company was not at that point even a hole in the ground. While the equity and the debt were successfully arranged, the wide distribution of shares diffused power in the equity shareholders so much that the contractors had effective control over the project companies as well as the contracting consortium. Because the shareholding group was widely distributed, the contractors could effectively issue claims for variation orders with little control by the non-contracting shareholders. This situation was remedied (after many showdowns) by the imposition of more management controls over Eurotunnel but not before cost overruns exceeded 100% of the original estimated cost of the project.

By permitting public flotation of equity shares in a project of this nature, the British and French authorities allowed the project to proceed but to the detriment of many shareholders unschooled in project finance. The shareholding public should not feel too sheepish, however, as they were in company with many of the world's top institutional investors and most of the top project finance lending banks. Since that time, it has been declared that lenders and investors are more knowledgeable and less naive. Many of the top institutional investors who are keen to invest in BOT projects will not get involved in a project unless they take absolutely no completion risk.

Lenders may be asked to take some of the completion risk by agreeing to fund a portion of the cost overruns up to a maximum amount. Anything above that amount would have to be financed by additional equity. The level of any standby loan and equity facilities is a function of the viability of the project and the reputation of the contractor to deliver a project on time and on budget. The short history of remeasured contracts and BOT projects has not been illuminating. Lenders and non-contracting shareholders should generally insist on fixed-price contracts for BOT projects, The importance of the risks of cost overruns and delays cannot be over-emphasized. For example, a cost overrun of 10% and a year's delay in completion at 10% interest will raise the project cost by 40%.

This fact emphasizes that pre-completion risks are often perceived to be greater than post-completion market risks for BOT projects. This is in contrast to most industrial projects in which the risk of product obsolescence and competitive market forces create greater risk during operation. Looked at in that way, BOT projects can be viewed as two distinct projects. The first phase is a high-risk construction project; the second phase is a relatively low-risk utility project. This dual-risk profile means that for equity investors, there is generally a high reward during the early phase (large capital gains followed by a lower reward in the latter phase (steadily increasing dividend flows). The two-stage nature of infrastructure projects should be reflected in the credit facility. Clearly, a utility such as a power station or railway, once in operation, should be able to command finer terms than those of pre-completion project loans because of the lower risk lenders would be asked to accept. Similar financial engineering issues can arise for all the other major credit and contractual arrangements associated with BOT projects. For example, in the Hopewell Navotas Power Project in the Philippines the offtaker was NAPOCOR, the state-owned power authority. NAPOCOR was in dire financial condition and therefore the central government of the Philippines had to guarantee its payment obligations to project lenders and add sufficient creditworthiness to the off-take arrangement. In other countries, the local power authority may have a sufficiently high standard of creditworthiness where government support is not necessary. Negotiations on the offtake agreement for a power project may centre on the strength of the off-take. Is it a tight take or pay contract? How are tariffs to be adjusted? What are the formulae for capacity and energy charges? All of these issues provide scope for financial engineering.

The purposes of financial engineering of credit and contractual agreements are to reduce the costs of the project and to enhance the project viability. Financial advisers should be able to justify their fee by the savings in project costs which their financial engineering produces.

Financial engineering through the use of financial instruments

The success of BOT project financing comes down to cashflow. In terms of structuring levels of debt and equity in projects, a common philosophy is to utilize as much debt as the project cashflows permit so as to realize an attractive return for the shareholders. There are no hard and fast rules as to the correct amount of debt and equity. While each project is different, the less equity in a project the greater the threats to the project cashflow. A more unstable cashflow means greater risk of non-repayment to the lenders and no dividends to the shareholders. Thus in order to enhance the return to shareholders while at the same time protecting to some degree against the risks to cashflow, more innovative financing instruments and techniques are required.

While specific financial instruments that can be applied to BOT projects will be discussed in more detail in Chapter 6, some discussion on financial engineering must entail a discussion of financial instruments.

One way to enhance the return to shareholders is the use of mezzanine finance in BOT projects. In its broadest sense mezzanine finance is the gap between senior debt and ordinary share capital. The choice of a particular type of instrument in the mezzanine layer of a financing package depends upon several factors.

(a) The project's prospective cashflow.
(b) The cost of the instrument.
(c) The legal and tax consequences of utilizing the instrument.
(d) The capital structure of the project company, existing and prospective,
(e) The risk/reward perceptions of the financing institutions involved.
(f) The size and purpose of the financing.

From the point of view of lending institutions, the attraction of providing mezzanine finance stems from the higher yield which can be obtained by the provision of this type of finance, particularly in light of the eroding margins on traditional lending. The returns expected by lenders for mezzanine finance obviously vary and depend heavily on the perceived risk of the project but in general will be upwards of 3% above more senior levels of debt. Higher risk instruments which more closely resemble equity in the mezzanine spectrum will command a considerably higher return on capital, usually in the 15–20% range.

On the debt side, because most capital market investors normally look for high-quality assets, innovative financing instruments for BOT projects tend to be issued with an underlying bank guarantee of the project risk. The advantages to the project of accessing the capital markets rather than conventional medium term bank finance include the following.

(*a*) The principal characteristics of capital market instruments is that they enable borrowers to broaden the base of institutions and individuals from which they can raise funds. Because the instruments are 'negotiable' they can be more easily traded.

(*b*) The wider range of investors which are thereby accessed reduces the cost to the borrower through competition and the different return expectations of the investors.

(*c*) The return to the investors on BOT projects are normally better than on more conventional investment instruments.

(*d*) Banks, increasingly under pressure to maintain adequate capital resources to support their risk assets, have responded to the challenge of the capital markets by developing their ability to place and trade the new instruments.

Borrowers need to consider a variety of factors in determining the most appropriate capital market instruments for their requirements. Factors such as:

- drawdown and repayment profiles
- currency mix
- the level of protection required against interest rate movements
- balance sheet structure.

Most BOT projects except in the more developed financial markets find it difficult to utilize sophisticated capital market instruments during the construction phase of the project. Increasingly, the ability of financial institutions to securitize and package project debt will mean more cost-effective financing of BOT projects.

References

1. NEVITT P.K. *Project financing*. Euromoney Publications, UK, 1983, 4th edn.
2. HOUSTON C.D.S. The Bristol Light Rail Project. *Proc. Instn. Int. Res. Proj. Conf. on Finance, Hong Kong.* October 1989.
3. VAN SCHALKWYK G. *Negotiating project financing: some how-to hints.* Toronto Dominion Bank, Toronto, 1984.
4. EMERSON C. *Project financing.* The Financial Times Business Enterprises Ltd, UK, 1983.

Chapter 6

Financing techniques

Introduction

Even in the most sophisticated markets, most BOT projects have been financed with straightforward equity and commercial bank debt. However, as bankers and investors become more familiar with BOT financing risks, innovations in financial instruments and BOT structures are being made. Competition drives innovation. Competition brings down the price that the sponsors bid to obtain the concession. As a result, cost savings have to be achieved elsewhere if the project's viability is to be maintained. Thus, there is a need for financial instruments and structures that achieve the sponsors' objectives. This chapter will not be a primer on basic corporate finance but assumes some fundamental knowledge of that subject. The purpose is to familiarize the reader with common parlance, financial instruments and techniques in BOT financing.

Equity in BOT projects

In the early stages of BOT project development, the projects were often contractor-driven. The contracting group (often made up of several contractors) would undertake to provide most of the equity for the project. As more companies saw the benefits of BOT projects and how they could fit into their general corporate strategy, the proportion of equity undertaken by the contractor diminished. Conversely, the stake taken by developers and pure investors increased. This generally suited the contractor whose major objective was to win the construction contract. Contractors were normally thinly capitalized and highly leveraged and preferred not to see large amounts of their capital tied up for many years as investments. Their preference was to recoup their capital quickly and move on to the next contract to be won. Thus marriage between contractors and longer-term developers/investors was an inevitable development in BOT projects. A further refinement of the process is the introduction of institutional investors whose major motivation is the return they obtain from the project's cashflows. This has had a positive significant impact on the structuring of BOT projects.

The introduction of long-term developers and investors in BOT projects was a consequence of the development of the BOT market. This was aided by the ultimate objective of the contractor and the constraints on contractors' capital. The benefits are a more realistic long-term approach to BOT projects and more careful scrutiny of the associated risks in a BOT project. For example, a contractor who took 100% of the equity in an early BOT project would have the profitability of the construction contract and the profitability of the venture as a measure of its return. The contractor might be willing to accept a lower than market return during the operational phase because of the anticipated profit in the construction contract. Developers who would consider the operation of the facility might earn a management fee during operation to supplement their overall return on investment or calculate the possible ancillary benefits of property development, but pure investors would have only the projected return on the project's cashflows. The introduction of pure investors into the equity of BOT projects adds a discipline that could easily be overlooked in earlier projects.

An example of varying equity returns

Let us assume a bridge project is to be undertaken on a BOT basis. The total investment cost is US$100 million (including capitalized interest). The concession will run for 20 years after completion of the bridge (assume two years' construction). Equity will represent 20% of the investment. The remainder is provided by a commercial bank loan on a non-recourse basis for 10 years at 10% interest. Equity will be held equally by a contractor, a well-known bridge operator and two insurance companies who view this as a good long-term investment. The projected return on the bridge is an internal rate of return of 18% for the entire concession. The value of the construction contract is US$75 million. The contractor will make a 10% profit on the contract. The operator will charge a 5% management fee on revenues for managing the project. Revenues will increase by 10% per annum. If we assume the contractor receives his profit at the end of the construction period (in reality the contractor aims to receive his profit throughout the construction period), then we produce these very different returns on equity investment. Keep in mind that each investor has put up US$5 million in equity.

	IRR return (22 Years): %
Contractor's return	44·10
Operator's return	33·25
Insurance company's return	18·00

If the contractor had taken 100% of the equity in this project, his total return would fall to 23·15% because it would diminish the impact of the construction contract profit. This example helps illustrate the dynamics of equity returns for BOT projects. Clearly, it is in the interest of the contractor to diminish his equity stake in the project and to increase the profitability of the venture from his perspective. However, the less equity the contractor takes the less control he has over the terms and conditions of the concession and the construction contract. That is why many BOT projects have been contractor-driven in the early phases of development. Subsequently, the contractor then reduces its share in the equity as the project goes forward. It is also easy to see why a contractor may naturally be less concerned with the terms and conditions of the operational phase of the project. The contractor may be willing to accept a lower tariff for the traffic because most of his profit has already been recouped before the first vehicle crosses the bridge.

In the event a developer takes over the operation of the facility, the returns that he can generate can be considerably higher than the project return. In reality, the concession company would probably undertake the management of the bridge itself, keeping the profits to return to its shareholders, but such an arrangement would not be unheard of for a power plant, waste treatment plant or other more complex projects.

The pure investor in the equity for BOT projects can generally expect to receive a return projected to be in the 15–25% range. This depends on the nature of the project, the country involved and the level of financial leverage. While this is an attractive return by comparison to many other investments, the pure investor finds itself on the bottom of the equity pile in terms of return and in the least control over risks. The pure investor insists on tight construction contracts and financially robust revenue projections and agreements. The pure investor adds discipline to the project structure by scrutinizing the terms and conditions of both the construction and operational phases of the project.

Another way sponsors of BOT projects differentiate their return from pure investors is by recognizing the value of their early development funds at a premium. Using the example above, let us designate the contractor and the developer as the sponsors of the project. Let us assume they spend US$1 million in developing the concept for the project (this would include basic design, traffic studies and financial advice). It is their intention to invite the two insurance companies to invest in the project once the basic proposal has been finalized. The sponsors believe that the value of their seed capital of $1 million should be doubled if the project comes to fruition because this capital was at risk before all necessary approvals have been obtained. The pure investors who would only invest once all the agreements have been reached would be asked to pay a premium for their shares, in this instance a 10% premium.

Value of sponsor development costs	$1 million
Value of risk capital	$2 million
Total value of required equity	$20 million
Sponsors' cash contribution	$9 million
Pure investors' cash contribution	$11 million
Sponsors' share in profits	50%
Investors' share in profits	50%
Sponsors' return	19.11%
Investors' return	17·03%

This is a simplified example. In reality, the sponsors' premium would depend on whether investors would still find this project attractive at the lower return. If not, the sponsors might have to discount the value of their venture capital return. Furthermore, the premium paid by the investors would be reduced as 80% of the sponsor's venture capital return would be funded by debt, thus reducing the investor's premium to 2% (20% of 10%).

Types of equity in BOT projects

Lenders to BOT projects want to see the sponsors put equity into their projects. There have been some prominent examples of BOT projects where minimal equity is invested, examples are the Sydney Harbour Tunnel and the Dartford Bridge Crossing, but as Nevitt[1] points out:

> Lenders look to the equity investment as providing a margin of safety. They have two primary motivations for requiring equity investments in projects which they finance:

1. Lenders expect the projected cashflows generated by the project to be sufficient to pay operating expenses, service debt and provide a very comfortable margin of safety to meet any contingencies which might arise. The more burden the debt service puts on the cashflow of the project, the greater the lenders' risk.

2. Lenders do not want the sponsors to be in a position to walk away easily from the project. They want sponsors to have enough at stake to motivate them to see the project through to a successful conclusion.

The usual form of equity in BOT projects is common shares all having equal voting rights, although in the North–South Highway project in Malaysia, subcontractors and the government employee pension fund subscribed M$1 billion (US$250 million) in redeemable convertible cumulative preference shares in the toll road company. Preference shares are not, however, used widely in BOT projects because of their nature. BOT projects need to minimize their obligations during the construction phase and the issuance of preference shares (even cumulatively) does not help a project in its early stages. More common is the issuance of different classes of common shares with different voting rights. In some BOT projects, the host government is given a golden share which provides them with a veto power in case of change of ownership or control of the project company. As host governments become more comfortable with the BOT process and are more prepared to relinquish control, this golden share obligation becomes less common.

Equity or quasi-equity instruments

A major reason why more exotic types of equity are not used is that BOT projects are complex enough at the early stages of development and intricate equity structures are distractions from the task at hand. As institutional investors become more comfortable with assessing the risks of a BOT project, there may be the possibility that they will find such alternatives to be attractive investments. Examples of these types of instruments are as follows.

(a) Preference shares — shares giving the investor the right to a fixed return through dividends.

(b) Convertible preference shares — shares giving the investor the right to a fixed dividend return and to convert to ordinary share capital at a future date.

(c) Redeemable preference shares — shares giving the investor the right to a fixed return and to obtain repayment of the investment at the end of a stated period.

(d) Unsecured loan stock — fixed interest loan stock that gives the investor the right to a fixed return and to obtain repayment of principal at the end of a stated period.

(e) Convertible unsecured loan stock — fixed interest loan stock with the right to convert to ordinary share capital at a future date.

These types of instrument may be used to construct a mezzanine layer of a financial package. The choice of a particular type of instrument depends upon:

- the project's projected cashflow
- the cost of the instrument
- the legal and tax consequences of utilizing the instrument
- the existing and prospective capital structure of the project company
- the risk/reward perceptions of the investors involved
- the size and purpose of the financing.

The most common form of mezzanine financing is the shareholder loan that may take on the characteristics of either debt or equity depending on the project and the factors stated above.

For institutional investors, the attraction of providing mezzanine finance stems from the higher yield that can be contained by the provision of this sort of finance. The returns expected by institutional investors for providing mezzanine finance obviously vary and depend heavily on the perceived risk of the project. In general, the rate will be upwards of 4% above the cost of senior debt. Higher risk instruments which more closely resemble equity in the mezzanine spectrum will command a considerably higher return on capital, usually in the region of 20% or more on an internal rate of return basis.

For project sponsors, the attraction of obtaining mezzanine finance from third parties stems from the lower levels of equity which it is necessary to provide in support of a project. This has the twin advantages of reducing the need for what is for most companies a scarce commodity, equity, and boosting the yield on the equity that is provided. Let us look at the impact of mezzanine finance through an example.

(a) Table 6.1 shows a project that costs US$1 billion to build. The debt to equity ratio is 70:30. The cost of bank financing is 10% per annum repayable over 10 years. Also, assume that cash available for debt service and dividends is US$200 million per annum.

   The equity investors in this project could look to a projected return of 16·43% in 10 years for this project.

(b) Assume the same project, but the shareholders can only raise US$150 million in equity. They do not want to relinquish control

Table 6.1 The impact of mezzanine finance: a US$1 billion example financed solely through equity and debt

Year	0	1	2	3	4	5	6	7	8	9	10
Debt	700	630	560	490	420	350	280	210	140	70	0
Equity	300										
Cashflow		200	200	200	200	200	200	200	200	200	200
Interest		102	91	80·5	70	59·5	49	38·5	28	18	7
Loan Pmt		70	70	70	70	70	70	70	70	70	70
Dividends		28	39	49·5	60	70·5	81	91·5	102	112	123

IRR (ten years) 16·43%

of the company. The bank lenders are not comfortable with their debt service ratios falling further. A mezzanine investor is found who would agree to buy redeemable preferred shares earning 14% interest p.a., repayable in the tenth year of operation. Table 6.2 shows what the cashflows and returns would look like.

The equity investors would have improved their return from 16·43% to 20·33% by using mezzanine finance for this project, while retaining 100% control of the company.

Table 6.2 The impact of mezzanine finance: a US$1 billion example incorporating mezzanine finance

Year	0	1	2	3	4	5	6	7	8	9	10
Debt	700	630	560	490	420	350	280	210	140	70	0
Pref. Stk.	150										
Equity	150										
Cashflow		200	200	200	200	200	200	200	200	200	200
Interest		102	91	80·5	70	59·5	49	38·5	28	18	7
Pref. Div		21	21	21	21	21	21	21	21	21	21
Loan Pmt		70	70	70	70	70	70	70	70	70	170
Dividends		7	18	28·5	39	49·5	60	70·5	81	91	12·5

IRR (ten years) 20·33%

Debt financing of BOT projects

Most BOT projects in the world have been financed primarily with commercial bank debt. Yet there are several alternatives available including the issuance of publicly rated bonds. This section will examine the major sources of debt financing for BOT projects, their limitations, relative advantages and issues critical to debt providers for BOT projects.

Commercial bank loans

Commercial banks were the first lending institutions to accept the concept of lending to a project based on the cashflows of the project with no or only limited recourse to the shareholders. The early developers of this type of lending were the oil and mining companies. It was reasoned that the techniques developed in lending to extractive industries could also be applied in many instances to infrastructure projects. From a lender's perspective, infrastructure projects were viewed as less technical and less risky. As banks painfully learned from their mistakes in early BOT lending situations, they refined their requirements for successful financing of BOT projects. The rapid economic developments in Asia in the 1980s and Latin America in the 1990s have allowed these techniques learned in home countries to be applied internationally. This, of course, added another dimension to the BOT lending analysis that is the element of political risk. Political risk will be discussed in more detail in Chapters 10 and 11.

It may be useful to look at a typical terms and conditions sheet for bank financing of a BOT infrastructure project (see Appendix). The 'term sheet' becomes the basis for the loan agreement and must naturally coincide with the other project agreements. While the term sheet is drawn from a real life example, we will use the example from earlier in this chapter and call the borrower the ABC Bridge Company Ltd. As you will recall, the shareholders were going to inject US$20 million in equity into the project and seek a loan from commercial banks of US$80 million. The arranging bank (the bank that structures and syndicates the finance) would seek to arrange financing on the terms detailed.

If we look at the important elements of this term sheet, it will serve to highlight the areas critical to lenders of BOT projects, the potential areas of conflict and how they are structured into acceptable project documentation.

The name of the borrower establishes the loan to the project company. The purpose of the loan is also clearly stated. The amount of the loan is also firmly established. The availability period establishes the period in which the loan can be drawn. Then, the project company can draw on the loan during the construction period but no later than two years after signing of the loan documentation. If there is any amount undrawn at the end of the construction period, it would no longer be available to the borrower and the amount of the loan would be reduced. The significance of the availability period is that if the amount is not fully drawn, but the contractor has not completed the toll bridge in the time permitted, the project company will not be able to draw down on the loan. If the project company wants to complete the project they must inject more equity. In this way, lenders exert some control over the project company and the contractor to complete the project on time.

The drawdown clause establishes minimum drawdowns. The reason for this is to ease the administrative burden of the agent bank. Each drawdown needs to be recorded and a separate interest rate established. Drawdowns in project loans are often tied to certain construction milestones that reduce the chances of too many drawdowns. It also ensures that the contractor and the borrower keep the project on track.

The commitment fee is payment to the lenders for their commitment to continue to lend to the project. The fee is paid on the undrawn portion of the loan. As construction progresses and the loan is drawn down, the amount of the commitment fee is reduced. At the end of construction, the loan amount will be fully drawn and the commitment fee payment will be zero.

The management fee is payable up-front upon loan signing and is a further inducement for the lenders to support the project. In larger transactions, the management fees can be divided between underwriting fees (which would normally be a smaller fee on the amount of a loan underwritten) and participation fees (a larger fee on the amount lent).

The interest rate is the price lenders charge for lending their money to the project. The spread is the lenders' profit. It is a reflection of the lenders' perceived risk in the project. In our case study, the lenders are most concerned with the project's risk during construction so their spread is 1·25% during the construction period. Once the project is completed, the lenders believe there will be less risk to them, so they lower the spread to 1% over their cost of funds. In our case, there is a further reduction in the lenders' perception of risk once the Cashflow Adequacy Test (CAT) is met. The greater the cashflow of the project, the more protection lenders have for their loans. Then, once the Debt Service Coverage Ratio (DSCR) exceeds 1·25 then the spread is reduced to 0·75%. There are many variations on spread strategy for project loans. For example, if the shareholders in the project company were particularly strong and gave their guarantee to the lenders during the construction period, the spread during the construction phase would be likely to be lower than the spread post-construction. Another example of spread variation is if lenders perceive there to be more risk in the project over time or that the project requires a longer duration than lenders may feel comfortable with. Lenders might then charge a higher spread during the latter years of the loan.

The loan principal repayment schedule in commercial bank loans for BOT projects is usually tailored to the cashflows of the project. In our case study, the repayments are graduated to reflect the fact that traffic would normally be expected to increase over time. The lenders want to see their loans repaid when possible and yet do not want to make loan repayment too burdensome to the project company. Another form of repayment is equal quarterly or semi-annual payments. This is more common for export credits or for projects where revenues peak more quickly such as in power or telecommunications projects. It is also becoming more common in BOT projects to see at least some financing with principal repayment at final maturity. In finance terms, this is called a bullet payment. Bank credit committees generally frown on bullet payments and the repayment schedule is more common in bonds and other capital market instruments. To be able to use capital markets instruments generally implies stronger creditworthiness than most BOT projects initially show. However, the use of capital markets instruments is a growing trend in the financing of BOT projects and will be discussed more fully later in this chapter.

In the case of the toll bridge, the definition of project completion is important as it triggers several events. From the lenders' perspective, it means the riskiest part of the project is completed. Lenders will often seek independent verification that the project is complete. In this instance, it is the independent engineer who certifies completion. For more technically complex projects, lenders may have their own technical adviser who will also verify completion. The lenders also insist on verification that the host government considers the project complete. Without government approval, both lenders and borrower may be ready to operate but will not be able to. Any significant delay at this stage can greatly affect the viability of the project because of the accumulation of interest on the debt. A critical factor, therefore, in the building of BOT projects is the maintenance of very regular contact with the host government. The lenders will also want to make sure that the toll bridge can handle traffic for a reasonable period without mishap. Again, this is more critical in BOT projects such as power stations and telecommunications projects where much more could go wrong. This time is usually called the 'test-run' or 'performance test' period. The project will not be certified completed until the bridge passes this test.

For the borrower, completion signals the commencement of revenue and a reduction in the cost of its debt. You will recall that the lenders agreed to lower their spread after completion and will lower it further once there is a sufficient level of cashflow protection. It is now that the shareholders will start to realize their investment return and must go about the business of operating a toll bridge.

The contractor's obligations to the project begin to fall away at this point. He will still be liable for any structural defects in the bridge for a period, but responsibility for the regular care and maintenance has passed to the project company. He has been paid the contracted amount, taken his profit and is ready to move on to the next project.

The cancellation clause is standard in many loan agreements and allows the borrower to cancel any portion of the loan that is not drawn by project completion date. If for example, the bridge was built for $10 million less than projected so that only $70 million was drawn, then the borrower could cancel the remaining $10 million worth of loans. If this clause were not there, even though the project company could not draw down on the facility because of the expiration of the availability period, they would continue to pay commitment fees on the total amount.

The DSCR is the most common financial ratio used in cashflow lending. It has many variations but it measures the level of protection the cashflows of the project provide for servicing of principal and interest on the debt. In the loan agreement, when the cashflow of the project exceeds 1·25 times debt service for a given year then the CAT has been met. This means a further reduction in the loan spread charged by the lenders. It is also a trigger for the payment of dividends. Lenders want to make sure that there is adequate protection for repayment of their loans before they allow shareholders to start making a return on their investment.

The security documentation is a critical part of the financing of BOT projects. It is the protection lenders will have if something goes wrong with the project either in the construction or operation phase of the project. In practice, the lenders are not seeking to exercise their rights under the security package at the first sign of trouble, but to use their security position as leverage to get the borrower and contractor to fulfil their obligations. Lenders normally do not have an interest in building or operating infrastructure projects. They will be prepared to do so if something goes disastrously wrong in order to protect their loans. In some developing countries where foreign lenders may lend to BOT projects, lenders would not be allowed to take over the project upon liquidation, so they will seek other assurances from the host government regarding their rights as lenders. The security package for lenders to BOT projects is usually much more extensive than shown above but this captures the essential elements of a common security agreement.

The provision that the lenders are named 'loss payees' under the insurance means that they will be paid on any claims arising from payment under the insurance policies taken out by the project company or the lenders. This puts the lenders in a stronger bargaining position in a significant insurance claim such as part of the bridge collapsing. As loss payee they will control how the funds from claims will be disbursed, whether to use it to repay the bank debt or allow the project company to rebuild the bridge. The rights of the borrower under the insurance policies are also assigned to the lenders. Adequate insurances are a crucial part of the security of lenders.

Beside insurances, the project company will assign its rights under the construction contract and the bonds the contractor puts up to the lenders. This is useful in the event that the lenders are forced to replace the borrower during the construction period. Furthermore, if the contractor defaults, the lenders will be assigned the proceeds of the performance and other bonds that the contractor has issued in favour of the borrower. The proceeds can be used to reduce the lenders' debt obligations. The lenders are also assigned the borrower's rights under the completion undertaking.

Shareholders of the project company also pledge their shares to the lenders. In some developing countries, it may not be possible for lenders to take possession of the shares. What lenders in such situations will get is the right to substitute another entity for the borrower. The most important assignment is the one for the toll road revenues and the other rights of the project company under the concession agreement. This establishes the primacy of the lenders to the cashflow and assets of the concession company.

The borrower will typically enter into covenants with the lenders which bind him to do certain things. Gerstell and McIsaac[2] define covenants as:

> Unconditional undertakings by the borrower that certain events will or will not occur during the term of the loan or the borrower will be obligated to repay the loan.

Covenants can be both positive (requiring the borrower or shareholders to take certain actions) or negative (prohibiting them from taking certain actions). In the case of the toll bridge, we have covenants that prohibit the borrower from pledging the cash to anyone else, restricting the payment of dividends and maintaining certain debt/equity ratios. There are also covenants which require the borrower to maintain adequate insurance throughout the concession period and which prohibit him from borrowing money from other sources or from changing ownership by the shareholders in the company. In this case, we also have a covenant that requires the contractor to maintain 25% of the equity until the project is completed. Another common covenant requires the borrower to submit regular financial accounts to the lenders.

The borrower is also required to maintain at least one account with the lenders in which typically a certain level of cash balance is maintained to provide comfort to the lenders for debt service. In our case, the company must leave the equivalent of six months' debt service requirement in the account. As debt service increases, the company will be required to augment the balance in the account. The effect of such a requirement is to provide lenders with more security and reduce the amount that investors can receive in dividends during the financing period. In more complex projects, the number of accounts that must be maintained by the borrowers multiplies.

After the loan is negotiated and signed, the borrower must still fulfil certain conditions before it can draw on the loan facility. Security documents must be properly executed and proof provided to the lenders. Corporate and government approvals and consents must be supplied to the lenders.

Other standard loan provisions are representations and warranties. These are assurances given by the borrower which if later turn out to be false, would force the borrower to repay the loan. There are also events of default which are a list of certain events that if they occur would trigger the borrower's obligation to repay.

Normally, lenders will want to be assured that their interest and fee payments are net of all taxes associated with lending to the borrower. The most common form of tax in cross-border lending is the withholding tax (which varies from country to country). There may also be stamp duties and other charges that the host government may impose on offshore borrowings. In that case, the borrower is obliged to pay those taxes and duties in addition to the interest and fee payments.

For governing law, as Gerstell and McIsaac[2] point out:

> It is important to choose a jurisdiction that has a substantial body of laws, and/ or judicial precedents governing financial transactions, experience in handling international financial disputes as well as a reputation for fairness in its courts.

The most common jurisdictions for BOT project loans are those of England and New York. The jurisdiction chosen is generally non-exclusive, i.e. the lender is free to sue in another jurisdiction if the law of another jurisdiction seems more attractive. Gerstell and McIsaac add that:

> If the loan is secured and the collateral is located in a foreign jurisdiction, local law regarding the creation and perfection of a security interest (in the assets of the borrower) must be consulted.

Use of counsel familiar with the chosen jurisdiction will also help ensure that the documents are in the proper form to be enforceable in the chosen jurisdiction. Lenders to BOT projects in countries other than their own may have to employ local legal counsel in addition to English or New York counsel.

Other common financing instruments in BOT projects

Export credits
In BOT projects in developing countries, a very common source of funding is export credit finance. Most developed countries have export credit schemes. These schemes share a number of common attributes and the common objective of promoting exports from their respective countries.

Capital market instruments
The following show the advantages of accessing the capital markets rather than conventional commercial bank finance.

(a) The principle characteristic of capital market instruments is that they enable borrowers to broaden the base of institutions and individuals from which they can raise funds. Because the instruments are negotiable, they can be traded easily (if there are buyers for the instrument).
(b) The wider range of investors which are accessed should in theory reduce the cost to the borrower (through competition and the different risk/return ambitions of the investing institutions). It also reduces the risk associated with borrowing from limited sources.
(c) From the point of view of these investing institutions, project finance offers them much higher returns than corporate bonds.
(d) Banks have responded to the challenge of the capital markets by developing their ability to place and trade the new instruments.

Multilateral agency loans
Institutions such as the International Finance Corporation, European

Development Bank, Asian Development Bank, the Inter-American Development Bank, the African Development Bank are all engaged in providing finance as well as project advisory services for projects in their respective regions.

References

1. NEVITT P.K. *Project financing.* Euromoney Publications, UK, 1983, 4th edn.
2. GERSTELL G. and MCISAAC C. *Project financing and BOT schemes: loan and security documentation.* Jakarta, 1991.

Appendix

Summary terms and conditions for the project finance facility

Borrower:	ABC Bridge Company Ltd
Purpose:	To finance the design, construction and operation of a tolled suspension bridge over the River Styx, linking Hither and Yon.
Amount:	A total facility of up to US$80 million.
Availability period:	The facility will be available until the earlier of project completion or 30 April 1996.
Drawdown:	Upon satisfaction of conditions precedent as specified in the Loan Agreement, drawdowns may be made in multiples of US$500,000 or the undrawn balance if less.
Commitment fee:	A commitment fee of 0·375% p.a. will be charged on the undrawn balance of the facility. The fee will be payable quarterly in arrears.
Management fee:	A flat fee of 1·00% payable up-front and distributed to the project lenders at the discretion of the arranger.
Interest rate:	Interest in respect of the amount drawn under the facility will be payable at the following margins over 3- or 6-month LIBOR as selected by the borrower.

Prior to project completion: 1·25% p.a.

After project completion but prior to satisfaction of the Cashflow Adequacy Test: 1% p.a.

After satisfaction of the Cashflow Adequacy Test: 0·75% p.a.

Interest will be calculated based on a 360-day year and will be payable at the end of each interest period.

Repayment:	Repayment of the facility will be by 16 unequal semi-annual instalments according to the schedule shown

below. Repayments will commence 6 months after the earlier of project completion (as defined below) or 31 October 1996 and will be based on the amount of the Facility outstanding on the last day of the availability period. The repayment schedule will be as follows, with each annual repayment payable in two equal amounts:

Year	Repayment: %	Cumulative: %
1996	5	5
1997	10	15
1998	10	25
1999	10	35
2000	15	50
2001	15	65
2002	15	80
2003	20	100

Final maturity:
Ten years from loan signing date in any event no later than 31 October 2003.

Prepayment:
The borrower may prepay all or part of the outstanding principal amount of the Facility at the end of any applicable interest period in minimum amounts of US$500,000, and integral multiples of that, or the balance outstanding under the Facility, if less. Any prepayments will be applied to repayment schedule on a pro-rata basis. Amounts prepaid may not after that be reborrowed.

Project completion:
Completion of the project will be deemed to occur when the lenders receive:

(*a*) Certification by the independent engineer and the borrower that the project has been completed and commissioned according to the project specifications and final approval by the Government Bridge and Road Department.

(*b*) Certification by the borrower and its auditors that sufficient funds are available to meet all liabilities incurred or due to be incurred by the borrower concerning the physical completion of the project, except liabilities arising under the loan facility.

(*c*) Certification by the independent engineer and the borrower that during a consecutive period of 30 days the whole of the bridge was open for public use and operated normally throughout that period. All necessary approvals of the Government and any other statutory body have been obtained.

Either the borrower or lenders may call for such certification at any time when, in their reasonable opinion, the project completion criteria have been, met.

Cancellation:	The borrower has the right to cancel without penalty or cost such part of the facility as has not been drawn by the time of project completion.
Debt service coverage ratio (DSCR):	The DSCR will be defined as the ratio of net cashflow before financing costs arising from operation of the bridge for any year to the debt service payments (including principal, interest and all fees) on the total senior debt of the borrower due and payable in respect of that year. The DSCR will be calculated at the end of each year of operation of the bridge.
Cashflow Adequacy Test:	The Cashflow Adequacy Test will be satisfied when the DSCR Test exceeds 1·25 for one full year of operation of the Bridge after project completion.
Security:	Project lenders will obtain various securities including but not limited to the following.

(a) The project lenders being named loss payees under the insurance policies.
(b) Assignment of the borrower's rights under the construction contract.
(c) Assignment of all relevant bonds provided by the contractor under the construction contract.
(d) Assignment of the borrower's rights under the completion undertaking.
(e) Pledge of shares in the borrower by all shareholders.
(f) Assignment of all toll revenues and all of the borrower's other rights under the concession agreement.

Covenants:

(a) A negative pledge in respect of funds in the cash retention account and all other assets not covered by the securities.
(b) No dividends will be payable by the Borrower until the Cashflow Adequacy Test has been met.
(c) The borrower will maintain adequate insurance cover with respect to the project, satisfactory to lenders, always while any amount is outstanding under the loan facility.
(d) The borrower will not borrow any amounts besides those drawn under the loan facility without the prior consent of the project lenders.
(e) No changes will be allowed in the ownership of the Borrower during the construction period without the prior consent of the lenders.
(f) The debt to equity ratio of the borrower shall not exceed 4:1 while there are any amounts outstanding under the loan facility.
(g) The contractor will agree to hold 25% of the equity of the borrower until the cashflow adequacy test is met.

Cash retention: account	All revenues of the company will be paid into a cash retention account. This account will be an interest-bearing account in the name of the borrower maintained with the agent bank. The borrower will be required to maintain balances equivalent to six months' debt service in the account while there are any amounts outstanding under the loan facility.
Conditions: precedent	To include:

(a) Total equity financing committed by the shareholders of US$20 million.
(b) All necessary approvals from the government and any other statutory authorities.
(c) Satisfactory review by project lenders of any amendments to relevant documentation including the concession agreement, shareholders agreement, construction contract, and all corporate documentation of the borrower.
(d) Satisfactory legal opinions from project lenders' counsel on the project documentation.

Taxes and other deductions:	All payments to be made by the borrower are to be free and clear of any present or future taxes, levies or duties or other deductions of whatever nature, imposed by the government or other official bodies.
Documentation:	The loan facility will be subject to the negotiation and execution of all project documentation satisfactory to all parties. The loan agreement will incorporate clauses currently standard in the syndicated loan market including provisions covering increased costs, alternate interest rates, events of default and information requirements.
Expenses:	All out of pocket expenses incurred by the Arranging bank and agent bank in connection with the arrangement and execution of this Facility shall be for the account of the borrower.
Governing Law:	The laws of England.
Agent:	XYZ Bank Ltd.
Arranger:	HSBC Capital Ltd.

Chapter 7

Estimating for major projects

Introduction

The whole basis on which BOT developments are founded is that a project promoter can finance, develop, construct and operate some public-sector service facility for which he can, for a pre-agreed concession period, charge some fee. At the end of the concession period the facility is handed to the relevant public authority at no cost, and the objective for the BOT promoter is therefore to ensure that the revenue stream arising from the project will provide a sufficient return to cover all of the financing, development and operating costs incurred, together with some acceptable level of profit to the investors. It is, therefore, obvious that, in order to decide whether or not the project represents a sound investment, the project promoter must make some predictions about the income which the completed development will realize during the concession period, and compare this with the predicted financing, development and operating costs. This calculation is likely to be complex, since both costs and revenue stream will be spread over a considerable period of time, typically 10–30 years.

The basic cost components of the budget for a BOT project will be:

(a) cost of land
(b) cost of construction including any enabling works
(c) cost of operation of the facility including periodic repair and maintenance and any refurbishment costs before handover
(d) financing charges
(e) cost of consultancy fees.

This chapter considers some factors which need to be recognized and quantified in the prediction of the initial development cost. Estimating techniques are considered in Chapter 8.

The income component will be generated by the anticipated revenue stream over the lifetime of the concession, and will require consideration of the whole life operating cost of the project. This issue is considered in Chapter 9.

Land costs

Costs involved in acquiring and assembling the land required will vary depending upon the policy of the public authority involved, the present use and ownership of the required land, and the relevant legal instruments and procedures relating to land acquisition and use which are available to the public authority concerned. In many cases the necessary land may be assembled and provided free of charge by the relevant public authority. Indeed provision of the land might well represent the public authority's input to, and financial stake in, the scheme, and this may, therefore, represent considerable support. As an example the land for the Hong Kong Tate's Cairn tunnel was provided free of charge by the government including the removal and resettlement of some 15 000 squatters.

In the early days of privatized infrastructure it was common for the land required for major projects such as railways, canals, etc. to be assembled by the government and ceded to the promoter in an attempt to provide speculators with some element of security and thus to encourage private participation in infrastructural development. Indeed it is reported[1] that:

> Land grants proved most effective in such large speculative ventures as the Indian railways and the trans-continental lines in the United States.

Although outright land grants may still be of use in encouraging the private sector to participate in projects which are seen as marginal or where the risks are perceived to be exceptionally high, nowadays BOT promoters will not normally gain any title to the land in the form of either leasehold or ownership rights, but will simply be granted some form of restrictive license to use the land specifically for the BOT project during the period of the concession. In the case of the Hong Kong Tate's Cairn and Western Cross Harbour tunnels for example the agreements are very specific in that the BOT promoter is given no title or ownership rights either to the land or to the completed tunnel. All that is granted is the right to operate the tunnel for the period of the concession and to collect the revenue. Restrictions such as this may be seen by funding organizations as limiting the security available to them in the event of default by the promoter unless the franchise agreement also contains some provision for assignment of the benefit.

Construction cost

A wide range of techniques exists for the forecasting of construction costs and prices, ranging from, at one extreme, simple unit cost-based predictions, to complex analytical estimating techniques at the other. The particular technique chosen in each case, and the degree of accuracy of the resulting prediction, will depend to a very large extent on the amount and quality of information about the proposed project which is available at the time.

Construction cost will normally form a substantial part of the cost equation for the project, although in most cases the construction cost will represent a smaller proportion of the total than the whole life operating and running costs. In the case of speculative BOT projects, there is a delicate balance to be struck between the time and cost to be spent on initial project appraisal and the likelihood that the project will eventually prove to be viable. Elliott and Allen[2] make the point very well:

> For large scale projects, particularly those dependent on innovation, it is almost impossible to produce all the cost estimates, sales forecasts, etc., with sufficient accuracy for a final implementation decision unless a fairly large amount of development work is first carried out on the project. For major engineering projects this pre-sanction design work could easily add up to a few man years of design effort. In terms of elapsed time it could spread over several months or even years. This type of work may be complex, requiring the attention of senior managers and skilled staff. . . . Thus the large scale or innovatory project requires a much earlier decision to be made — long before it is possible to produce sanction estimates of high accuracy — in order to minimise abortive work. This first decision as to whether or not to proceed with a project must be taken very early in the project life cycle, as part of the initial study phase. The facts about the project that have to be presented to the decision makers are the same as those in the final decision stage, but of course the accuracy of such things as cost and sales estimates is only indicative, e.g. with a one in five chance of not being wrong by more than ±33%. . . . Obviously it must be clear that the project has a good chance of being proved viable but it must be realised that this is based necessarily on predictions that are subject to wide margins of error.

It is therefore highly likely that:

(a) the tendency will be that only those projects which are seen to be clearly viable at an early stage will eventually come to fruition

(b) engineering design will be kept as simple as possible; innovative engineering in this context usually represents increased risk.

Promoters are not likely to want to spend considerable sums of money on complex and detailed appraisal of borderline projects, and therefore the importance of accurate early stage cost estimating based on very limited information cannot be over-emphasized if good potential opportunities are not to be thrown away. What is, therefore, required is a way of providing 'quick and dirty' estimates of likely construction costs, backed up by more accurate, and time-consuming techniques for monitoring the budget throughout the progress of the design on those projects which are seen to be initially viable. Estimating techniques are considered in some detail in Chapter 8.

The relationship between time and cost

The existence of a relationship between time and the cost of construction work cost is well recognized, and there will always be some optimum time for completion of a project at lowest cost. Completion ahead of the optimum time will require uneconomic working, perhaps shift working and other acceleration costs, whereas completion after the optimum time will mean that the construction resources have been used less efficiently than they might have been.

In the case of a BOT project time will normally be a very significant factor in the overall equation. The prediction of time and cost for the construction stage of a BOT project is therefore a delicate balancing act between the costs of accelerated completion and the additional revenue generated. The situation is also complicated by the fact that funders will expect to see a contract with a fixed time-frame, and extensions of time for the construction contract will, therefore, be most unwelcome.

Any estimate of price for construction work must therefore pay due attention to the time requirements and proposed construction methods, and estimating must, therefore, be carried out hand in hand with project planning. Cost information cannot be meaningful unless it is related to a time frame. Spon,[3] in the context of civil engineering work, sees the preparation of the plan as a necessary prerequisite to the estimate:

> To prepare a price for a civil engineering project, then it is necessary to have regard to the method to be adopted in executing the work, draw up a detailed programme and then cost out the resources necessary to prosecute the chosen method.

The purpose of the pre-tender plan

The basic purposes of the pre-tender plan are to identify how the work is to be carried out in order to meet the required time frame. The project timescale will also indicate the length of time 'preliminaries' items such as site establishment will be required and, in conjunction with the associated resource data, will allow the estimator to develop a provisional cash flow forecast. This information can then be used to forecast the financing requirements of the project and any consequent costs. It is also probable that the estimator will be required to provide comparative assessments of different ways of completing the work, and of the additional costs involved in meeting the required time scale as against the cost of achieving the optimum time/cost balance. This calculation, or perhaps commercial judgement would be a better term, can incorporate many subjective factors.

Value engineering

Most BOT schemes require an optimum balance of earliest possible completion at lowest possible cost. The achievement of this optimum will require examination of a wide range of alternative solutions to the problem, and it is highly likely that the consortium with the most innovative solutions will be able to submit the most competitive bid.

BOT projects are, therefore, highly likely to benefit from some kind of value engineering or value management study. A number of formal value engineering techniques exist, see for example Kelly and Male,[4] but all involve the project participants taking part in some kind of session designed to maximize the creativity of the whole project team. While a variety of techniques exist to aid this process, the most widely used techniques are built around some kind of brainstorming activity where the basic concepts and functions of the various parts of the project are progressively re-evaluated. No suggestions are considered too wild or outrageous at this stage, and all suggestions are recorded. The second stage of the process requires evaluation of the output from the first stage, and research apparently shows that good creative suggestions are just as likely to come from those without specialist subject knowledge as they are from subject specialists.

The optimum time for a value engineering study is sometimes considered to be as early in the design process as possible after the design problem has been initially analysed, since it is at this stage that the maximum potential exists for cost and time optimization. Consortia launching pre-emptive bids for public sector work might, however, be wise not to show all of their cards at once, particularly if government rules require competitive bidding. The Tate's Cairn Road Tunnel in Hong Kong is a case in point. The Nishimatsu/Gammon joint venture launched a pre-emptive bid to construct the tunnel on a BOT basis, with completion within 42 months. The Hong Kong Government was, however, bound to seek competitive tenders, and Nishimatsu/ Gammon, despite having floated the idea, were, therefore required to tender in competition with five other consortia. Amendments and refinements to their design during the competition stage made it possible for them to submit a successful bid on the basis of a 37 month construction period.

Consortium and joint venture bidding

Most BOT projects are large and/or complex projects, and many are located in the less developed areas of the world. Bidding for such projects will normally involve contractors acting as part of a consortium or joint venture, and this will almost certainly pose particular problems because:

(*a*) the projects themselves are usually large and often complex
(*b*) projects may pose special risks in terms of their cultural, geographical and political environment
(*c*) tenders for normal construction work are usually prepared by one company acting alone and in competition with other similar firms, and many construction contractors are, therefore, not accustomed to tendering as part of a larger team
(*d*) a substantial number, perhaps most, consortia and joint venture organizations are set up to handle specific one-off projects, and it is therefore, usually necessary to re-establish the necessary management and administrative organizations afresh for each new project.

It is, therefore, evident that the risk element in joint venture/consortium arrangements is usually much more complex than in a traditional tendering situation. This section considers some of the more important issues which arise for contractors participating in joint venture or consortium projects, particularly during the pre-contract stage, and it is, therefore, necessary to consider questions such as the following.

- What are the requirements for a successful joint venture?
- What are the potential pitfalls?

In some cases the consortium itself may become large and complex. Consider, for example, the consortium formed for the construction of the Channel Tunnel. The main contractor in this case was Transmanche-Link (TML), who were awarded a contract to design, construct and commission the whole transport system. TML was itself a joint venture between two separate consortia, one British (Translink) and one French (Transmanche Construction). Each of these consortia in turn consisted of five construction companies as follows:

Translink	Transmanche Construction
Balfour Beatty Construction Ltd	Bouygues SA
Costain Civil Engineering Ltd	Dumez SA
Tarmac Construction Ltd	Societe Auxiliarire D'Enterprises SA
Taylor Woodrow Construction Ltd	Societe Generale D'Enterprises SA
Wimpey Major Projects'	Spie Batignolles SA

This project also highlights the point that some projects are so large that no one company was big enough to take on the whole project. Young,[5] reporting on a case study of the project, makes the point that:

> The five UK joint venture companies when combined had 21% of the UK construction industry which in 1990 came to £48·467 billion. This is an indication that no one company alone could take on the Channel Tunnel contract by itself, which when it was awarded stood at £4·7 billion (1985 prices) and is currently worth £9 billion (1992 prices). Average turnover per day for TML is a staggering £3 million which reinforces the use of joint ventures.

Requirements for a successful joint venture

The first and most important requirement for a successful joint venture is that the project must be economically and technologically viable. Given these criteria, the requirements for a successful joint venture partnership are much the same as those for any other kind of partnership and indeed for any construction. The following factors taken from Smith[7] have been identified by a number of authors as being some of the major factors which are especially important in consortium and joint venture projects and which must therefore, be born in mind when attempting to estimate the scheme costs.

A well-organized cohesive team
The development of a strong 'team chemistry' must be developed through the pursuit of common goals and activities. It could be argued that the prime aim in all construction joint ventures should be to achieve a high degree of synergy, a situation where the combination of the separate factors is brought together in such a way that the eventual result achieved is greater than the sum of the parts.

Implicit in this idea is the notion that there must be mutual trust between the various parties, and mutual agreement about what the eventual goals, both of the consortium as a whole and of the individual firms, actually are. In order that these things can come about various supporting mechanisms are required. Essentials would include good communication links between the joint venture partners, good managers and management skills and a true willingness to participate in a shared activity for the benefit of all involved. Some of these things can prove difficult to achieve, particularly when personnel are seconded to the joint venture on a part-time basis while still being employed within their parent companies. The need for strong, sensitive and professional management of the joint venture vehicle is clear if the potentially disparate elements of the team are to be successfully welded together into a cohesive unit.

Precise and comprehensive contracts and agreements

Another important consideration is that the risks, costs and benefits of the project are shared equitably amongst the members of the consortium. This factor is obviously of vital importance in the case of very large projects, where the cost of preparing the bid can in itself be almost astronomic. Torrance *et al.*[6] suggest that the partners to the joint venture should each have equal shares, and in the case of the British Channel Tunnel Consortium, Translink, each of the members provided finance, management expertise and specialist knowledge, and each held a 10% stake in the project as a whole. Profits and losses were, therefore, to be shared equally amongst the consortium members.

While the rationale for this is easy to see, it is apparently not necessarily a prerequisite. Young[5] also reports that, in the case of the French joint venture, Transmanche Construction:

> Two of the member companies had a larger stake than the other three. Bouygues SA had a bigger stake than the rest. This was mainly due to its financial size and its ability to take on more responsibility and risk than the other four companies. The three smaller companies were more specialised and concentrated on certain technically demanding sections of the work.

It seems likely that each joint venture needs individual consideration, and would be good practice to structure the agreement in such a way that the company able to take the biggest share of the risk should also take the biggest share of the potential rewards.

It is evident that a series of well-drafted contracts and agreements is essential. The agreements must be drawn in such a way that they define precisely the roles and obligations of each of the parties, together with the allocation of their respective risks, rights, liabilities and benefits, but which also encourage the various participants to behave as a team without conflicts of interest or differing goals. The drafting of such agreements is obviously a very demanding task, but agreement on these points is essential if the contractors are to be able to adequately price the risks they are expected to carry.

Relevant knowledge and experience
The selection of suitable partners for a joint venture is obviously of paramount importance. Taken together the various members of the consortium must possess all of the expertise necessary to complete the project but without unnecessary redundancy, and they must all be prepared to work together for the good of the team as a whole.

Many joint venture bids are put together by groups of people either on the basis of personal contacts or by firms who have worked successfully together in the past. As an example consider the case of the joint venture team which submitted the successful design and build bid for a major hospital project in Scotland. In this case the initial opportunity was identified by an architect in private practice, who then approached a personal contact employed by large building contractor whom he knew had extensive experience in the construction of major hospitals. The building contractor brought on board mechanical and electrical sub-contractors and consultants with whom he had worked successfully before, and assumed the lead role of 'bidder' for the project. Structural engineering and quantity surveying consultants were also added to the team.

Potential problem areas for joint venture agreements

Management issues

The main potential sources of friction between the parties to a joint venture agreement are relatively easy to identify. Many potential areas of conflict, particularly those relating to arguments over individual members' contributions and obligations together with their share of potential risks, benefits and liabilities can and should be forestalled through careful drafting of the joint venture agreement, but there may be other potential areas of conflict which are not so easy to foresee. Among the more important identified by Torrance et al.[6] are as follows.

(a) Divided loyalties, where managers assigned to the joint venture may feel that the interests of the joint venture as a whole conflict with the interests of their parent company.

(*b*)　Attempted interference in the management and decision making process of the joint venture company from individual parent companies.

(*c*)　Changes of policy inside the joint venture members' parent organizations may lead to attempts to change the terms of the joint venture agreement. This may be especially important in the case of joint ventures involving governments, such as those set up as BOT projects. These projects are extremely sensitive to political stability, and a change of government policy can result in very serious disruption of the joint venture agreement. An extreme example is that of the Suez canal opened in November 1869 under the terms of a 99-year concession from the Egyptian Government but which was later nationalized before the end of the concession period. Less extreme and perhaps more common examples of governmental interference might include changes in taxation policy or financial controls, or political instability.

(*d*)　Lack of trust between the joint venture partners can reduce the efficiency of the management and decision-making process, and can also lead to partners being wary of sharing information, techniques and technology. It is conceivable that there might be particular problems here in the case of international joint ventures where cultural differences between the parties, if not fully appreciated and understood by all concerned, could give rise to considerable misunderstanding and consequent lack of mutual trust. Differences of perception, values, attitudes and expectations must be identified early on in the venture, and agreements must be reached which are accepted by all parties to be a fair compromise by all concerned. Torrance *et al.*,[6] reporting on the preliminary results of research into national and international joint ventures, state that:

> In particular, with regard to the cultural dimensions of joint ventures, the findings are emphasising the need for greater understanding of and allowances for two main cultural dimensions. That is, the external cultural features of the societies from which the joint venture partners are drawn. It is essential to clearly distinguish those common features of beliefs, values and attitudes which generally exist within the different cultures. In addition, the professional ethics and practices, together with normal business practices must be identified arising from each culture. Where differences exist, these must be clearly understood and accepted by all the parties involved and agreement reached over

how allowances are to be made in order to accommodate these differences.

Young,[5] however, in her description of how the cultural differences issue was apparently successfully resolved in the Channel Tunnel project, appears to indicate that the issue was not really a problem at all.

It is apparent that no special arrangement was made between the UK companies in order to accommodate cultural differences in language, technology and managerial approach of the French contractors. . . . To ensure that business practices between the British and French companies were as compatible as possible, exchanges of personnel were cultivated whilst accepting that there were differences in culture and attitudes.

It would seem that the important thing is to explore, in as much detail as possible, what cultural differences might cause problems before signing the joint venture agreement.

Commercial issues

Reference has already been made to the need for the joint venture agreement to identify and record each party's contribution to the venture, and their respective shares of the potential risks, profits and losses. These are issues upon which each party must make its own detailed assessment prior to commitment to the venture. It is, therefore, vitally important that each party evaluates these factors from its own purely selfish point of view, and in order that this may be done the joint venture sponsor, usually the 'lead bidder' must provide all of the necessary information.

In the case of a simple joint venture such as that for the submission of a design and build bid the decision might be relatively easy. The possible loss to a participating consultant, an architect for instance, will be limited to his costs incurred in preparing the necessary design information, and he must balance this potential loss against the probability of his consortium submitting the winning bid. His assessment of whether or not his consortium stands a good chance of submitting the winning bid will be governed by his assessment of his other partners, particularly perhaps the lead bidder, and also by his assessment of the strength and number of competitors.

For contractors entering into a long-term joint venture such as a BOT arrangement, the risks are much more difficult to assess. The following are typical potential risks in BOT projects.

(*a*) Construction risk including time delays, cost overruns, etc.

(*b*) Infrastructure problems including the availability of transport links, public utility services, etc. This is especially important in the case of projects in the developing world.

(c) Market risks including the availability of raw materials, accuracy of market demand forecasts and stability of the market price for the project's product.

(d) Political risk including taxation, financial controls, labour relations regulation, political stability, etc.

(e) Operating risk. This will require a comprehensive life cycle cost study of the operation and maintenance costs of the project.

(f) Foreign currency risks. The entire stability of the project may be threatened by unexpected currency fluctuations affecting the prices of imported or exported goods and materials. Such fluctuations can have serious effects upon the project's ability to service the debt. Foreign currency exposure in developing countries is a major concern.

(g) Insolvency risk including insolvency of the sponsor, joint venture partners, suppliers, etc.

Risks and their mitigation are considered in more detail in Chapters 10 and 11, but assessment of these factors will also require the preparation of a detailed financial model, considered in more detail in Chapter 9, upon which the sensitivity of changes to any or all of these factors can be tested.

Parties to joint ventures of this type will typically attempt to limit their risk exposure through the formation of a separate joint venture company which will assume the whole of the liabilities of the project and in which the principal partners to the deal will simply be shareholders. The company will be established in such a way that, in the event of the joint venture incurring losses, there is only limited recourse to the parent companies' assets.

References

1. THE WORLD BANK, *Infrastructure for development*. Oxford University Press, New York, World Development Report 1994.
2. ELLIOTT D.B.L and ALLEN M.W. (WEARNE S. (ed.)). Selection and Sanctioning. *Control of engineering projects*. Thomas Telford, London, 1989.
3. SPON. *Spon's civil engineering and highway works price book*. E & F.N. Spon, UK, 1994, 8th edn.
4. KELLY J. and MALE S. *Value management in design and construction*. E & F.N. Spon, London, 1993.

5. YOUNG B.A. A joint venture in the UK construction industry — the Channel Tunnel. *Proc. Int. Conf. on Project Management*. Guangzhou, China, 1992.
6. TORRANCE V.B., ALI M.Y.I., FATANI A.J. and SMITH A. Research into national and international joint venture projects of UK construction companies. *Proc. Int. Conf. on Project Management*. Guangzhou, China, 1992.
7. SMITH A.J. *Estimating, tendering and bidding for construction*. Macmillan, 1995.

Chapter 8

Estimating techniques

Introduction

This chapter considers the techniques commonly used to estimate the costs of construction work, methods of collecting the necessary basic historical cost data, allowances to cover unforeseen contingencies and some aspects concerning the potential accuracy of early stage cost estimates. This chapter does not aim to be a detailed text on estimating methods — a deeper consideration of the issues can be found in Smith.[1]

The major techniques in common use, in increasing order of potential accuracy, are:

(a) cost per functional unit
(b) cost per unit of floor area
(d) elemental cost estimating
(e) analytical estimating.

The first two techniques generally make use of historical data to produce 'ball park' figures quickly and with little effort, and are, therefore, those usually used for early stage cost predictions. Elemental estimating is normally used for more detailed cost monitoring during the design stage, whilst analytical estimating makes use of current cost data and would normally be used when firm design information is available and the works can be quantified with some degree of accuracy. Note, however, that the use of historical costs derived from past projects has a very significant drawback since, by their very nature, they reflect the state of the construction market at the time the previous projects were let. They cannot, therefore, take account of the market situation at the time the new project will be let, and they, therefore, need to be adjusted to take account of dynamic market factors. This adjustment will obviously be very subjective.

Cost per functional unit

Perhaps the most obvious way of forecasting the probable cost of a proposed new construction project, particularly in the early stages when little firm information is available, would be to look at how much similar projects have cost in the past. If, for example, a contractor has previously built a power station of a certain size and level of specification, and is lucky enough to be invited to build another project of similar size and specification but on a different site, he ought to be able to use the historical cost data from the first scheme to give a reasonably accurate prediction for the construction cost of the new project even though no detailed design information is yet available for the new scheme. The historical data would of course need to be adjusted for the effects of time (cost inflation), and for different site and market conditions, but nevertheless the data should be sufficient to give at least a guideline cost for the new scheme.

It is, however, rare to get two schemes which are exactly the same, and if we are to consider the use of historical data of this kind we are, therefore, forced into a position where the best we can hope for is to find one or more previous schemes which are, in some respects, similar to the proposed project, and somehow to adjust the cost data to suit the new scheme.

Perhaps the simplest way is to express the historical costs in terms of some functional unit, in the case of a school, for example, costs could be expressed per student place, for a hospital in terms of cost per bed, for a hotel in terms of cost per guest room or for a motorway in terms of cost per mile or kilometre. Using this very rough and ready method the historical costs of previous schemes, suitably adjusted for time, can be used to prepare early stage cost estimates for the construction of similar schemes in the future. The estimates will, of course, be subject to a large margin of error, perhaps of the order of ±30%, but they will nevertheless be useful in setting outline budgets.

This, and the other following price forecasting techniques described, are fairly well developed in the case of building projects, but are much less so for civil engineering since the costs for this type of work are considered to be much more dependent upon the detailed programme and working methods to be used. There has consequently been a tendency to postpone any attempt at detailed estimating for civil engineering work until the tendering stage, relying up to that point on estimates prepared on the 'cost per mile' basis previously outlined. According to Spon:[2]

The result has been a growing pressure on the part of project sponsors for an improvement in budgetary advice, so that a decision to commit expenditure to a particular project is then taken on firmer grounds. The absence of a detailed pricing method during the pre-contract phase also inhibits the accurate costing of alternative designs and regular cost checking to ensure that the design is being developed within the employer's budget.

This would appear to be fertile ground for further research. This uncertainty, and the potential accuracy of pre-contract estimates is obviously of great concern to BOT promoters.

Costs per unit of floor area

In the case of building works an improvement on the cost per unit technique is to convert the costs from a range of similar buildings to costs/unit of floor area — normally either a cost per square metre or a cost per square foot. If a sufficient number of schemes were to be analysed, then a cost data bank could be created which could then be used to predict a probable range of costs for new projects. It might then, for example, given a new hotel, be possible to say that past experience shows that hotel buildings ought to cost between say £1000 and £1200 per square metre. The costs would, of course, have to be adjusted to a common time base, and perhaps some adjustment made for location, but in theory at least the more previous projects available the more accurate the prediction for the new project ought to be.

In practice this cost/unit area approach is very widely used for early cost appraisal of buildings, and given an outline brief which, for example, calls for 3500 m² of offices, shops and flats in a mixed development it would be possible to apply some average overall cost assessment derived from previous schemes, say £600 per square metre, to give a predicted cost for the project of about £2·1 million.

Of course, the estimate cannot be very accurate because there are so many unknowns, and so it is really not a good idea to give single point estimates of this type. The cost at this stage would be more likely to be given as a range, say ±30% (i.e. £1·5−£2·75 million). It is, however, sometimes unfortunate that the lowest figure quoted at this early stage often tends to be the one everyone remembers, and thus all too often becomes the cost limit for the project; the cost target against which the architects, engineers and contractors must work, and the project then becomes strongly finance-led.

In the case of a mixed development such as that mentioned above (flats, offices and shops) the accuracy of the estimate might be improved as the design develops by using different costs per square metre for each of the different types of accommodation, hence in the 3500 square metre scheme described above we might have:

$$
\begin{array}{lll}
\text{Shops} & 500 \text{ m}^2 \times £300 & = £0\cdot15 \text{ million} \\
\text{Offices} & 2000 \text{ m}^2 \times £700 & = £1\cdot40 \text{ million} \\
\text{Flats} & 1000 \text{ m}^2 \times £400 & = £0\cdot40 \text{ million}
\end{array}
$$

Total estimated cost £1.95 million

Again the total cost ought to be given as a range to indicate the degree of potential accuracy, perhaps in this case, for example, $\pm 15\%$ (i.e. £1·65–£2·25 million).

This cost per square metre approach using historical cost data from previous contracts is very useful, particularly during the early design stage. It is quick, simple and anyone can understand it, but the level of accuracy tends to be low due to the following disadvantages.

(*a*)   No two projects are ever exactly alike.

(*b*)   All of the previous costs must be adjusted to a constant time base.

(*c*)   Some predictions need to be made about the current market environment and the effect it is likely to have on the new project, but it is also necessary to know what effect market forces had on the projects used as a base.

(*d*)   With only a cost per square metre to work from we have no indication of any problems which might be posed by the site or the design of the new building.

(*e*)   The basic cost per square metre approach makes no allowance for the cost effects of the proposed procurement methodology.

It is also evident that if historical cost information is to be used to attempt to estimate the cost of new, as yet undesigned projects, then the previous projects need to be analysed in much more detail than simply calculating the cost per square metre of floor area. In choosing the projects to use as a historical base it is obviously essential to choose buildings of roughly the same type and standard of specification, but in addition we also need to know, at least, about the procurement method and the degree of risk which tendering contractors were being asked to bear; about the degree of competition; the project start date and the tender period in order that we can make some adjustment for the time delay; about any abnormal costs attributable to the site and something about the constructional form and design approach. Since no two buildings are ever exactly alike it is necessary to develop some mechanism to allow comparison of the costs of apparently different buildings with each other and for this we need an understanding of the way in which design variables affect project cost.

Although a detailed consideration of the above factors is beyond the scope of this text, it might be useful to look briefly at the following two aspects:

- methods of relating historical costs from a number of schemes to a common time base
- the effects of changes in some simple design variables relating to the building geometry on the project economics.

Updating of costs from previous schemes to a common base

The most common way to relate the costs of different schemes to a common base is through the use of some type of index. The followng two types are common.

(a)   An index measuring changes in construction cost by measuring changes in the market prices of the principal resources used (labour, materials, plant costs, etc.).

(b)   An index measuring changes in the level of tender prices for construction work.

Both may be useful, and both have advantages and disadvantages.

An index of building cost

Indices charting the movement of prices of individual resources have two primary advantages:

- they are easy to construct
- the basic data is readily available and widely published.

The method first requires the selection of some suitable base date from which to construct the index, and this initial starting point is conventionally given an index number of 100. Subsequent price movements, in particular resources are then measured by comparing the price at any future date with the price at the base date and expressing the result as an index number. The formula for constructing the new index is then:

$$\text{New index} = \frac{\text{New price} \times 100}{\text{Initial price}}$$

So if, as a simple example, we take an index to measure changes in the price of ready mixed concrete:

base date say January 1980 index 100
price at base date £21 per m^3
price in January 1994 £41·5 per m^3

$$\text{Index at January 1994 is therefore } \frac{£41·5 \times 100}{£21} = 197·61$$

Using this technique it is possible to track the movement of the prices of the individual inputs to the construction process with considerable accuracy, but to be of any real use for total project cost prediction, it is necessary to combine the price movements of all of the individual components into an index to represent the project as a whole. This is not as easy as it may at first sight appear, since the prices for the different resources tend to vary at different rates, and the different inputs have different significance in different projects depending upon the particular combination of resources used. For example, the price of concrete would be a very significant factor in a concrete bridge, while the price of steel might be relatively less significant, but the balance of priorities would be changed significantly in the case of a bridge constructed mainly of steel.

It is, therefore, necessary to construct some mechanism to assign a weighting to each of the inputs to the construction process to indicate their relative importance in each individual structure, and this is conventionally, done according to the approximate quantity of each resource in any particular project.

Having assigned a weighting to each component resource, the results of the calculations for all of the component resources are then combined in order to arrive at an index number for the project as a whole as shown in the following formula:

$$\text{Building cost index} = \frac{\sum\limits_{\text{no. of items}}^{1} \left(\dfrac{\text{Current price}}{\text{Original price}} \times 100 \times \text{weighting} \right)}{\sum\limits_{\text{no. of items}}^{1} \text{Weightings}}$$

There are a number of potential improvements which could be made to refine this approach, but the above gives a general idea of the basic technique.

As stated above the main advantage of this technique is that the basic price movement data required for each of the component parts is readily available, and it can, therefore, give a good indication of overall movements in the price of the underlying resources. The major disadvantage of relying on this technique as a predictor of construction price, however, is that the method is only concerned with measuring variations in the market prices of the inputs to the building process. In any competitive tendering situation the market forces acting upon the individual contractors involved in the tender auction are likely to be a significant factor, and this is not reflected in the index. Although the approach can give a very accurate guide to the movement of contractors' costs, the use of a cost-based index alone as a predictor of construction price is not reliable.

A tender-based price index

The second type of index is one which attempts to measure the movement of tender prices. The general technique is to compare prices for selected measured items in tender Bills of Quantities with prices current at some suitable base date and which are set out in a comprehensive master schedule. The cumulative variation in price between the project in question and the base schedule is then expressed in the form of an index.

Obviously the ideal would be to compare all of the prices for the whole project with the rates in the base schedule, but in practice this would be extremely time-consuming. Research has shown that, in a typical construction project the Parieto principle applies, with a large proportion of the total cost, often as much as 80%, covered in a small proportion, often as low as 20%, of the measured items. It is, therefore, possible to achieve acceptable standards of accuracy by using a sampling process from the items in the project Bills, and research originally done some 20 years ago by the Directorate of Quantity Surveying Services based in the United Kingdom Department of the Environment has shown that for building projects a sample of the most significant items in each trade up to a total of 25% of the total trade cost is sufficient to give an acceptably accurate indication of the pricing level. This sample of items is then re-priced using rates from the base schedule and by comparing base prices with tender prices an index number is derived.

Obviously if the index numbers obtained are to be used to attempt to predict future changes in tender prices then the greater the number of projects which can be analysed the better. In the United Kingdom the Royal Institution of Chartered Surveyors (RICS) Building Cost

Information Service[6] claims that a sample of about 80 projects is required in each quarter to give statistically reliable data. It is highly unlikely that any one construction organization will have this volume of information available every quarter and, therefore, the results obtained must be treated with some caution, but over time the technique can give a reasonable indication of trends in the movement of tender prices.

A tender-based price index of this type therefore has considerable advantages over a cost-based index in that:

(a) it measures the change in the price of construction work to the client taking into account the market forces which affect the tendering process
(b) it is easy to operate once the base schedule has been prepared and it is ideally suited to computer operation
(c) it is largely independent of building type and function and allows tender price trends for dissimilar buildings to be compared.

Considerable care is required in using tender price indices as indicators of inflationary trends. Indices such as these are only approximate guides, and they may be badly skewed by the particular projects used to compile them. Walker,[3] in his discussion of the problems, surrounding the funding of Hong Kong's new University of Science and Technology, gives a graphic illustration of the problems which the indiscriminate use of indices can cause.

Application of indices in cost estimating

Historical indices may then be plotted on a chart, and a number of mathematical techniques are available to project likely future values. Once the relevant indices have been calculated they can be used to update historical scheme costs to a common base using the formula:

$$\text{Percentage variation} = \frac{(\text{current index} - \text{original index}) \times 100}{\text{original index}}$$

The process is illustrated in the following simple example:

Date of tender of existing project — June 1993
Proposed date of tender for new project — January 1997
Tender price index June 1993 = 705
Anticipated tender price index January 1997 = 770

121

Percentage increase to be applied June 1993 – January 1997 =

$$\frac{(770 \, - \, 705) \, \times \, 100}{705} = 9.22\%$$

Effect of building geometry on project cost

The above techniques can provide the required 'quick and dirty' estimate for an initial decision to be made as to whether to proceed further with the project or not. If the decision is taken to proceed then the anticipated project development costs must be monitored, as the design develops in order to ensure that the original budget predictions remain valid. The cost predictions therefore need to be 'fine tuned' as progressively more detailed information becomes available. In the case of civil engineering (roads, tunnels, etc.) the process will depend almost entirely upon some form of elemental unit rate estimating, but building work tends to be more complex and there are a number of factors to do with building geometry which may have a significant effect on cost and which need to be considered during the design development stage. While much of the building geometry will be dictated by the constraints and orientation of the site, it is still worthwhile considering, in outline at least, the effects of factors such as building shape, scale, storey height and overall building height on the economics of the project.

The plan shape of a building may have serious effects upon the project cost, since the more complex the shape becomes the greater the quantity of external wall required to contain the same floor area. Similar problems arise with scale, for example a square building 20×20 metres on plan and 3 metres high will require 240 m^2 of external wall to enclose a floor area of 400 m^2, and each square metre of floor area thus requires $0 \cdot 6$ m^2 of external wall. A similarly shaped building $100 \times 100 \times 3$ metres high will, however, only require 1200 m^2 of wall to enclose a floor area of 10 000 m^2 and each square metre of floor area then only requires $0 \cdot 12$ m^2 of external wall. It is, therefore, obvious that simply to use a cost per square metre of floor area rate for a new building without considering plan shape and scale could potentially be very inaccurate. Historical costs per square metre of floor area alone are thus seen to be a very blunt instrument indeed, and some additional mechanism is needed to describe the geometry of the building. There have been a number of attempts to develop mathematical formulae to model the cost efficiency of various building shapes, and several alternative methods are listed in Ferry and Brandon.[4] One very simple and popular approach at early design stage is to use ratios such as, for example, the ratio of external wall area/floor area to represent the envelope shape, and the ratio of internal partition area/floor area to represent the extent of internal subdivision.

Using a basic cost per square metre of floor area also takes no account of the storey height, and changes in the storey height of buildings of a constant floor area will obviously give rise to changes in the wall/floor and partition/floor ratios and thus to changes in the overall building cost. Changes in storey height will also affect other vertical elements such as services, staircases, structural frame, etc.

In addition to all of this high-rise buildings are almost always more expensive to build per square metre of floor area than low-rise ones. Seeley[5] reports a Department of the Environment study in the UK which showed the costs of local authority office blocks '... rising fairly uniformly by about 2% per floor when increasing the height above four storeys'.

The following are the basic reasons for this.

(*a*) High-rise structural forms are generally more expensive than low rise, and may also require special foundation solutions.

(*b*) Building services in tall buildings usually require special consideration. For example, it may be necessary to install pumps for the water systems, high speed lifts, special fire protection systems, etc.

(*c*) The necessity to provide dedicated building services and/or fire refuge floors at intervals of, say, every 10–15 floors.

(*d*) Construction of high-rise buildings will usually demand specialized construction equipment, and construction costs will generally be more expensive than for a low-rise solution.

On the other hand, however, these effects may easily be offset by the need to make the maximum use of highly priced land, and the increased costs of high-rise solutions may be completely negated in the context of the overall development equation.

Improving the accuracy of the estimate

Accuracy can be improved, particularly in respect of the vertical elements like walls, but also for elements like roofs and foundations which on multi-storey buildings are shared between a number of floors, by calculating the cost per square metre of the components themselves rather than the cost of the whole building per square metre of floor area.

The cost of foundations could therefore be expressed as a cost per square metre of ground floor area, the roof as a cost per square metre of roof area, the external walls as a cost per square metre of external wall area and so on.

The rates and quantities derived in this way are known as element unit rates (EUR) and element unit quantities (EUQ) respectively. It is, however, self evident that derivation of this level of information requires a much more detailed analysis of the previous projects to identify the costs and areas for each functional element of the building. A comprehensive library of historical cost information, in the form of detailed cost analyses, is, therefore, a very important quantity surveying resource. The RICS Building Cost Information Service publishes a detailed guide for the preparation of cost analyses for buildings to an established standard,[6] and also provides a forum within which subscribing members can submit cost analyses for their own projects for inclusion in a central computer database, the whole of which is then available for all subscribing members to access. No such national database exists for civil engineering projects.

Elemental cost estimating

Elemental cost estimating is normally carried out in parallel with the development of the design, and is, therefore, usually considered to be an ongoing activity which continues in parallel with the design process, with the objective of monitoring, evaluating and progressively refining the probable cost of the work throughout the design stage, hopefully to a progressively increasing level of detail and accuracy. The process is, therefore, one of attempting to cost the evolving design.

The process basically involves measurement of the work to a progressively finer degree of detail. The measured items are then priced, either by using Bill rates from previous schemes or by building up unit rates from basic principles using an analytical estimating technique. Since the process is an ongoing one in parallel with the design, the final and potentially most accurate pretender estimate will be prepared by pricing the project Bill of Quantities while the project is out to tender.

Use of appropriate computer techniques can be very helpful in permitting alternative design options to be quickly modelled and evaluated, and they may also provide facilities for some sensitivity testing of the model. At the very lowest level a simple spreadsheet programme can be extremely useful.

Analytical estimating

The estimating and cost forecasting techniques previously considered rely mainly on the use of historical cost data, but as the design develops and more information becomes available it may be more useful to try, as far as possible, to use analytical estimating methods using current costs and prices.

Two major analytical techniques are in common use. 'Unit rate estimating' uses pre-determined output rates for labour and plant, in conjunction with a price per unit for materials, to calculate a rate per unit (m, m², m³, nr, etc.) for some measured item of work, and this unit rate is then set against a total measured quantity. 'Operational estimating', on the other hand, aims to calculate the total cost for a complete work package by determining the total resources (labour, plant, materials and time) needed for completion of the whole operation.

Synthesis of unit rates

In principle the synthesis of unit rates simply requires that the estimator adds together the costs of all of the resources required to complete a given item of work.

The calculation of unit rates is therefore largely an arithmetical process, and many estimators now use computer-based spreadsheet programs as a matter of course.

One major problem lies with estimating the production rates of labour and plant, and this problem is perhaps most marked in civil engineering where costs vary greatly depending upon the working methods employed. General 'rules of thumb' for estimating labour productivity have long been used in the construction industry, and it is perhaps as a consequence of this that there is still a common belief that all estimators have an in-depth, encyclopaedic and accurate knowledge of production rates for all items of construction work. Ashworth and Skitmore,[7] for example, refer to estimator's standard outputs being contained in a 'black book' which, they maintain, is rarely if ever amended or revised. Those estimators who don't possess a personal 'black book' can gain some guidance on production rates for a huge variety of construction tasks from generally available price books such as those published by Spon, Wessex and Laxton.

While there is no doubt that 'standard' production information of this type is useful in providing a general idea of possible production rates, it is important to understand that the figures given are, at best, single-point averages of averages derived from a sample of projects, and therefore represent only a guide to the average work-rate which might be achieved under ideal conditions. No indication is given of the possible spread which might occur on either side of the average. While there is little doubt that, in order to be effective, the estimator must have a good idea of the kind of average production rates which might be achieved, and the 'black book' or the standard price book can perhaps give some guidance in this respect, it is also plainly nonsense to pretend that any forecasts based on such general information would prove to be accurate in every, or even any, specific case.

The obvious way to assess labour productivity accurately might appear to be to collect data from completed work, and it is often said that the monitoring and coordination of such site feedback ought to be part of the estimator's role. The estimator, however, faces a number of severe problems associated with the collection of site feedback. On the whole, site feedback to the estimator is both erratic and of doubtful accuracy, and it is no doubt for these reasons that research appears to show that estimators tend not to place great reliance on the information they do receive.

Operational estimating

Operational estimating techniques attempt to forecast the cost of completing an entire construction operation, rather than attempting to forecast the cost of work by formulating unit rates for each measured item of work, and they, therefore, require the prior preparation of both a method statement and a programme for the work. In some ways the preparation of an operational estimate involves the same basic activities as the preparation of a unit rate, in that the estimator must assess the cost of all of the resources required to complete the work. In this case, however, the number and type of resources, and the time for which they are required, will be dictated by the project programme and the activity method statement.

The advantages of estimating the cost of complete operations, as opposed to preparing unit rate analyses for measured work items, are the following.

(a) When compiling an operational estimate the estimator has a much clearer and more complete picture of the whole task to be done than is usually possible when attempting to build up a price from unit rate analysis based on measured quantities.

(b) Where the work involves extensive use of plant it is often difficult to apportion the costs among a group of measured items. It is for this reason that the operational method is generally preferred for large civil engineering schemes.

(c) It may be necessary to consider the interrelationship of a number of trades or particular combination of resources involved in a particular operation or activity. The use of unit rate methods can mask these interrelationships, but the use of operational methods, in conjunction with the proposed method statement allows them to be explored in detail. Operational methods also allow easy comparison of alternative methods of carrying out the work.

(d) The production rates used in the cost prediction are based upon a carefully prepared programme rather than on supposedly 'standard' outputs. The estimate can, therefore, take account of variations in production rates due to uneconomic or out of sequence working, discontinuous work flow etc.

Worked examples of operational estimating are included in CIOB[8] and in McCaffer and Baldwin.[9]

Contingency allowances

It is normal practice in any estimate to make some allowance to cover the extent of the perceived risk inherent both in the project and in the estimating process, and this allowance is termed the contingency sum. In the past contingency sums have often been simply an educated guess, or at best have been estimated in a fairly unsystematic way on the basis of the estimator's past experience, and it has subsequently been shown that, when operating in this way, estimators are more likely to underestimate rather than overestimate the sums required. Contemporary developments in risk analysis now mean that risks can be quantified with much more accuracy, and Barnes[10] describes a rather more scientific technique for the assessment of contingency sums using probability analysis based on risk assessment.

One of the biggest risks as far as the accuracy of the early stage estimate is concerned is the degree of technological risk associated with the project. Hindsight shows that technological risk is almost always underestimated, and projects which are technologically innovative have a significantly greater chance of overspending the budget. In the context of BOT projects the promoter will be looking for certainty of cost from an early stage, and there may be a temptation, at least in the case of more marginal schemes, to take a chance and reduce the initial budget in an attempt to make the scheme appear more viable. It is, therefore, most important that designers of BOT schemes balance the use of innovative high technology solutions against the possible risks of disruption to the project budget. It is perhaps for this reason that few BOT schemes employ innovative engineering design.

Accuracy of early cost forecasts

Provided that the original underlying assumptions were reasonable, and that the development of the design does not result in the cost allocated for each of the elements in the cost plan being exceeded, the forecasts generated by the techniques described above should provide an acceptably accurate estimate of project cost for contractors to use as a basis for BOT proposals where the design may be significantly incomplete, at least in detail, at the time of bid submission.

There has been considerable research into both the accuracy of quantity surveyors' early forecasts of construction cost, and also into the factors which influence accuracy, spread over the past 30 years, but the main effort in this field has been concentrated in the past decade or so. Skitmore et al.[11] present a good review of the current literature, and state that they have found that the results of previous studies were in many cases contradictory and widely different. As regards the accuracy of early stage cost predictions for building work, the overall mean seems to be around ±15% at early design stage, reducing to ±8% or so at tender stage, but the coefficient of variation is very large.

So far as civil engineering work is concerned Barnes[10] quotes figures of ±33% at feasibility stage, while Thompson,[12] reporting on earlier research, says:

> ... the average increase in value (between pre-contract estimate and tender) of civil engineering contracts utilising bills of quantities has been shown to be 10·5%.

There is, however, significant evidence that forecasts of final out-turn cost often go astray with potentially disastrous consequences for all concerned. The World Bank,[13] for example, discusses the Highway of the Sun, from Cuernavaca to Acapulco in Mexico where the US$2 billion final cost was more than twice the original estimate giving rise to the need for tolls five to ten times higher than those for comparable distances in the United States. Predicted traffic flows failed to materialize, and the Mexican Government has been forced to take a number of steps including extending the concession life to render the project viable. The problem may be even worse for schemes which display a high level of technical innovation. Examples quoted by Skitmore *et al.*[11] include the Humber Bridge (estimate £19 million final cost £120 million) and the National Westminster Tower (initial estimate £15 million final cost £115 million) both in the United Kingdom, and the Sydney Opera House (estimate £2·5 million, final cost £87 million) in Australia. These are, of course, exceptional cases, but they do serve to illustrate the point that early estimation of construction cost is an art as much as a science. No estimate can be any more accurate than the design information which it attempts to quantify, and early-stage cost estimates should therefore be regarded as indicators of an order of cost rather than firm and precise statements.

Probablistic estimating

It has been convincingly argued by some that the potential accuracy of estimates based on historical cost data can be improved by taking account of the fact that the range of historical information available forms some probability distribution. Estimates should therefore be produced on a probablistic basis rather than as definitive single point estimates. The issue is considered in some depth by Flanagan and Stevens.[14]

Production of estimates of this type can be made easier through the use of a computer database and appropriate statistical manipulation software. There is, however, little evidence that probablistic techniques are widely used in practice, and this area would again seem to be a fertile area for future research.

References

1. SMITH A.J. *Estimating, tendering and bidding for construction.* Macmillan, 1995.
2. SPON, *Spon's civil engineering and highway works price book.* E & F.N. Spon, 1994, 8th edn.
3. WALKER A. Building the future. Longman, Hong Kong, 1994.
4. FERRY D.J. and BRANDON P.S. *Cost planning of buildings.* BSP, 1991, 6th edn.
5. SEELEY I.H. *Building economics.* Macmillan, 1991, 3rd edn.
6. RICS, *Standard form of cost analysis: principles, instructions and definitions.* The Royal Institution of Chartered Surveyors, London, 1989.
7. ASHWORTH A. and SKITMORE R.M. *Accuracy in estimating.* The Chartered Institute of Building, UK. Occasional paper No. 27.
8. CIOB. *Code of estimating practice,* The Chartered Institute of Building, UK, 1983.

9. MCCAFFER R. and BALDWIN A.N. *Estimating and tendering for civil engineering works*. Granada Publishing, London, 1984.

10. BARNES N.M.L. (WEARNE S. (ed.)). Financial control of construction. *Control of engineering projects*. Thomas Telford, London, 1989.

11. SKITMORE M., STRADLING S., TUOHY A. and MKWEZALAMBA H. *Accuracy of construction price forecasts*. University of Salford, 1990.

12. THOMPSON P.A. (WEARNE S. (ed.)) Financial control of public works. *Control of engineering projects*. Thomas Telford, London, 1989.

13. THE WORLD BANK. *Infrastructure for development*. Oxford University Press, New York, 1994.

14. FLANAGAN R. and STEVENS S. (BRANDON P.S. (ed.)). Risk analysis, in *Quantity surveying techniques: new directions*. BSP Professional Books, Oxford, 1990.

Chapter 9

Life cycle costing and financial modelling

Introduction

Previous chapters have considered some of the more important issues to be considered in the cost evaluation of a BOT project, both in terms of establishing the initial financial viability of the scheme, and in cost planning/cost monitoring the design process. A number of techniques have been described. In the case of a BOT project, however, it has already been established that, in order to be economically viable, the revenue generated by the project during the period of the concession must be high enough to cover all of the costs involved. These costs will include the initial development cost, financing costs, maintenance and running costs, an acceptable return to debtors and shareholders, payment of any premium to the host government, and an acceptable level of profit for the operator. This, therefore, means that the cost/revenue equation must be considered for the whole life cycle of the concession. The extended life of a BOT scheme also means that many of the factors are subject to considerable uncertainty and variability, and in order to assess the effects of possible changes in the key project variables it is, therefore, necessary to construct and test a financial 'model' of the whole project life cycle. Note that there are a wide range of decision analysis tools used to test the economic viability of development projects (see also Chapters 3, 5 and 6). It is not intended here to discuss the various types of analysis which might be used, merely to show how financial models can be constructed and used through some simple examples.

This chapter, therefore, begins with an outline consideration of financial modelling, and goes on to discuss some aspects of operating and maintenance costs, and the time value of money. The chapter concludes with a discussion on the problems and difficulties which can arise in considering costs over an extended project life cycle.

Financial modelling

Financial models are defined by Pfaff[1] as '... mathematical constructs which can be used to help better understand, control, examine, or manage the financial affairs of an individual or institution'. There are, therefore, an infinite range of types of financial model, and the type of model used in any particular situation will obviously depend upon purpose for which the model is required. Financial models of various kinds are used in the initial estimating stages of BOT projects (see also Chapters 7 and 8), but this section considers the financial models conventionally used in the consideration of a BOT project throughout the whole life cycle. Such models are most likely to be used either

(*a*)   to allow the project participants to investigate the overall likely financial performance of the project as an investment throughout its life cycle and to test that model under a variety of conditions (i.e. to test the overall financial viability of the scheme)

(*b*)   to enable the comparison of alternative methods of construction or the use of alternative materials.

Such models usually work by modelling cash flow, and the model, therefore, needs to incorporate cost data for the whole of the projected life cycle (normally the term of the concession) together with all of the variables which may have an effect on the financial performance being measured. Note, however, that while it is relatively easy to model quantifiable financial data, it is very much more difficult to model the effects of those more subjective risks which might affect a project with a life span of several decades. These factors are none the less important, and the results generated by financial models based on quantitative data will need to be interpreted in the light of these more subjective factors.

The development of sophisticated computer spreadsheet programs has made the generation of financial models of this type much easier, and packages such as LOTUS 1-2-3 are adequate for the construction of some very complex models. This text is not intended to be a primer on the use of spreadsheets, and it is assumed that the reader is already familiar with the basic principles of the technique, but Pfaff[1] is a useful reference for those without the necessary computing skills.

Models to investigate overall financial performance

A simplified example of a cash flow model, produced using the LOTUS 1-2-3 spreadsheet, is shown in Table 9.1. The project is a simple toll

Table 9.1 *Simplified example of a cash flow model for a toll bridge:* £ × 10³

		1	2	3	4	5	6	7	8	9	10
Traffic flow	2 500 000 movements per annum										
Toll	£1										
Year		1	2	3	4	5	6	7	8	9	10
Fixed expenditure											
Development and construction		(5000)	(4500)								
Repay loan				(563)	(563)	(563)	(563)	(563)	(563)	(563)	(559)
Finance charges				(540)	(473)	(405)	(338)	(270)	(203)	(135)	(66)
Annual maintenance/ operation				(350)	(350)	(350)	(350)	(350)	(350)	(350)	(350)
Resurface						(400)					(400)
Total		(5000)	(4500)	(1453)	(1385)	(1718)	(1250)	(1183)	(1115)	(1048)	(1375)
Income											
Toll fees				2500	2500	2500	2500	2500	2500	2500	2500
Cash flow		(5000)	(4500)	1047	1115	782	1250	1317	1385	1452	1125

Internal rate of return to equity investors   12·52%

bridge. In this example the land is to be provided free of charge by the host authority, and the concession period will be ten years from the date of commencement of construction, with an expected design and construction period of two years. Initial development and construction costs are estimated to be £9·5 million, of which £4·5 million is to be debt financed through a financial institution, with the remainder being raised from equity partners. Repayment of the loan is to be made annually in arrears in equal instalments over the period of the concession, with an interest rate of 12% per year on the reducing balance. The equity partners will gain the return on their investment from profits generated during the period of the concession. Periodic resurfacing costs are assessed as £400 000 in years five and ten, and annual maintenance and running costs at £350 000. Traffic flows are assessed at an average 2 500 000 vehicles per year with a toll of £1·00. In this particular model all costs and revenues are expressed in present-day money, the assumption being that inflation will have an equal effect on both costs and revenues throughout the concession period. The internal rate of return is calculated from the cash flows by the spreadsheet software using the @IRR command.

This model is very simplistic in a number of areas. It does not, for instance, take any account of taxation, the initial expenditure for design and construction work is conveniently assumed to be evenly spread over the two-year period, with the equity contribution being spent first, and the debt provision would normally be drawn down on a monthly, quarterly or half yearly basis as the construction proceeds. None the less the model does give an idea of the approach, and the incorporation of more complex features is simply an extension of the approach shown. The model shown in Table 9.1 is sufficient to indicate that simple 'what-if' scenarios can be quickly tested in order to investigate the effect of changes in key variables on financial performance. Tables 9.2 and 9.3, for example, show the effect of variations in traffic flows 10% above and 10% below the target respectively, retaining the toll at £1·00.

The ability to rapidly investigate the effects of changes in the key variables on the financial performance of the project is of fundamental significance for two reasons. Firstly, it is important to know which variables have the most significant effect on overall performance. Secondly, BOT projects are generally considered to be inherently risky, and one of the major problems with long-term projects is that the data become less certain the further ahead the predictions are made. Sensitivity testing of the model is, therefore, a very important process in order to define the limits of the 'envelope' within which profitability of the project will be considered to be satisfactory. The simplest approach

Table 9.2 *The effect of traffic flow variations on cash flow: £ × 10³*

Traffic flow	2 750 000 movements per annum									
Toll	£1									
Year	1	2	3	4	5	6	7	8	9	10
Fixed expenditure										
Development and construction	(5000)									
Repay loan		(4500)	(563)	(563)	(563)	(563)	(563)	(563)	(563)	(559)
Finance charges			(540)	(472)	(405)	(338)	(270)	(203)	(135)	(66)
Annual maintenance/ operation			(350)	(350)	(350)	(350)	(350)	(350)	(350)	(350)
Resurface					(400)					(400)
Total	(5000)	(4500)	(1453)	(1385)	(1718)	(1250)	(1183)	(1115)	(1048)	(1375)
Income										
Toll fees			2750	2750	2750	2750	2750	2750	2750	2750
Cash flow	(5000)	(4500)	1297	1365	1032	1500	1567	1635	1702	1375

Internal rate of return to equity investors   17·05%

Table 9.3 The effect of traffic flow variations on cash flow: £ × 10³

| Traffic flow | 2 250 000 movements per annum | | | | | | | | | |
| Toll | £1 | | | | | | | | | |
Year	1	2	3	4	5	6	7	8	9	10
Fixed expenditure										
Development and construction	(5000)	(4500)								
Repay loan			(563)	(563)	(563)	(563)	(563)	(563)	(563)	(559)
Finance charges			(540)	(473)	(405)	(338)	(270)	(203)	(135)	(66)
Annual maintenance/ operation			(350)	(350)	(350)	(350)	(350)	(350)	(350)	(350)
Resurface					(400)					(400)
Total	(5000)	(4500)	(1453)	(1385)	(1718)	(1250)	(1183)	(1115)	(1048)	(1375)
Income										
Toll fees			2250	2250	2250	2250	2250	2250	2250	2250
Cash flow	(5000)	(4500)	797	865	532	1000	1067	1135	1202	875

Internal rate of return to equity investors   7·44%

is to run the model a number of times, changing each of the key variables in turn in order to test which of the variables has the greatest effect on project profitability.

Computer-based probability analysis techniques such as Monte Carlo simulation can also be used, and a number of packages are readily available. In this case all of the variables are described to the model in the form of probability distributions, and the model is processed many times using values taken at random from the various probability distributions given. The resulting projections of project financial performance will also be given as a probability distribution, and this can obviously give a much better picture of likely project performance than can be obtained from single-point deterministic estimates. It may, however, not be sufficient to consider each variable in isolation, since some variables will often be interrelated. In the model given, for example, it is highly likely that there will be some interrelationship between the traffic flow and the toll charge, i.e. beyond some threshold figure increases in toll charges are likely to give rise to reduced traffic flows as travellers find alternative routes. It may, therefore, be necessary in some cases to build more complex models which include these interrelationships. (Risk analysis methodologies are discussed in more detail in Chapter 11.)

Models to evaluate the true value of alternatives

The second use of whole life cost models is to evaluate the true costs of alternatives over a project, or a product, life cycle. This may be useful during the project design stage, where it is necessary to make a choice between increased initial capital cost for some component as against an expected reduction in ongoing running or maintenance costs. A further use of this type of technique is when attempting to choose whether an asset should be retained and refurbished or demolished and replaced. Life cycle costing is frequently used in the economic analysis of business alternatives, and only an overview of the technique is given here. (A more comprehensive treatment of the technique may be found in Fabrycky and Blanchard,[2] but see also Flanagan et al.[3] and/or Hoar and Norman[4] for a more readable treatment of life cycle costing applied to construction.)

A cash flow approach is again used, but a further complication, when attempting to compare the true value of different options for costs and benefits spread over a long period of time, is that some of the costs will fall to be paid now whereas other costs, and the whole of the revenue stream, will fall due at various times in the future and will thus be affected by inflation and interest rates. Additionally some of these future costs and revenues will be lump sums (e.g. on a toll road resurfacing costs may be planned to occur at regular intervals), whereas the costs of, for example, toll booth operators and traffic policing, together with virtually the whole of the revenue stream, will be ongoing throughout the concession period. These points, therefore, require further consideration.

The time value of money

In order that different combinations of costs and benefits occurring over an extended period of time can be adequately compared, techniques are required to enable conversion of all future expenditure and revenue to some common base. The usual technique is to convert all future financial transactions to their present day values, i.e. in the case of future costs to calculate the amount which it would be necessary to commit today to meet the anticipated future expenditure at whatever point in the future it is going to occur. A similar approach is also taken for future benefits. In other words the amount of future transactions is discounted to present-day values. The technique obviously requires some assumptions to be made with regard to future interest and inflation rates, and these are considered later.

As a simple example assume that, for budgeting purposes, it is necessary to calculate the present-day provision to be made for the replacement of some piece of plant in a year's time at an estimated present day cost of £105 000. If it is assumed that money invested today will earn a real rate of interest (i.e. the difference between the actual interest rate and the predicted inflation rate) of say 5% per year then it is obvious that an investment of £100 000 today will provide the necessary £105 000 in a year's time, a 'simple interest' calculation for which the formula is:

$$E = C(1 + r\%)$$

Where: E is the amount of the future expenditure

C is the capital needed to invest

$r\%$ is the real interest rate.

Turned around, the amount which needs to be invested now for some expenditure in the future is obviously:

$$C = E/(1 + r\%)$$

Consider now a slightly more complex example where the cost is due two years in the future. The same technique may be applied except that now account must be taken of the interest earned in the second year on the initial capital plus the interest earned in the first year:

$$E = C(1 + r\%) + r\%C(1 + r\%)$$
$$= C(1 + r\%)^2$$

and this equation may be extended for any number of years (n) to give the general formula for compound interest:

$$E = C(1 + r\%)^n$$

The amount of money to be invested today to cover some expenditure (E) at a point (n) years in the future is thus:

$$C = E/(1 + r\%)^n$$

Therefore, if there is a need to replace some piece of plant in ten years' time at a predicted present-day cost of £105 000, given a real rate of interest of 5% the sum to be invested today is:

$$105\ 000/(1 + 5\%)^{10} = £64\ 460$$

In other words the value of the future expenditure is discounted to the value in today's money, i.e. the present value of £105 000 payable in ten years' time given an interest rate of 5% is £64 460. Similarly, if revenues are regarded as negative expenditure, then the present value of an income of £105 000 receivable in ten years given a 5% discount rate is only £64 460.

This is all very well for items which occur as occasional lump sums, but what about those transactions which arise on a regular basis at a constant rate throughout the life cycle? What is needed here is a formula to enable calculation of the present day cost of spending some amount of money at regular intervals, say every year, for (n) years. It is common to treat costs of this kind as if they fall due at the end of each period, so if the amount required is constant each year, then the amount required in the first year is:

$$C = E/(1 + r\%)$$

Similarly we know that for the expenditure arising in the second year we need to commit:

$$C = E/(1 + r\%)^2,$$

for the third year

$$C = E/(1 + r\%)^3 \text{ etc.}$$

The total therefore to provide for a constant expenditure (E) in each of (n) years is therefore:

$$C = E/(1 + r\%) + E/(1 + r\%)^2 + E/(1 + r\%)^3 \ldots + E/(1 + r\%)^n$$

This is a geometric series which reduces to the formula:

$$C = E((1 + r\%)^n - 1)/r(1 + r\%)^n$$

So given a continuing expenditure of £50 000 per year each year for the next 10 years and a discount rate of 5%, then the amount of money to be committed now is £386 086. In this form the calculation is known as the year's purchase or YP.

All of this information is available in published valuation tables, but can in any case be simply calculated using a computer spreadsheet.

Using these techniques it is obviously possible to calculate all of the expenditure and income flowing into and out of a project, discounted to present-day values and, more importantly, to be able to compare the true cost of alternative approaches over their whole life cycle. The technique is known, predictably, as discounted cash flow (DCF).

Discounted cash flow — an example

Figure 9.1 shows the general idea. In this case the problem is to compare the true whole life costs of alternative claddings to a power station turbine hall, to be constructed as a BOT project with a concession life of 20 years. Cladding type 1 has an initial cost of £5 million, will last for 20 years, and will require routine maintenance every 5 years at an estimated cost of 7·5% of the initial installation cost. Cladding type B has an initial cost of £8 million, has a life of at least 30 years but is forecast to require repairs at an estimated cost of 2·5% of the initial cost immediately prior to hand over at the end of the 20-year concession. The

Cladding type 1

Initial cost	£5 000 000	
Maintenance at 5 years	7·5% × 5 000 000 × 0·91	339 649·05
Maintenance at 10 years	7·5% × 5 000 000 × 0·82	307 630·61
Maintenance at 15 years	7·5% × 5 000 000 × 0·74	278 630·52
Replacement at 20 years	5 000 000 × 0·67	3 364 856·67
Total whole life cost	£9 290 766·86	

Cladding type 2

Initial cost	£8 000 000	
Maintenance at 20 years	200 000 × 0·67	134 594·27
Total whole life cost	£8 134 594·27	

Figure 9.1 Comparative whole life costings for cladding options

discount rate is assumed, for the purpose of this example, to be 2%. Factors affecting the choice of discount rate are considered later.

Note that all future expenditure is discounted to present-day values by taking the future expenditure at present day prices and multiplying by the value of £1 in 5, 10, 15 or 20 years respectively at the relevant discount rate. This information is obtainable from published tables or by calculation from the formulae given earlier.

In this case the option with the higher capital cost but lesser maintenance cost would seem to be the best buy. There are, however, fairly serious limitations which must be considered in any life cycle costing study, particularly when the two alternatives are reasonably close together as in this case. The limitations are considered later, but a question which deserves further consideration is the choice of discount rate.

Choosing the right discount rate

Life cycle cost predictions are frequently made net of inflation, with the discount rate taking account of both future inflation and interest rates. Choice of the correct discount rate is, therefore, of fundamental importance. Long-term interest and inflation rates are very difficult to predict with any degree of accuracy, but there is generally considered to be a relationship, usually roughly stable, between the inflation rate and market investment rates such that a real rate of interest (i.e. a positive rate of return net of inflation) is available somewhere, and in the absence of any other information this is the rate usually used as the discount rate in DCF calculations. Note, however, that the relationship between interest and inflation rates may vary over time.

The discount rate therefore takes account of both inflation and the prevailing interest rate, sometimes taken as the bank base rate, in order to give an effective rate of interest. The formula for calculation of the discount rate (d) is:

$$d = [(1 + b)/(1 + i) - 1] \times 100$$

where: b = bank base rate
i = prevailing inflation rate

The proof for the derivation of the formula may be found in Kelly and Male.[5]

It follows from the above that the question of what particular discount rate to use for any specific project is a matter of individual professional judgement and may vary from project to project depending upon the way the project is to be financed. In the case of projects financed from borrowings for example the appropriate rate is obviously the actual cost of borrowing the money, usually net of inflation, but different criteria may apply in the case of equity finance.

Interest rates and inflation rates will also, of course, vary over time, but the relationship between the prevailing inflation and interest rates is generally considered to be roughly stable and the discount rate should, therefore, stay within a fairly narrow range.

Limitations

Life cycle cost analysis suffers from a number of limitations which must be recognized and understood if the results of the technique are to be used intelligently. The techniques attempt to predict the future, and the future is by its very nature uncertain. Much of the data relates to future costs and benefits which may be subject to unforeseen factors. In many cases, such as the example given in Figure 9.1, only small changes would be required to the key variables (initial capital cost, repair costs, etc.) to give a totally different answer. In addition predictions about future interest and inflation rates are in themselves risky, and the longer the term of the concession the riskier the process becomes.

Notwithstanding the above, financial modelling of the kind described here is useful, and many of the risks can be minimized by the use of sensitivity and probabilistic analysis. In the final analysis, however, the results of such models should be used as only part of the data available to the decision-maker in reaching his decision. Ferry and Brandon[6] point out clearly the dangers of using such models as the sole basis for decision making.

References

1. PFAFF P. *Financial modelling*. Allyn and Bacon, 1990.
2. FABRYCKY W.J. and BLANCHARD B.S. *Life cycle cost and economic analysis.* Prentice Hall International, Englewood Cliffs, New Jersey, 1991.
3. FLANAGAN R., NORMAN G., MEADOWS J. and ROBINSON G. *Life cycle costing theory and practice.* BSP, Oxford, 1989.
4. HOAR D. and NORMAN G. (BRANDON P. (ed.)). Life cycle cost management. *Quantity surveying techniques — new directions.* BSP, Oxford, 1990.
5. KELLY J. and MALE S. *Value management in design and construction.* E & F.N. Spon, London, 1993.
6. FERRY D.J. and BRANDON P.S. *Cost planning of buildings.* BSP, Oxford, 1991, 6th edn.

Chapter 10

Risks and their mitigation

Risks are unavoidable in any construction project. The degree of risk that a contractor is exposed to depends on the contractual arrangement and the role that he takes. The wider his scope of work, the more risks he assumes. For example, a design and build contractor is assuming more risks than a contractor building to an architect's design. It is not difficult therefore to envisage that the promoters of a BOT project are faced with a daunting array of risks, many of which they would not assume under a traditional public sector project.

Apart from the contractor, other participants are also faced with substantial risks. Lenders, in particular, are risk sensitive. For example, in Turkey, the Akkuyu nuclear reactor power plant was put forward as a BOT project by a Canadian atomic energy specialist company, AEC, as long ago as 1984. The project stagnated with no one prepared to finance it, and this later resulted in the withdrawal of the proposal.

In this chapter, the nature of the risks inherent in BOT projects will be discussed and some mitigation measures will be suggested.

Types of risks and their mitigation

The risks inherent in a BOT project have commonly been grouped under three headings — financing risks, political risks and technical risks. The chapter on financial engineering explains that these risks occur at different periods and, therefore, grouping by stages of a project is also possible.

Financing risks

Foreign exchange and interest rate fluctuations
Foreign exchange risk is especially relevant to developing countries, which have to import equipment and substantial amounts of materials

using foreign currencies for settlement. However, the income arising from the use of the completed facilities or the sale of products (say electricity) are in local currency. Yet repayment of foreign loans has to be in foreign currencies. Therefore, project sponsors usually have to seek remittance and convertibility guarantees from the host government in order that the necessary transactions can be effected and the project revenues including dividends can be remitted freely. Reluctance on the part of governments to give these guarantees or to curtail restrictions inevitably discourages foreign investment in a country's infrastructure. Fortunately, solutions other than guarantees have evolved. For example, in the Shajiao 'B' coal-fired power station project in China, the Hong Kong developer is being paid for the power generated 50% in the local currency, Renminbi (RMB), and 50% in foreign currencies converted from RMB at predetermined exchange rates. The developer uses the local currency to purchase coal from China at predetermined prices. In other cases, an offshore 'escrow account', effectively a trust fund established and funded by the proceeds generated from the venture, can be set up to which all project revenues and foreign loans are paid. Such an arrangement can avoid the risks of expropriation and ensure a smooth flow of capital and revenues to all parties concerned during the concession period.

Foreign exchange fluctuations can also be detrimental to financial soundness by affecting the prices of input and output, as well as loan repayment. Likewise, an upward movement of interest rates will affect the repayment ability of the project company. However, it is unusual for lenders to agree on fixed exchange rates and interest rates in a lending package and, therefore, other hedging facilities have to be sought. In the Malaysian North–South Highway project (the largest BOT scheme in Malaysia) the government provided the project company with the guarantee that it would make up the shortfalls if any adverse exchange rate movement exceeds 15% on its offshore debt, or if any adverse interest rate movement exceeds 20% on its floating rate offshore debt, or when it would otherwise be unable to pay its debts as certified by its auditors. These guarantees instilled confidence in the funders that the project company would be able to service its debts under extremely adverse conditions in the money market.

Market risks
Changes in market price, demand and sources of raw material supply will inevitably affect the construction and operation of projects, let alone profitability. In industrial projects, lenders want to ensure the sale of the product so that there are sufficient revenues to repay their loans.

Suppliers are, therefore, required to guarantee supply quantities and prices and even to secure the promise of alternative supply sources. The government, or more usually, the wholesale purchasers (such as utility companies), could guarantee their obligations by take-or-pay or take-and-pay agreements to purchase the product on defined terms and price.

Power stations offer common examples of these supply and offtake agreements. In its various BOT power projects in China and the Philippines, the Hopewell Group secures its fuel supply from the utility or joint venture partner associated with the projects during the 'co-operation period'. In the case of the Philippine projects, the local utility company supplies fuel at no charge, while in the Chinese projects, fuel is supplied at a fixed price or on terms which effectively protect the group from the effect of any increases in the cost of fuel. On the offtake side, the local equity or cooperative joint venture partners of the project companies established by the Hopewell Group in China and the Philippines either pay a charge based on the available capacity of the plants or purchase at a pre-agreed price a specified minimum amount of the electricity generated by the plants during the cooperation periods. Such contractual obligations have been guaranteed by state entities or governmental authorities for at least the period during which the project financing is outstanding.

Income risks

For transport projects, the initial traffic forecast may be overoptimistic, either due to wrong assumptions, or to the availability of alternative routes, or to an insufficient connecting road network. Income from direct tolls may then fall short of expectations and hence the cash flow of the sponsor is jeopardized. An example is a 6000 km toll road project in Mexico reported in the World Bank's *World Development Report* 1994.[1] As a result of hasty traffic and cost projections prepared by a Mexican government agency, the project was pushed ahead. State-owned banks failed to perform proper project screening and appraisals before lending to the concessionaire, who proposed a short concession period. In order to earn a return within the short concession period, tolls charged were four times higher than those in the United States. With such high tolls, roads users naturally preferred using old roads, despite doubled travelling time. Thus the expected traffic failed to materialize. This factor, coupled with cost overruns of more than 50%, meant that the Mexican Government had to take remedial measures. These included extending the concession periods from 10 or 15 years to 30 years and banning heavy vehicles from using the old road network.

Figure 10.1   Eastern Harbour Crossing

Another example is the initial operating period of the Eastern Harbour Crossing (EHC) in Hong Kong (Fig. 10.1). Despite the opening of this new cross harbour facility in September of 1989, car drivers still habitually used the already congested Cross Harbour Tunnel (completed in the 1970s), resulting in a shortfall of expected traffic through the EHC.

Figure 10.2 shows the comparison of traffic flow between the two later BOT tunnels and the highly successful prototype Cross Harbour Tunnel in Hong Kong (Fig. 10.3). Before the EHC was completed in September 1989, traffic was forecast at 40 000 vehicles per day against a design capacity of 90 000 vehicles a day. However, actual traffic turned out to be less than 20 000 per day when EHC opened. Such a shortfall cast doubt on the viability of the project in the initial year of its operation. After an active promotional campaign, traffic flow steadily increased to about 60 000 vehicles per day, but it took two years for this to happen, and the EHC still compared unfavourably with the Cross Harbour Tunnel, which has a throughput of 120 000 vehicles per day against a design capacity of 90 000. The Hong Kong government considered imposing an additional tax on users of the original Cross Harbour Tunnel in order to direct more traffic to the EHC. However, such a move would create a differential toll structure to the possible detriment of the Cross Harbour Tunnel operator and the public. Considering the fact that

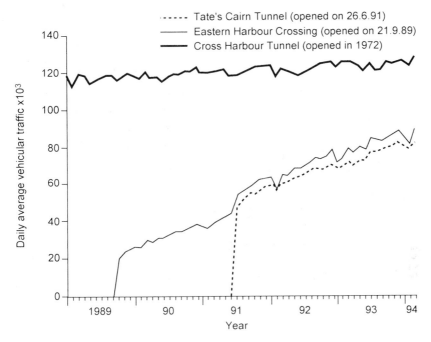

Source: *Traffic and Transport Digest,* Transport Department, Hong Kong

Figure 10.2   Comparison of traffic flow 1989—94

the government had previously given an undertaking to the EHC's operator that no passage tax would be imposed within the initial years of its operation it is obvious that injustice would have resulted had the tax proposal not been scrapped.

The situation with the EHC improved, however, soon after the opening of the connecting Tate's Cairn Tunnel (a BOT tunnel with design capacity of 100 000 vehicles per day), which feeds the EHC with north to south traffic (Fig. 10.4). Traffic flows through both tunnels have been moving in tandem with each other and there has been an increasing trend towards both reaching their respective design capacities in the near future.

Both of the above examples indicate the possible detrimental effect of an alternative route forming direct competition. The EHC—Tate's Cairn example shows the benefit that can be brought about by complementary routes. BOT projects can be interdependent for their success, and this illustrates the importance of good planning.

Very few governments have in fact guaranteed 'no second facility' to promoters, as it would generally be against public interest to do so. A notable exception is the Channel Tunnel, where the respective

Figure 10.3   Busy traffic through the first Cross Harbour Tunnel in Hong Kong

Figure 10.4   Tate's Cairn Tunnel under construction in Hong Kong

governments promised Eurotunnel, the promoter, that there would be no other fixed link across the English Channel before the year 2020 in order to avoid undermining the returns to investors.

For privatized road projects under the DBFO scheme, the UK government encourages private financing by reimbursing project companies with 'shadow tolls' based on recorded traffic flow rather than having to take tolls directly off road users. This gives a much better guarantee of return to funders because direct tolling would be difficult due to the great number of interconnecting roads, which make switching to alternative untolled routes easy for drivers.

Other incentives provided by governments to attract investors in these risky undertakings have been seen in two other BOT projects.

(a) The Sydney Harbour Tunnel Company was guaranteed a minimum traffic toll income. Under the so-called 'Ensured Revenue Stream Agreement', the project company, The Sydney Harbour Tunnel Company, will receive a guaranteed cash flow based on agreed projections of tunnel and bridge traffic (minus tunnel receipts). If cross-harbour traffic falls below 10% of the forecast demand, the state government would have to pay for the shortfall.

(b) In the case of the Malaysian North−South Highway, the Malaysian government undertakes to provide additional finance to PLUS, the concessionaire, in the event of a drop in traffic volume in the first 17 years of operation creating cash-flow problems.

Cost overrun risk

When construction costs exceed original estimates, either due to inflation or excessive design changes, drawdowns from loans may not be able to match the payments due to contractors. This may also cause lenders to question the continued viability of the project. Additional sources of finance may have to be sought. A typical example is the Channel Tunnel project, which had its construction costs priced partly on a lump sum, and partly on a target cost basis. This project ran hideously over budget, with an estimated final project cost of US$15 billion (£9·75 billion), doubling the initial estimate of US$7·4 billion (£4·8 billion).[2] These huge cost overruns even caused the financing banks to threaten to take over the franchise before it was eventually opened on 5 May 1994.

The Malaysian North−South Highway also suffered a hefty cost overrun, with the final cost estimated at US$2·5 billion, or 75% above original estimates. The increase was attributed to inflation, unplanned additional work and early implementation of planned enhancements.

Tiong[3] suggested that cost overrun risk can be mitigated in the ways described below.

Additional capital injected by project sponsors. Eurotunnel, the concessionaire for the Channel Tunnel project, had gone through several major equity offerings to meet its ever increasing construction bills. The founder offer in 1986 raised US$71 million (£46 million), followed by a private placement raising US$317 million (£206 million). In 1987 the public share offering raised US$1.18 billion (£770 million) and the 1990 rights issue raised US$872 million (£566 million).

Standby credit facility from original lenders. In the Shajiao 'B' Power Station project, the Chinese government assisted the developer in the arrangement of an 'emergency loan facility' to provide funds in the event of force majeure.

The Malaysian government set aside 10% of the total investment cost as a standby element for their North—South Highway project.

Fixed price contracts from contractors. Most BOT projects are based on lump-sum fixed-price turnkey construction contracts. Typical examples include the Dartford Crossing in the UK and the Tate's Cairn Tunnel in Hong Kong. The effectiveness of fixed-price contracts in containing construction costs within budget depends very much on the degree to which the host government can avoid uncertainty and changes to performance specifications and design standards.

Sponsors' escrow fund for completion. A US$160 million (A$223 million) interest-free loan was extended to the project company for the Sydney Harbour Crossing, funded out of tolls paid on the existing Sydney Harbour Bridge during the construction period.

Political risks

Political risk is often the most significant risk faced by foreign investors and lenders in the developing world because of the likelihood of dramatic overnight political change. Such changes can jeopardize projects at a critical stage. There are two main types of political risks, which are discussed below.

Sovereign risks
This may be due to a change of government composition. One of the contributing factors to the abandonment of the Channel Tunnel project in 1975 was the 1974 change of government in the UK from Conservative

to Labour, which left the project without any effective political sponsorship. A further example is the case of the Thai rail and highway project awarded to Hopewell Holdings, where fears that the project could be delayed were sparked by a military coup in Thailand in 1991. In Canada, the privatization contract for the redevelopment of Terminals 1 and 2 at Toronto's Pearson International Airport was scrapped following a change of government after the general election in 1993. Immediately upon assumption of office, the new Canadian government called for a review of the controversial contract, which was said to be too lucrative to be put into private hands.

A further sovereign risk is the possible change of legislation. Any government is at liberty to amend or repeal legislation as it sees fit. These changes may arise due to purely domestic considerations, such as changes in economic policy, or they may be part of wider constitutional issues. Sponsors of BOT projects sometimes manage to obtain agreements from the host governments to restrict such changes but their value is doubtful against a government which is determined to change the ground rules. Nevertheless, most governments are interested in having more than one infrastructure project supported by the private sector, and they, therefore, would not wish to deter future investment by capricious behaviour.

A more subtle risk in this connection, especially in developing countries, is the volatility of promises given under strong personal influence. An example is the uncertainty which faced the Bangkok rail and highway project when top officials in the ousted government were removed following the 1991 coup.

Instability risks
This type of risk can range from labour unrest and embargo of construction equipment to outright expropriation. Construction companies could be forced into bankruptcy by a political decision to stop work. The same can happen with war and hostility between countries. Major political uprisings can also take away financiers' interest in otherwise lucrative projects, at least temporarily. For example the Tiananmen Square incident in China on the 4 June 1989 caused the syndication of loans for the Guangzhou-Shenzhen-Zhuhai super-highway to be delayed until 1991.

Tiong[3] and Nevitt[4] suggest the following ways in which protection can be sought by investors in BOT projects in potentially unstable countries.

(*a*) Obtain the government's agreement to allow the project sponsors to freely exploit the particular investment for a given period of time. However, if investors rely too much on this sort of agreement, they are betting heavily on the long-term stability and consistency of the policies of the host government.

(b)   Form a consortium of international investors and lenders so that expropriation of the project facility will result in default of a number of international loans and jeopardize the country's credit rating to an unacceptable degree.

In Thailand, the Second Stage Expressway in Bangkok was taken over by the government in 1993 after a row over revenue sharing and operation of the completed expressway. In response to this, the syndicate of more than 40 Thai and international banks withdrew financing for the US$1 billion scheme. Although the discordance was eventually settled by the sale of majority stake held by the original sponsor, Kumagai Gumi, a cloud of doubt surrounded the project financing community as to the viability of further schemes.

(c)   Take out a political risks insurance policy. Government agencies such as the Export Credits Guarantee Department (ECGD) in the UK or other multilateral development agencies such as the World Bank (through an affiliate called the Multilateral Investment Guarantee Agency — MIGA) offer various guarantee schemes. In the United States, agencies such as the Overseas Private Investment Corporation (OPIC) provide coverage for investment abroad. Insurance covers have also been made available to offer protection of initial costs against government non approval and delay in completion due to physical loss.

(d)   Negotiate for a financial undertaking by the host government. Lenders normally insist that host governments provide some coverage for outstanding debt and other financial obligations for uninsurable force majeure events. Both the Bangkok Second Stage Expressway and the Gazi power project in Turkey have concession agreements containing these protective features.

Technical risks

Construction difficulties

Unforeseen soil conditions and breakdown of equipment are common occurrences on any construction site, especially for large civil engineering projects. Usually, these will have repercussions on cost and time but the effects are usually surmountable with today's technology.

For example, during the construction of the Eastern Harbour Crossing in Hong Kong, unexpected weakness in the harbour bed caused severe flooding and erosion of the tunnel's foundation. This resulted in some interim delay but engineers and contractors were able to overcome the problem eventually and finished ahead of schedule. Construction contracts under BOT arrangement are usually of the Design and Build type, which do not provide redress for contractors against adverse geological conditions. Against the constraints of lump-sum fixed-price contracts, contractors normally either include a substantial risk allowance in the price or they simply gamble and hope for the best.

Completion delays

Projects can be delayed due to all sorts of reasons, but poor interface co-ordination and late design changes are very common. For example, the Channel Tunnel project was allegedly delayed by late changes in the signalling system specification and the shuttle design. Out of the seven year construction contract, a delay of one year resulted. As BOT projects rely on the income from the completed facilities to service their debts, the rolled-up interest from a delayed project can be substantial and can seriously damage the project's profitability. At one time, financiers of the Channel Tunnel were reluctant to commit further loans when the above-mentioned delay resulted in substantial cost increase.

Project sponsors need to take positive steps against events like these. In particular they need to ensure suitably designed and implemented organisation structures, especially in respect of project management. They can also commit the contractors to lump sum contracts, using proven technology and agreed milestone schedules, which define contractually the timing and relationship of critical stages of the projects with payment incentives. Less positive measures include the imposition of heavy liquidated damages based on expected loss. Contractors could also be required to provide completion guarantees and performance bonds. In the latter case the risk of cost increases due to late completion is borne by insurance companies or banks, for which a premium is charged.

Operation risks

During operation of the facilities the revenue generating capability may be hindered by equipment breakdown or the discovery of defects in the work. Proper training of local operators for operation and maintenance is obviously essential, as is the stipulation of adequate contractual provisions for maintenance and the making good of defects by the contractor. Maintenance bonds will also provide a source of funds for the remedial work. More positive steps include careful choice of operator, and where possible involvement of the operator in the design and commissioning phases. The sponsor must ensure that the operator has adequately provided for management of the operation and maintenance of the completed facilities over the entire concession period.

Risk pattern

As mentioned at the beginning of this chapter, different risks relate to different stages of any BOT scheme. Echoing the views expressed in the chapter on financial engineering, any infrastructure project can be viewed as two distinct projects: a relatively high-risk construction project and a relatively low-risk utility project.

After commencement of construction, the risks begin to increase sharply as funds are advanced to purchase materials, labour and equipment. Interest charges on loans to finance construction also begin to accumulate. Force majeure risks are particularly acute during the construction and development phases of a project.

These risks peak in the early operational years when the projects are under the greatest pressure due to peak debt servicing when the highest interest burden occurs. Once the project is running to the business plan, the revenues are collected from toll fees, debts are paid and the project sponsors recover their investment with profits. This is in contrast to most industrial projects where the risks of product obsolescence and competitor response usually lead to market risks predominating especially when the operation and maintenance costs are high and the concession period is short. It is important that this pattern of risk distribution be appreciated by those parties demanding returns from the projects. In the case of investors, they should not expect dividends to be paid out of the proceeds until such time as the risks have levelled off. Likewise the lenders' agreement should be sought to effect repayment according to a progressive schedule. Governments usually take this factor into consideration in structuring the concessionaires' obligations. For example, in the case of the Tate's Cairn Tunnel in Hong Kong, the government stipulated that royalty payments are due from the franchise holder, payable in two stages:

(a)   2·5% of the operating receipts for a period of five years after the road operating date
(b)   5% of the operating receipts thereafter for the duration of the franchise.

In another example, the Malaysian North–South Highway, the government's fixed-interest loan is repayable over 25 years, with a grace period of 15 years.

Risk allocation

From the discussion of mitigation in the previous sections, it appears that reducing the risks to one party generally entails passing the risk to other parties.

Therefore, what the project sponsors are actually doing is evaluating the level of acceptability of each risk and seeking to allocate the unwanted risks to the different parties involved. A 1994 UK DoT study into the risks posed by DBFO road projects is reported by Middleboe[5] to have identified almost 300 separate areas of risk. Middleboe also reports that 'Government has laid down that roads can only be taken on through DBFO or shadow tolls if 'significant' risk is transferred to the private sector and the cost of transferring the risk is less then the imputed value of the risk.' The term 'significant' is not defined, and a comparison of the contractor's assessment of the cost of assuming the various risks on any particular scheme with the value of the risk as assessed by the Government will apparently form one of the criteria for assessment of tenders. Accurate assessment and pricing of specific risks is, therefore, becoming an increasingly important factor for contractors to consider in projects of this type.

The allocation of risk to parties like the contractors will normally be at some additional cost to the project. Similarly, coverage of risks by insurance policies also entail premiums, which eventually form part of the project costs. Apart from this cost consideration, regard should be given to the risk-taking attitudes of the participants for an equitable sharing of risks to result.

Contractors' attitudes to BOT risks

There are mixed views amongst contractors towards participating in BOT projects. Surveys carried out by Industrial Market Research Ltd in the United Kingdom in 1989[6] and the Chartered Institute of Transport in 1993[7] indicate that contractors demonstrate their risk perception in a number of ways. The following paragraphs assembled from these reports show this.

High tendering cost
Often, contractors tendering for private transport infrastructure projects

spend in excess of US$1·5 million for feasibility studies, investigation, design, planning and estimating. If they have to incur these levels of cost and still compete with four or five other contractors the risk is generally not considered worth taking.

There should be a clear statement of intent, instead of contractors being simply informed at the end of the bidding process that the project will not go ahead. If abandonment is inevitable, refunding of bidding costs should be made possible.

Lack of exclusivity

Contractors are wary about the risks of their innovative proposals being put out to competitive tender without gaining exclusivity or preferential treatment from other competitors.

The issue of intellectual property has also caused concern with companies being unwilling to 'invent' schemes only to lose the opportunity to build them since someone might have 'stolen' the idea. A generous reward scheme is needed to encourage the initiation of schemes.

Expected return

Major contractors in the UK were mostly involved in existing public sector infrastructure projects at the time of the 1989 survey. To justify their involvement in private sector investment, the report said that they would have to achieve higher levels of return, a quicker pay-back or achieve other spin-off benefits such as development gains or business for other companies within their organization.

The 1993 report suggested that a market for private investment could be created by the transfer of a network of roads (the main subject of the report) to tolled status within the public sector, the creation of a number of companies owning significant shares in the network and the subsequent privatization of those companies.

Long-term equity interest

Many contracting companies see themselves solely as contracting companies and do not want to have a lot of money tied up in long-term projects. Those who have participated are looking to liquidate their shareholding at the earliest possible opportunity. The 1989 survey quoted one contractor as saying: 'We will put in the seed corn equity upfront, we'll get the project up and running from an operational point of view and then we'll pull out.'

The 1993 report suggested that government should not overlook the possibility that the best outcome could be to procure the project in the public sector by means of design/build competition, put it into use and subsequently sell it off on the basis of established cash flow.

Government's commitment

Contractors stated that they would only be prepared to take the perceived increased risk in privatized projects if the government takes a positive stance on the subject rather than 'playing with the issue on a piecemeal basis'. The 1989 survey revealed a general consensus view amongst the leading United Kingdom contractors that the private sector was expected to take the whole burden of risk, and this made many of them wary about their involvement in previously untested areas. Contractors were found to believe that their participation in private schemes had an inherently higher level of risk than that incurred when operating as a contractor to government.

The 1993 report analysed some alternative procedures and practices and suggested that it would generally be advisable for the government or sponsoring authority to take the project through planning consent or parliamentary approval before seeking co-investment bids.

Financiers' attitudes towards BOT risks

In the UK, the Channel Tunnel and Dartford Crossing attracted a large number of bankers in arranging and underwriting loans. There was therefore a general feeling that the major clearing banks will dominate the major privatization deals. However, the 1989 research commissioned by Touche Ross[6] gave the consensus view that the banks did not adopt a proactive role in this respect leaving the contractors to be the prime movers. One of the reasons cited for this rather passive approach is the long gestation period of these projects.

The research further revealed that all of the financial institutions which had been involved in privatized schemes had incurred high opportunity costs, frequently with the banks only being paid if their consortium was successful. Indeed banks believed that their risk position was far worse than that facing contractors, since if a privately funded project ends up as a public sector project, banks receive no reward for their labours, whilst the contractors still have a chance of obtaining the construction work. Banks were also concerned that the traditional planning procedures would limit the finance available for these private sector projects as the banks could not afford to have money committed throughout the protracted time it takes to get major schemes to fruition.

The research reported a number of suggestions put forward by the financial organizations on how government could improve matters. These were:

(a) giving concessions to the originator and then getting competitive bids for construction
(b) creating a fund for bid costs
(c) putting in equity rather than giving grants (sharing of profits in the long term)
(d) giving concessions in perpetuity, giving choice of refinancing at a later date
(e) more freedom in operational pricing.

More recent development in the UK of DBFO private road contracts sees the requirement for contractors to put up at least 5% equity, thus giving lenders some protection against contractors' default.

The pessimistic views of UK financiers are also reflected by the comments of some bankers who had experienced the Channel Tunnel saga. Bennett[2] writes:

> While no major players have departed the business as a result of Eurotunnel, many of the banks within the syndicate are unlikely to lend again to a risk carrying venture.

Barry (Project Finance director of a leading bank) is quoted as saying:

> In the future they will certainly be more circumspect about committing funds to a large infrastructure project and many of them would find it difficult to get credit approval.

The situation in Asia is, however, more encouraging. Many developing Asian countries such as Vietnam, China, Thailand and the Philippines are building up their infrastructure using the BOT approach. Project finance represents a profitable lending opportunity for banks since the margins they earn can be well above those of similar-sized corporate loans. More banks in Asia will want to add some project finance loans to their portfolios, especially those related to much needed facilities such as power and transportation.

Participants in developing countries are more receptive of risks than their counterparts in developed countries. One simple reason is that the former are prepared to take higher risks with the expectation that the rewards are high in developing countries. Participants in developed countries are more concerned about the long-term earning profile of their investments rather than jumping at quick and volatile profits.

Having understood the risk-taking attitudes of the major players, the structure of any BOT project should be designed in such a way that risks and rewards are allocated according to the parties' willingness to bear them.

References

1. THE WORLD BANK. *Infrastructure for development*. Oxford University Press, New York, World Development Report 1994.
2. BENNETT R. Morton's folly. *Euromoney*, 1993, June, 59–63.
3. TIONG R. *The structuring of build-operate-transfer construction projects*. Technological Monograph, Nanyang Technological University, Singapore, 1992.
4. NEVITT K.P. *Project Financing*. Euromoney Publications, London, 1989.
5. MIDDLEBOE S. The risk factor. *New Civil Engineer*, 26 May 1994, 10.
6. TOUCHE ROSS. *Private sector investment in public sector infrastructure*. Industrial Market Research Ltd, 1989.
7. CHARTERED INSTITUTE OF TRANSPORT. *Mobilising private investments*. 1993.

Chapter 11

Risk analysis

Introduction

The previous chapter identifies the types of risk inherent in BOT projects and introduces some of the mitigation measures by way of practical examples. This chapter is intended to give a broad overview of the techniques for analysing project risks, which form an integral element of the risk management function.

The reasons for carrying out risk analysis are many. First of all, a rigorous risk analysis is necessary before a project is embarked upon in order to establish its financial and technical feasibility. It can help to screen out financially unsound projects and get minds working together early enough to overcome foreseen technical difficulties. An increased understanding of the project risks leads to the formulation of more realistic plans in terms of cost estimates and programmes. Knowing the magnitude of the possible impact that may be caused by the contingent factors, the parties can seek for better allocation of the risks through the agreement of suitable contract clauses, procurement of insurance or other risk response measures. Apart from these, a more positive and rational risk-taking attitude will result from a carefully prepared risk analysis as the risk-takers know where they stand.

Risk analysis embraces qualitative and quantitative techniques. Much has already been written on the techniques used for estimating cost and project duration, and it is not intended to repeat that subject here. Instead, attention is drawn to techniques applicable to the analysis of other types of risk which might apply to BOT projects.

Qualitative analysis

Qualititive analysis is a means of identifying the main risk sources or factors. A list of them is prepared and an assessment of the consequences on cost, time and performance is made. An idea of how such a list can be compiled may be drawn from the classification schemes suggested by Tiong,[1] Beidleman *et al.*[2] and Woodward *et al.*[3].

Tiong suggests that BOT risks can be classified into the following.

(a) Construction phase — completion delays, cost overruns, force majeure, political risk, infrastructure risk (referring to other facilities in direct competition with the BOT project in question).

(b) Operational phase — raw material supply, market, performance/technical, operations/maintenance, foreign exchange, other contingencies.

Beidleman *et al.* use a slightly different terminology with an additional phase.

(a) Development phase — technology risk, credit risk, bid risk.
(b) Construction phase — completion risk, cost overrun risk, performance risk, political risk.
(c) Operating phase — performance risk, cost overrun risk, liability risk, equity resale risk, offtake risk.

Woodward *et al.* adopt a different classification approach, dividing BOT project risks into global risks and elemental risks. Global risks are those having a wider circle of influence whereas elemental risks are those specific to a particular project. The detailed classification scheme is as follows:

Global risks
(a) Political — government, technology
(b) Legal — framework, type of agreement
(c) Commercial — market, input, currency
(d) Environmental — impact, ecological.

Elemental risks
(a) Technical — physical conditions, construction, design, technology
(b) Operational — operation, maintenance, training
(c) Financial — form of financing, evaluation, ownership, return, currency
(d) Revenue — demand, toll/tariff, development.

Although the above-mentioned risk frameworks seem to give discrete keywords to represent individual risk factors or sources, many of them are interdependent. For example, financial risk is largely outside the control of the private sector, but the taking on of this risk by the private sector will have a favourable incentive effect on project cost elements which are largely subject to controllable risk, such as construction and performance. The impact upon the project as a whole must, therefore, be carefully considered.

Apart from the use of a checklist, the identification stage relies on a mixed use of intuitive judgement, brainstorming meetings and personal experience of the risk analysts. Databases of common risks that have occurred in the past are usually referred to.

Once identified, the probability of occurrence of the risks can be assessed into the broad categories of 'high' or 'low' and their possible impact classified as 'major' or 'minor'. Immediate response action should then be taken for highly likely occurrences having major impact should they materialize. Note that a low probability of occurrence does not necessarilly give rise to a minor possible impact. Significant consequences may arise from low-risk items. Consider, for example, the possibility of a 1 in 100-year storm occurring on a tunnel project which involves working on a river bed. The probability of the risk event occurring is very low, but the effect if it happened could be disastrous.

Depending on the size or complexity of the project, it may be necessary to revisit the identification phase after the assessment phase to identify any consequential 'secondary' risks. A secondary risk may result from a proposed response to an initial risk and might, therefore, render the initial response unsuccessful. For example, in order to avoid foreign exchange risk, a concession company in a developing economy may opt to raise local finance for a transport facility. If a substantial cost overrun occurs, local financiers may not be able to extend their lending to fully meet the increased cost, especially when they are committed to subsequent projects.

Quantitative analysis

Experience has shown that qualitative analysis of risks usually leads to the need for some quantitative analysis. Quantitive analysis is a process involving mathematical models and analytical techniques, often using computers, to evaluate and quantify the impact of risks on the final cost and timescale of projects. However, such techniques may be difficult to apply to the analysis of events which fit better to a relative scale rather than an absolute one. A number of different techniques are available, the choice of which is dependent on the type and size of project, the availability and accuracy of information or data, the cost of the analysis and the time constraint, as well as the experience and expertise of the analysts. It should be noted that mathematical models and techniques can be useful indicators of trends and problems for attention, however, they should not be relied on as the sole guide to decisions.

Having cited the necessary general caveats, it is intended to give an elementary account of two quantitative techniques which may well find applications in BOT projects.

Sensitivity analysis

Sensitivity analysis is a deterministic modelling technique which is used to test the impact of a change in the value of an independent variable on the dependent variable. Basically, it is trying to provide answers to 'what if' questions. It also helps to identify factors that are risk sensitive by testing which components of the project have the greatest impact upon the project outcome.

The methodology is simple. First of all, a base case estimate should be formulated using data which are current or normally has a high likelihood of occurrence. Then, step-wise changes (including positive and negative directions) are introduced in the independent variables one by one to test their effects on the dependent variables. Sometimes, especially where synergizing or offsetting effects are envisaged, change of more than one independent variable can be introduced to test the combined effect of the changes. When all the beneficial cases are considered at the same time, the best case scenario will emerge. Likewise, when all adverse cases are combined into the model, the worst case scenario will emerge. In reality, the best case and the worst case rarely occur. Nevertheless, the worst case scenario does provide a reference bottom line for determining the minimum acceptablility of the project.

To demonstrate the application of sensitivity analysis to BOT project, a hypothetical project is illustrated by way of two tables (see Tables 11.1 and 11.2). Assuming that an expressway project has been made the subject of a privatization scheme, calculations have been made to estimate the project outcomes and financial requirements, which include such dependent variables as maximum loan amounts, timing of maximum loan, cover factors (defined as the total net present value of after-tax cash flow divided by the outstanding loan balance), internal rate of return (IRR), etc. These estimates are made based on current data and up-to-date forecasts of such independent variables as capital expenditure, operating expenditure, forecast traffic volume, currency

Table 11.1 *Sensitivity analysis: results of adverse cases*

Runs	Base case	(i)	(ii)	(iii)	(iv)	(v)	(vi)	(vii)	(viii)	(ix)
ASSUMPTIONS										
Operating expenditure increase	—	7·5%	—	—	—	—	—	—	—	7·5%
Capital expenditure increase	—	—	10%	—	—	—	—	—	—	10%
Delay: months	—	—	—	6	—	—	—	—	—	—
Traffic volume increase/(decrease)	—	—	—	—	(10%)	—	—	—	—	(10%)
Currency appreciation/(depreciation)	—	—	—	—	—	(10%)	—	—	—	(10%)
Interest rate p.a. increase/(decrease)	—	—	—	—	—	—	10%	—	—	10%
Inflation above base case	—	—	—	—	—	—	—	3% p.a.	—	3% p.a.
Equity raised 1994–96: $ × 10⁶	200 p.a.	—	—	—	—	—	—	—	100 p.a.	100 p.a.
RESULTS										
Maximum amount of loans: $ × 10⁷	180 p.a.	190	230	180	200	190	195	220	190	300
Date of maximum amount of loans	12/1994	12/1994	12/1994	12/1994	12/1994	12/1994	12/1994	12/1994	12/1994	12/1995
Concession period cover factor	4·0	4·3	3·7	4·6	4·0	4·5	4·3	3·5	4·4	2·3
17-year cover factor	2·0	2·1	1·9	2·2	1·9	2·2	2·2	1·8	2·2	1·2
15-year cover factor	1·8	1·8	1·6	1·8	1·6	1·8	1·8	1·5	1·8	1·0
12-year cover factor	1·2	1·1	0·9	1·2	1·0	1·2	1·1	0·85	1·1	0·5
Date of final repayment	12/1998	12/1998	12/1999	12/1998	12/1999	12/1998	6/1999	12/1999	6/1999	12/2002
Average loan life: years	6	6	7	5·5	6	6	6	7	6	9
Concession IRR: %	15·7	15·5	15·0	15·8	14·5	15·7	16·0	14·3	16·0	12·0

N.B. As this is a sample showing methodology rather than actual details, data are fictitious

Table 11.2 Sensitivity analysis: results of beneficial cases

Runs	Base case	(x)	(xi)	(xii)	(xiii)	(xiv)	(xv)
ASSUMPTIONS							
Operating expenditure increase	—	—	—	—	—	—	—
Capital expenditure increase	—	—	—	—	—	—	—
Delay: months	—	—	—	—	—	—	—
Traffic volume increase/(decrease)	—	10%	—	—	—	—	10%
Currency appreciation/(depreciation)	—	—	10%	—	—	—	10%
Interest rate p.a. increase/(decrease)	—	—	—	(10%)	—	—	(10%)
Inflation above base case	—	—	—	—	0·5%p.a.	—	0·5%p.a.
Equity raised 1994–96: $ × 10^6	200 p.a.	—	—	—	—	300 p.a.	300 p.a.
RESULTS							
Maximum amount of loans: $ × 10^7	180 p.a.	170	180	180	165	180	150
Date of maximum amount of loans	12/1994	12/1994	12/1994	12/1994	12/1994	12/1993	12/1993
Concession period cover factor	4·0	5·2	4·5	4·6	5·0	4·3	5·7
17-year cover factor	2·0	2·5	2·2	2·3	2·5	2·0	2·6
15-year cover factor	1·8	2·1	1·8	1·9	2·0	1·6	2·1
12-year cover factor	1·2	1·4	1·2	1·2	1·4	1·0	1·4
Date of final repayment	12/1988	6/1988	12/1988	6/1998	6/1998	6/1998	12/1996
Average loan life: years	6	5	5·5	5·6	5·10	5·30	4·30
Concession IRR: %	15·70	16·70	15·70	15·60	16·40	15·60	17·30

N.B. As this is a sample showing methodology rather than actual details, data are fictitious exchange rates, interest rates and inflation rates. When completed, these estimates form the base case scenario.

A revised estimate of the project outcomes is then performed assuming that operating expenditure increases by 7·5% from the base case scenario (Adverse case (i)). It can be seen that the maximum loan requirement is increased, cover factors are decreased, average loan life is extended and IRR is reduced.

Similar calculations are performed, taking an adverse assumption against each independent variable in turn. The results are recorded and compared to reveal the change that produces the largest effect on the project outcomes. Taking a consistent magnitude of adverse change across the independent variables (10% in most cases), the largest reductions in IRR are caused by reductions in traffic volume and inflation. All changes represented by cases (i) to (ix) are then superimposed together to produce the worst case scenario, which brings the IRR to a point as low as 12%. If this level of return is still acceptable to the promoter, this project is almost certainly viable.

Similar exercises are carried out making beneficial assumptions against each independent variable (cases (x) to (xiv)). Again, traffic volume turns out to be a very sensitive factor as far as the IRR is concerned. All beneficial cases are then superimposed together to form the best case scenario, giving an IRR of 17·3%. The difference in IRR between the worst case and the best case is about 5%. This is the expected range embracing the actual IRR when the project is implemented.

A limitation of sensitivity analysis is that each risk is considered independently without quantifying their probabilities of occurrence.

Probability analysis

Probability analysis is a more sophisticated form of risk analysis. It overcomes the limitation of sensitivity analysis by specifying a probability distribution for each risk and then considering effects of the risks in combination. Like sensitivity analysis, probability analysis also results in a range of values in which the final outcome would lie.

Probabilistic analysis commonly uses sampling techniques such as 'Monte Carlo' simulation. This method relies on the random calculation of values that fall within a specified probability distribution. For simplicity, a triangular distribution may sometimes be taken as an approximation to a normal distribution. The overall result is derived by the combination of values selected for each one of the risks. In order to obtain the probability distribution of the project outcome, the calculation is repeated many times, up to 1000, using a computer. The following hypothetical example demonstrates the principles and procedures.

Assume that a promoter of a BOT power plant project has come up with the following estimated costs, revenues and possible concession periods together with their associated probabilities (amounts shown are in millions).

Capital cost	$14 000	$15 000	$16 000	
Probability	0.30	0.60	0.10	
Annual operating cost	$2000	$2200	$2400	
Probability	0.30	0.50	0.20	
Annual revenue	$4400	$4500	$4600	$4700
Probability	0.10	0.30	0.40	0.20
Concession period	10 years	15 years	17 years	
Probability	0.40	0.30	0.30	

For each of the above variables, a histogram or probability distribution diagram (Fig. 11.1a) can be drawn up. Based on this diagram, a corresponding cumulative frequency diagram (Fig. 11.1b) can be plotted for each of the variables. In this example, the annual revenue variable is used to demonstrate the technique and similar treatment can be performed on other variables.

Firstly, a series of numbers (two-digit in this case from 00 to 99) is assigned to each of the discrete revenue probability intervals. The number of different two-digit numbers in the range is allocated to the probability of achieving its associated revenue on a proportional basis. Therefore, the numbers 00–09 are allocated to the revenue estimate of $4400 million; the numbers 10–39 are allocated to annual revenue of $4500 million and so on.

Secondly, using a table of two-digit random numbers (such as those in the Tables of Random Sampling Numbers by Kendall *et al.*) random values of annual revenue can be selected. Taking the first four random numbers from the tables (23, 15, 75 and 48), the values of revenue can be read off easily from the cumulative frequency distribution diagram. Thus, the revenues of $4500 million, $4500 million, $4600 million and $4600 million respectively are selected. Likewise, four samples are taken for each of the three other variables using this simulation approach. The results are depicted in Table 11.3.

The rates of return are calculated by using the formula (Net annual revenue/capital cost = D/A) and looking up annuity tables (such as Perry's valuation tables: annuity $1 will purchase using single rate).

If a large number of samples is taken (above 100), a frequency

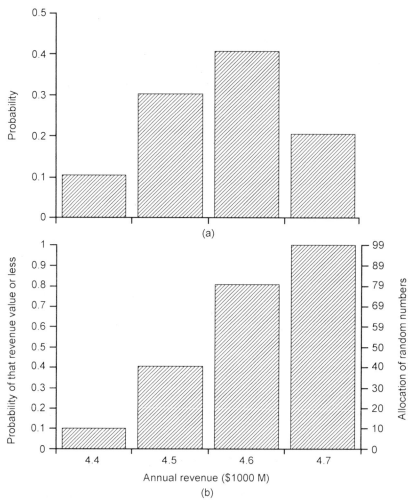

Figure 11.1 (a) Probability distribution histogram for annual revenue; (b) cumulative probability diagram for annual revenue

distribution for the rates of return can be drawn. Thus, a range of rates of return and their probabilities can be established. In addition to a single yield figure, a measure of the chance that any yield rate falls within the range is an important decision criterion for the BOT project promoters.

Monte Carlo simulation can be applied prior to a project commencing and can also be used for strategic control of the project during construction since the project can be re-simulated at any time.

Table 11.3 Sample results by Monte Carlo simulation

Sample number	Capital cost $ × 10⁹	Annual revenue $ × 10⁹	Annual operating cost $ × 10⁹	Net annual revenue $ × 10⁹	Concession period (year)	Rate of return: %
	(A)	(B)	(C)	(D=B−C)		(D/A)
1	14	4·5	2·0	2·5	10	0·1786	12·5
2	14	4·5	2·0	2·5	10	0·1786	12·5
3	15	4·6	2·2	2·4	17	0·1600	14·5
4	15	4·6	2·2	2·4	15	0·1600	13·5

Political risk analysis

Lenders and investors to a BOT project are concerned about the political stability of the host country in which the project is located. Most banks and multinational corporations have developed some sort of country risk analysis if they are involved with lending or cross-border operations in more than a handful of countries. There are two types of systems in common use, namely those for risk assessment, and those for risk rating. Some organizations combine the two systems with the risk assessment system itself automatically generating country ratings. The techniques range from qualitative analysis such as simple checklists, through complicated statistically based scoring systems, to sophisticated techniques such as multivariate analysis.

The qualitative approach relies on the experience of experts who have the knowledge and analytical ability to assess the different political risk factors. A checklist containing comprehensive questions and/or statistics is prepared, answered and collated before final judgement is made by experts. Typical headings for questions would include economic, strategy, foreign exchange generation, opposition groups, external factors, etc. Answers to these questions can include subjective judgement.

The basic idea of a scoring system is that a set of statistical indicators (for example, GDP growth rate, current account deficit/receipts and inflation rate) are chosen and scores are assigned to values of each indicator. These scores can be weighted and then summed to obtain a total score, which can be used to derive an overall rating with some level of objectivity (see Chapter 2 for examples).

With multivariate analysis, the variable factors of political risks are interrelated through either addition, subtraction, multiplication or division. These mathematical manipulations result in a political risk indicator. In order to assess total political risk, the different indicators are weighted against each other. The difficulty of this approach lies in finding suitable quantifiable variables for each political factor, and the weighting of the different indicators. Therefore, this method should be restricted to individual specific aspects of political risk such as expropriation or nationalization. The quantitative method can lead on to the scenario approach which, in essence, tries to envisage how political risk may develop under different sets of assumptions.

References

1. TIONG R. BOT projects: risks and securities. *Construction management and economics*. E. & F.N. Spon, 1990, 8, 315−328.
2. BEIDLEMAN C.R. *et al*. On allocating risk: the essence of project finance. *Sloan Management Review*, Spring 1990, 47−55.
3. WOODWARD D. *et al*. Risk management of BOOT projects. *Project*, 1992, Mar., 10−11.

Bibliography

EVERSETT J.E. Risks and rewards in BOOT projects. *Proc. Conf. on BOOT Projects*. Budapest, May 1993, 87−97.

KRAYENBUEHL T.E. *Country risk: assessment and monitoring*. Woodhead-Faulkner, 1988.

PERRY J.G. *et al*. Risk and its management in construction projects. *Proc. Instn. Civ. Engrs*, 1985, 1, June, 499−521.

Chapter 12

Legal framework

Objectives of legal framework

For any privatized infrastructure to succeed, it must have a proper legal structure and the interrelationship between the participants must be well defined so as to achieve a balanced allocation of risks between the parties and thereby accrue the benefits required by government and private sector participants. The functions of a legal framework include:

(a) the definition of the overall concept and structure of the project including project finance and taxation issues
(b) establishment of enabling legislation and the regulatory systems on environmental protection, planning and user charges
(c) controlling undue competition
(d) facilitating the negotiation of the respective rights and obligations and preparation of the associated documentation; allocating risks and identifying insurance requirements
(e) establishing procedure for the resolution of disputes.

As the coverage is so wide and involves both public interest and private interest, the legal framework can be classified into several levels for the purpose of further discussion.

Levels of legal framework

Level one: international treaty

When an infrastructure project involves more than one nation, a treaty is required. A classic example is the Treaty of Canterbury, 1986, signed between the governments of the United Kingdom and France for the Channel Tunnel project. Another more recent intergovernmental agreement paved the way for the second crossing between Malaysia and Singapore.

In the case of the Channel Tunnel, the object of the treaty is to demonstrate the two governments' commitment to facilitating the project and providing the necessary undertakings; to make provision for international machinery to safeguard the governments' interest in matters such as safety and the environment during construction and operation; to deal with matters of national jurisdiction, and to establish arrangements for arbitration in the event of disputes over interpretation of the treaty between the two governments and with the concessionaires. The treaty will also enshrine the private sector nature of the link and the concessionaire's right to compensation in the event of political interference or cancellation by either government. The treaty is supplemented by a number of protocols and exchanges of letters setting out in detail the arrangements outlined in broad terms in the treaty. Protocols are required, for example, to cover policing, immigration, customs, and animal and plant health control. The substance of the treaty is embodied in the Channel Tunnel Act 1987 to convey the necessary jurisdiction on private rights in the UK.

Level two: concession agreement

This is necessary to establish the rights and obligations of the concessionaires to carry out the development, financing, construction and operation of the infrastructure system. Amongst other things, a concession agreement contains basic terms such as the definition of the project, the concession period and the conditions upon which the concession would be withdrawn. Initially, because the project company does not yet exist or, if it has been formed, has little financial substance (or staff), the promoting group will deal directly with the government. When the project company has been capitalized, the promoters will be allowed to assign the contract or there will be a novation between the project company and the government.

The concession agreement can be granted by way of a statute, as in the case of the Eastern and Western Harbour Crossings and the Tate's Cairn Tunnel in Hong Kong. It can also be granted to the concessionaire under a private contract, as in the case of the Malaysian North–South Highway. According to Jewkes,[1] the rights of the concessionaires vary greatly with the form of grant used. The differences are depicted in the following.

Mechanism for adjustment
Parties to a private contract may easily alter, amend or relax the terms of the concession granted to such a contract, except where the alteration

would render the contract illegal. The terms of a concession granted under statute may usually only be altered or varied by the enactment of further legislation which can be costly and time-consuming. For example, according to Hong Kong Ordinance (Chapter 215), any adjustment of toll levels for the Eastern Harbour Crossing needs to be approved by the Governor-in-Council and go through the process of statute amendments.

Remedies for breach

Under a private contract, any breach of the concession by the government, such as the improper termination of the concession, would entitle the concessionaire to damages and, in some cases, specific performance of the terms of the concession. However, these remedies may not be available to the concessionaire under statute. Under English law jurisdictions, the concessionaires would be required to enforce their rights by applying to the courts for judicial review of the government's action or inaction under the concession and the powers of the courts to grant relief to the concessionaires are discretionary. However, under other jurisdictions, for example in the Philippines (Bill No. 1285 and Republic Act No. 6957) and Greece (Law 2052/1990), provisions exist in the legislation to compensate the concessionaires in the event that termination by government takes place.

Third parties' actions

For a concession granted under private contract, only the parties to the concession can enforce its terms. If it is granted under statute, third parties may potentially have a right to apply to the courts for an order requiring the government to comply with the provisions of the statute or to perform certain public duties.

Reserved power of the government

Government often reserves to itself certain discretionary powers of approval in relation to matters which are the subject of concession in order to effect the necessary control. For example, the Eastern Harbour Crossing Ordinance in Hong Kong gives the Director of Highways the powers to approve design and method of construction as well as construction contracts. Yet the statute itself restricts the scope of these power expressly. Also, the rules of administrative and public law under English jurisdictions require any officers of the government to exercise any powers of discretion fairly, impartially and within scope. Complainants may call for a judicial review of the manner in which the power of discretion was exercised.

In the case of a discretion given to or reserved by one of the parties under a private agreement, the manner in which the discretionary power is exercised is restrained either by express provisions, for example, agreement to arbitrate on engineer's power, or other channels of dispute resolution.

Level three: agreements for the internal regulation of the concessionaires

This level of the framework is to regulate the relationship of the participants in the project company and may include the following documentation.

The consortium agreement
According to Chow,[2] the expression 'consortium' refers to any grouping, typically formed on a 'one-off' basis, which is governed by a contractual agreement. At the feasibility stage, promoters, which can include contractors and financiers, may form a consortium to push the scheme forward. A consortium agreement regulates the relationship between the members of the promoting group by laying down the authority and responsibility of the promoters vis-à-vis each other. This agreement is usually replaced by the shareholders' agreement upon the establishment of the project company.

The shareholders' agreement
This governs the relationship between the members who have invested in the project company after incorporation, and will include items such as their respective percentage interests, the Memorandum and Articles of Association of the project company, its directors, dividend policy and restrictions on the disposal of shares until completion or repayment of loans. The agreement also regulates the responsibilities of the shareholders with regard to further equity injection and the sanctions which exist if one or more parties fail to make available the requisite funds. Government may also wish to take an equity position in the project company, holding what are commonly called 'golden shares'.

Level four: agreements for external dealing by the project company

Loan agreement
The loan documentation will impose various conditions on the borrower, that is the project company. Apart from the usual loan terms

175

these conditions may include limits on payment of dividends, requirements for working capital, financial covenants as to the ratios of debt to equity, limits on changes to the concession agreement or the construction contract, etc. Lenders may require various commitments from participants of the project company. For example, a contractor may have to pay interest on the accrued loan for delay in completion irrespective of whether extension of time is granted under the construction contract. An 'independent checker' may be required by the lenders to monitor the construction progress as a condition for disbursement of loan advances.

Consultancy agreements

The project company may wish to employ its own consultants to monitor the works of the design build contractor or the appointment of consultants may stem from a requirement of the concession agreement aiming to ensure compliance with government specifications and regulations. In the former situation, the consultant plays the role of an engineer under a standard form of civil engineering contract. In the latter case, the consultant will act in the capacity of an independent checking engineer, whose terms of employment may be influenced by government's requirements. For example on the Tate's Cairn Tunnel project in Hong Kong, the independent checking engineer had to ensure that the 'in-principle approvals' of the Director of Highways were implemented by the contractor. Other consultants may include financial advisers, who are usually from merchant banks, and legal advisers, who are instrumental in establishing the legal framework, especially those private agreements mentioned in this chapter. Their conditions of engagement are based on the respective practices of the financial and legal professions.

Construction contract

This is usually a design build or turnkey type of contract executed by the project company (as the employer) and the contracting arm of the prime sponsor. Lenders will like to see that this contract is a lump-sum contract but target-cost contracts have been used (for example on the Channel Tunnel project). These contracts frequently insist upon the transfer to the contractor of many responsibilities and risks which, on more conventional traditional projects would be borne by the employer. Heavy liquidated damages may be stipulated to induce on-time completion. Performance guarantees in terms of time/cost/quality will be sought. Due to their special position, contractors in BOT projects frequently accept more onerous conditions than in other types of contract. The stringency of these conditions can be exemplified by two cases:

Malaysian North — South Highway. The conditions for the construction contract were modified from the third edition of the FIDIC standard form. However, there were substantial amendments in the following areas.

(a) *Ground conditions.* The Contractor will be solely responsible for interpreting the site investigation and topographical survey information supplied by the project company and will, therefore, be unable to claim additional time or cost resulting from unforeseen ground conditions.

(b) *Weather.* Contractors will be required to allow for all weather conditions in their prices and programmes and will not be entitled to an extension of time for any adverse weather conditions.

(c) *Notice requirements for claims.* Contractors have to comply with stringent time limits and procedures for the notification and submission of claims.

(d) *Lump-sum works.* Usual civil engineering contracts provide for remeasurement of work which is subject to uncertainties. In this particular contract, approximately 60% of the value of the construction works was carried out on a fixed-price lump-sum basis, irrespective of the actual quantities executed except to the extent that they related to variations or additions to the contract required by the project company. The balance of the work, though remeasurable, is subject to a maximum cap or ceiling, beyond which the Contractor is made to bear the additional costs. In so doing, the risk of cost overruns is essentially transferred to the Contractor. This would not normally be construed as equitable under normal circumstances.

(e) *Control of progress.* Milestone dates are built in the work programme. Failure by the Contractor to meet these key dates will invoke the liquiduated damages provisions as well as call on the performance bond. One special penalty in connection with the previously mentioned shareholding is the ability of the project company to require the Contractor to surrender its holding of preference shares in the project company at a fixed price in the event of default by the Contractor.

Sydney Harbour Crossing. Under this design and build contract, the scope for adjustment of the contract sum is very limited. The Conditions of Contract stipulate the following events as the only grounds for increasing the Contract Sum:

(*a*) injunctive or other proceedings or relief under the law brought against the joint venture or its sub-contractors

(*b*) changes in law which affect the design or construction of the Tunnel, except those relating to the awards of industrial tribunals

(*c*) failure of the Commissioner to comply with the lease

(*d*) other imposed requirements by Authorities which are different from those prevailing at lease date.

Operational input agreement

This is used in production facilities to ensure a long-term steady supply of the essential raw materials in order to maximise efficient operation. For materials from a nation's supply, this agreement will be executed with a state-owned body. Ideally, the supply quantity and price should be fixed to ensure stability of production cost and output. An example is the Shaijiao 'B' Power Station in the Peoples' Republic of China, where the Promoter, Hopewell Power (China) Ltd, secured a fixed-price contract for the supply of coal fuel from the northern part of China.

Operational output agreement

This is again used in production facilities to ensure the sale of products or by-products, such as the electricity generated and the coal ash produced by a BOT power station. They can either be in the form of a 'take-or-pay' agreement, which imposes an unconditional obligation on the purchaser to pay irrespective of supply conditions, or the less stringent form of 'take-and-pay' agreement, where a payment obligation only arises when products are actually rendered. Again, taking the Shaijiao 'B' power station as an example, the Chinese power authority agreed to purchase a minimum quantity of electricity from Hopewell on a 'take-and-pay' basis at a fixed price per kilowatt hour over the 10-year cooperation period.

Operating and maintenance agreement

In the event that the project company is not going to operate and maintain the completed facilities, for example, where an experienced co-promoter is available, this agreement will govern the relationship between the project company and the operator, and may be in the form of a sub-franchise.

An example is the Hong Kong Eastern Harbour Crossing, where the operation of the rail tunnel is put in the hands of the Mass Transit Railway Corporation, the operator of the existing subway system.

Table 12.1 summarizes the main functions of various agreements and the parties involved. Since each BOT project has its own special circumstances, it is not possible to be definite about what documents will be required in all cases, not to mention the standardization of them, except perhaps by headings.

Case studies of the legal framework of selected BOT projects in different countries

The Eastern Harbour Crossing (EHC) and the Tate's Cairn Tunnel (TCT), Hong Kong

Following the precedent of the Cross Harbour Tunnel, · a highly successful privatized project, the Hong Kong Government decided, in the mid-1980s, to award the second harbour crossing, the Eastern Harbour Crossing, and its associated 4 km land tunnel, the Tate's Cairn Tunnel (Fig. 12.1) to private consortia by international tendering. Upon notification of their respective successful bids by the Hong Kong Government, both of the sponsoring consortia had to set up separate corporate entities to receive the franchises and to enter into numerous agreements with the government, lenders, shareholders, contractors and other related parties. Before the commencement of construction enabling legislation was enacted, namely the Eastern Harbour Crossing Ordinance (Ordinance No. 47 of 1986), and the Tate's Cairn Tunnel Ordinance (Ordinance No. 50 of 1988). Basically, the two pieces of legislation are similar in form except for the major distinction created by the fact that EHC effectively had two franchises separately granted to the Road Company and the Rail Company, whereas for the TCT a single franchise was granted to the Tate's Cairn Tunnel Company Ltd. The two separate yet similar Ordinances include, *inter alia*, the following rights and obligations of the franchise holders.

(a) The franchise periods for the road tunnels of EHC and TCT are each of 30 years, commencing from the start of construction. The franchise period for the rail tunnel of EHC is 18 years commencing from the rail operating date.

(b) For the EHC, the rights to keep in place the railway works and to operate the railway were to be transferred by the Rail Company to the Mass Transit Railway Corporation (MTRC), which is the operator of the existing subway system in Hong Kong. In return for this transfer, a separate Operating Agreement further stipulates pre-determined rental payments from the MTRC to the Rail Company.

Table 12.1 *Summary of documentations forming legal framework of BOT projects*

	Agreement	Parties	Main functions/content
Level 1: Internal agreement	Treaty	2 or more countries	Internal agreement; demonstration of governments' commitment
Level 2: Government agreement	Concession agreement	Government/project company	Grant of rights to finance, build operate, and to collect charges
Level 3: Internal agreements	Consortium promoters	Promoters	Define relationship of agreement before establishment of project company
	Shareholders' agreement	Project company/ shareholders	Define capital structure and relationship of shareholders
Level 4: External agreements	Loan agreement	Project company/ lenders	Terms of loans, securities and restrictions
	Consultancy agreement	Project company/ consultants	Scope of consultancy services and renumeration
	Construction contract	Project company/ contractor(s)	Scope of work, terms on time, quality and cost
	Operational input agreement	Project company/ suppliers	Terms of supply
	Operational output agreement	Project company/ purchasers	Terms of sale
	Operation agreement	Project company/ operator	Terms of operation and leases

(c) A majority of directors of the franchise holding companies shall be persons who are ordinarily resident in Hong Kong. The government has the power to appoint two directors to the board of the franchise holding companies.

(d) The amounts of issued and fully paid up capital of the franchise holding companies are stipulated.

(e) For the EHC, the government was entitled to a 5% shareholding in the TCT before the route opened to traffic, increased to 7·5% thereafter. This is because TCT feeds traffic to the EHC as they form parts of a trunk route from north to south of Hong Kong. (Although the government is not a shareholder in the TCT, it is entitled to a periodic royalty payment rated at certain percentages of the operating receipts.)

(f) The completion periods stipulated for EHC and TCT were 42 months and 37 months respectively from the start of construction. Extension of time was allowable for certain uncontrollable events, which specifically excluded want of sufficient funds. Failure to meet these completion periods could result in revocation of the franchcises granted.

(g) Winding up of the franchise holding company or revocation of the franchises will result in the determination of its rights and

Figure 12.1 Busy traffic along the approach road to Lion Rock Tunnel before Tate's Cairn Tunnel was opened in Hong Kong

obligations. Upon this happening, the assets of the defaulting company shall vest in the government. The defaulting company was liable to compensate the government for, *inter alia*, any expense incurred in putting the sea-bed, any land or any uncompleted construction works in a satisfactory order to enable the construction works either to be maintained in a state in which they can be continued at a future time or abandoned as the Director of Highways shall determine. The government would, however, pay to the company the value of the vested assets by agreement, failing which arbitration could be invoked.

(*h*) The Director of Highways was vested with the power to approve the design, methods of construction and construction contracts. Failure to comply with the approval requirements will cause the cessation or demolition of the construction works.

(*i*) Power of making by-laws for the regulation of traffic inside the tunnels is granted to the franchise holder to ensure safe and efficient operation.

(*j*) The power to collect tolls from users of the road tunnels is the most important right as far as the franchise holder is concerned. The actual toll levels are detailed in the schedules forming part of the ordinance. Change of toll levels can be effected by agreement with the Governor in Council or failing that, by resort to arbitration under the arbitration ordinance. Guidelines are given to arbitrators to ensure that the companies are reasonably but not excessively remunerated having regard to altered circumstances.

Apart from the statutory instruments mentioned above, a host of documentation was used to establish the legal framework. Among them were the shareholders' agreement, the project agreement which embraces the construction works agreement between the government and the franchise holding companies. In addition, the latter executed construction contracts with their principal contractors and loan agreements with their financiers. Diagrams depicting these legal relationship between the parties for EHC and TCT are shown in Figures 12.2 and 12.3 respectively.

Dulles Toll Road Extension, Leesburg, and other projects in the USA

The privately financed Dulles Toll Road forms a 14-mile extension of a currently state owned and operated toll road from suburban Washington, DC to the Dulles Airport. It cost US$250 million.

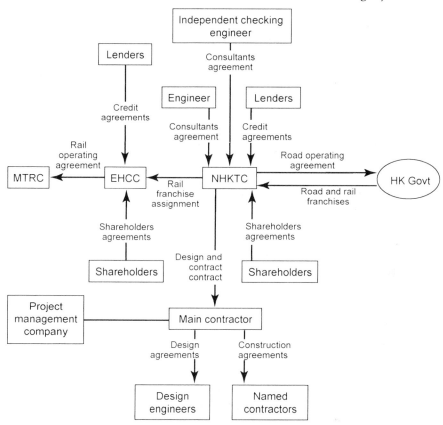

Figure 12.2 Legal relationship of parties to the Eastern Harbour Crossing, Hong Kong

Reportedly,[3] it was the first BOT highway in the US. To enable the project to be privatized, the Legislature of Virginia enacted the Virginia Highway Transportation Act of 1988, which permitted the private financing, construction and operation of toll roads.

Apart from procuring local, state and federal permits pertaining to the environmental impact and design standards, the concessionaire, the Toll Road Corporation of Virginia (TRCV) was required to obtain approval of the road alignment and design from the Virginia Commonwealth Transportation Board. It also needed to obtain approval for a financing plan, rates of return and toll rates for the receipt of a Certificate of Authority from the Virginia State Corporation Commission (SCC), which was established to regulate financial operations. Approval for increasing the toll is subject to factors such as debt coverage and the rate of inflation. The technical aspects, including detailed standards for highway design, maintenance and operations, were looked after by the

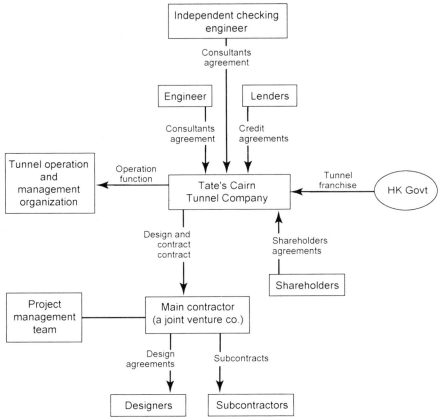

Figure 12.3 Legal relationship of parties to the Tate's Cairn Tunnel, Hong Kong

Virginia Department of Transportation via the so called Comprehensive Agreement.

TRCV acquired a right of way (ROW) for the alignment through compensation and ground lease, without using 'eminent domain', which was the condemnation powers authorized to state agencies for acquisition of ROW in private partnership projects.

Construction was carried out using a guaranteed maximum price (GMP) contract, which included a liquidated damages clause to guarantee timely completion, and an incentive cost savings clause. The concession period is 40 years.

Other American BOT projects are being promoted, although the US has been described as a late and reluctant starter for this procurement approach. In California, Assembly Bill No. 680 authorized the California Department of Transportation (CALTRANS) to contract several privately developed public transportation projects. CALTRANS will support the projects in a variety of ways: by accelerating the planning process, negotiating equitable leases and rates of return on investments, exercising eminent domain to acquire ROW and by reducing tort liability potentials after projects are constructed. One toll road project worth US$2.4 million has been completed thus far. Privatization legislation has been considered or passed in Arizona, Minnesota, Illinois, Missouri, New Jersey, Texas, Massachusetts and others. In the State of Massachusetts, consideration has been made to allow a third-party contractor to build, maintain and operate the toll collection system for the 7-mile Central Artery-tunnel network in Boston after its completion around the year 2000, and plans are on the drawing board to privatize the operation of the new third harbour tunnel and depressed Central Artery even though the construction was funded mainly by federal sources. In Essex County, all state highway maintenance is now in the hands of a private contractor.

Terminal 3 of Lester B Pearson International Airport in Toronto, Canada

This is the first privatized airport terminal in Canada. It cost US$433 million and was completed in 1991. It was jointly developed by Canadian developer Huang & Danczkay and Lockheed Terminal Inc. of Canada under a private long-term ground lease from Transport Canada, the federal body for management of airports in Canada.

No enabling legislation was required for this privatization project, other than a revision to the Air Services Fees Regulations that excluded Terminal 3 from Federal terminal fees and charges. According to a Task Force Report, current legislation enables the responsible federal body, in this case Transport Canada, to enter into term dispositions that would enable local entities to achieve the objectives of decentralization.

Unlike other jurisdictions which put a heavy emphasis on price regulations, price guidelines for fees charged to the public for the use of this Terminal were limited to those prices in effect at opening day. From that time on, market forces have dictated prices. Airlines fees are primarily cost based and concessionaires bid competitively for space in the Terminal.

An interesting fact about this project is that the concession was transferrable subject to the federal body's approval. Thus, Terminal 3 had changed hands recently to another private sector consortium while the original developer has used the money to develop other projects.

References

1. JEWKES R. Legal considerations in privatized infrastructure projects. *IFAWPCA* Supplement, *Asian Architect & Contractor*, 1989, July.
2. CHOW K.F. *Construction joint ventures in Singapore.* Butterworth, Singapore, 1985.
3. ATKINSON C.R. *Private development of transportation infrastructure: assessing feasibility, risks and financial strategies.* MIT, unpublished MSc dissertation, 1991.

Chapter 13

Procurement options for infrastructure projects

Introduction

Previous chapters have examined BOT from various perspectives. As mentioned earlier, BOT is not a panacea for all infrastructure problems. If the project is not well conceived, BOT may not produce the desired results and, therefore, decision makers have to look at all the options available for the procurement of infrastructure before deciding to adopt the BOT approach.

When considering infrastructure procurement options, inevitably the basic line of thought goes back to the decision of 'to privatize or not'. This chapter tries to summarize the rationale for and against privatization, followed by a discussion on non-privatized alternatives and the possible variants of the BOT model.

Assuming that a decision had been made to privatize certain infrastructure, another question that would need to be addressed is how to choose the best undertaker. This chapter, therefore, ends with a suggested methodology for the evaluation of proposals from the private sector.

Pros and cons of privatization

Privatization is a policy decision having wide repercussions on the political and social arena. From a government viewpoint, the following are generally perceived benefits of privatization.

(a) It can relieve the financial and administrative burden of the government in undertaking and maintaining the much needed infrastructure.

(b) By introducing commercial discipline and possibly, competition, the economic efficiency and productivity of the projects are enhanced.

(c) Usually a vigorous cost benefit analysis and viability study will be carried out by the private sector to ensure profitability. Positive results add justification to the need for the facilities, whereas poor response from the private sector reflects an uncertain demand for the facilities.

(d) As early income is desired by the private sector, a shorter time for the realization of the completed facilities is more probable.

(e) As the expertise of the private sector can be utilized, the public sector establishment size can be reduced.

(f) By stimulating private entrepreneurship and investment, the rate of growth of the economy is expected to accelerate.

(g) The risks of finance, construction and operation are transferred to the private sector.

For a balanced judgement in deciding whether to privatize or not, governments need to take the following disadvantages into consideration.

(a) There is a trade-off in allowing the private sector to operate facilities and receive income, which means long-term revenue to the government is reduced or postponed in return for reduced risk taking.

(b) The traditional state control of infrastructure is diluted, with a possibility of the government monopoly position being shifted to the private sector. An effective legal framework is, therefore, necessary to protect the public interest.

(c) The quality of products produced or services rendered may be difficult to guarantee. This potential drawback can be mitigated by competent monitoring of the private sector's work. Usually, users of facilities have a certain power of influence over the quality standards, especially if cheaper alternatives exist.

(d) The imposition of toll charges on previously free facilities may bring about public objection, which may be politically undesirable.

(e) In order to attract investment, governments may have to provide incentives in the form of relaxation of taxation requirements and so on which violates the consistency of established policy. Relaxation of foreign exchange regulation may undermine the country's balance-of-payment positions and credit rating.

(f) Government may have to take over unsuccessful ventures before maturity of the franchise.

The general public may, however, look at the move towards privatization in a different light. They may view the merits of privatization as:

(a) relieving the otherwise probable imposition of tax burden for the development of needed infrastructure
(b) providing needed infrastructure in shorter time, and relieving congestion or electricity blackout etc
(c) providing more efficient services
(d) creating job opportunities which are not possible without private initiative in a sluggish economy
(e) giving rise to non-user benefits such as eased congestion on adjacent route or the provision of housing as a result of development right granted on transport infrastructure.

The public may also view the demerits of privatization as:

(a) giving rise to a potential monopoly situation
(b) creating unemployment or loss of security benefits in the public sector if privatization involves the transfer of management and ownership to private operators
(c) creating hardship to users, especially those in the lower income group. (An example is the toll roads in Cheras of Malaysia. This toll had amounted to 12% of the average income per head of regular users before subsequent reduction upon their sustained objection.[1])

After considering these wider political and social issues, the answer is still not immediately obvious. The reason is that the success of privatization models such as BOT relies on the intrinsic profitability of a proposed scheme as well as the sustainability of the financial sector in a given environment. In other words, most privatizated projects are demand-driven and not source-driven. When there is a low demand for a facility, government cannot push it forward to the private sector. On the contrary, the private sector are often proactive in making privatization proposals to government when they see a possible niche in any sector.

Before adopting the privatization approach, it is imperative that non-privatized options are thoroughly considered.

Non-privatized procurement options

Governments in developed countries are commonly accustomed to procuring public infrastructure facilities with funding from capital reserves. A variety of contractual arrangements is possible, but the most common forms are the conventional type (with separate design and construction teams), and design and build.

Governments in developing countries also use these procurement approaches but there is a more frequent reliance, on loan financing in the form of supplier's credit or buyer's credit. In the case of supplier's credit, a contractor concludes two contracts with the client: a contract to supply and construct and a separate loan agreement linked to the construction contract. The contractor obtains financing from his own banks, secured by a repayment guarantee from the government of the country where the client is located. To add further protection, the contractor may procure credit insurance from his own country. In the case of buyer's credit, the client concludes a supply and construct contract with a contractor on the basis of cash payment terms. The client obtains the necessary loan from a local or overseas financial institution, which lends on the strength of a repayment guarantee from the government of the client's country. The overseas lenders may also obtain credit insurance from their own countries.

With the necessary finance in place, the client may appoint its own design and supervision consultants and procure construction services from a contractor using competitive tendering or negotiation. This is usually called a conventional or traditional arrangement. As lump-sum fixed-price contracts are favoured by most commissioning entities, little overlap of design, tender, and construction can take place. Nevertheless, when tenderers all bid based on the same set of design information, bid evaluation is simple and easy. Quality of performance is comparatively more reliable as independent supervision is normally available.

With design and build (D & B), the client only needs to specify performance requirements to contractors, who submit tenders on prices as well as design proposals. Tenders are more difficult to evaluate as different designs are involved. Nevertheless, after the award of the contract, the client need only communicate with the D & B contractor, who can no longer deny responsibilities and pass the buck to someone else. Fast track construction is possible with D & B since overlapping of design and construction can take place. Quality of performance is dependent on the degree of monitoring by the client and the competence of the contractor.

Under the BOT arrangement, turnkey contracts are commonly executed between the project sponsors and the contractor, who may well be a project sponsor himself. The reasons for this arrangement are both practical and strategic. On the practical side, a contractor/sponsor, through his own consultants, should have carried out feasibility studies, detailed investigations and design before he submits any proposal to the government. Often the design is well advanced into the engineering phase, thus making it natural for the contractor to continue with the design role. Strategically, a contractor/sponsor would also like to retain his control over the design. The distinctions between 'pure' D&B contracting and BOT incorporating turnkey contracts are depicted in Table 13.1.

Variants of the privatized approach

Build Own Operate Transfer (BOOT)

Essentially a BOOT project is when a government grants a private-sector organization a concession to build a facility, own it, operate it during the concession period, and then transfer it back to government. It differs from BOT in the ownership element, but the distinction is getting blurred in many cases as the two names are used almost interchangeably on the premise that transfer would eventually take place. A typical example of a BOOT contract is the Dartford Crossing, a toll bridge across River Thames in the UK. The concessionaire for this project was also granted the toll collected from existing tunnels to finance the new construction.

Build Own Operate (BOO)

This type of project differs from BOT in that the promoting group designs, finances, constructs, and operates a project, but with a plan to syndicate all or a portion of its equity after completion. Thus, the concession company retains ownership and operates the project indefinitely, continuing to derive revenue from it. A BOO scheme might provide more incentive for the project sponsors (hence the owners) to maintain the facilities during the concession period. Yet, except for the scenario that a lower user charge might result from the perpetual ownership, a BOO scheme is not generally welcome by host governments. The BOT arrangement offers more flexibility in that the host government can negotiate a new agreement for continued operation and maintenance with the original concessionaire/operator.

Table 13.1 Comparison of 'design and build' and 'BOT-turnkey' method of contract procurement

Factors	Design and build (government owned)	BOT (by private sector)
Procurement	Contractor undertakes the design and construction of a project to meet performance requirements	Consortium undertakes to finance, design, build and operate a project and return ownership to the government after a fixed concession period
Suitability	Can be used in any type of project	Used where the completed project can generate revenue such as tolls for repayment of loans and profits thereafter
Contract	Design and build contract between government and contractor	Concession agreement made between government and concession company encompassing design and build obligations
Finance	Borne by government from public funds, bonds or loans	Borne by projects sponsors of the concession company from equity and loans
Contract sum	Fixed-price lump-sum contract agreed between government and contractor before award of contract	Fixed-price lump-sum turnkey contract agreed between concession company and contractor
Payments	Contractor receives interim payments from government as the works proceed	Contractor (usually himself a project sponsor) receives interim payments from the concession company, which will not have revenue until the project is completed and in operation

Table 13.1 Continued

Factors	Design and build (government owned)	BOT (by private sector)
Risks (political, financial and technical)	Shared between contractor and government. Government can re-appoint by use of performance bond if the contractor is in default	Shared among project sponsors without recourse to government. Government can step in if they fail to complete the project as stipulated
Time for completion	Agreed in contract, government safeguards by imposing liquidated and ascertained damages (LD) in case of delay	Completion guarantee by concession company. Government can take over the project if concession company fails to complete on time. Contractor liable for LD for delay
Operation	By government or sale of operation franchise through private competition	By concession company or an operator, who is usually a project sponsor
Defects	Borne by contractor within the defects liability period (DLP)	Borne by the turnkey contractor or the concession company
Maintenance beyond DLP	Borne by government or the franchised operator	Borne by concession company within the concession period

193

Design Build Finance Operate (DBFO)

This acronym has been proposed for eight major road construction projects in the UK. One such project is a £200·5 million plus (US$380 million) contract for the A1–M1 link road and associated works in West Yorkshire. Basically, the arrangement is BOT in essence, but with the promoters' renumeration paid through a shadow toll instead of direct tolling of motorists. This shadow toll is paid by the UK government based on traffic flow measured by stretching sensing cables across the road. This gives a much better guarantee of return to promoters as traffic would otherwise tend to switch to alternative untolled routes, given the existence of a great number of interconnecting roads in the UK. Although shadow tolling would mean that the government would eventually have to foot the bill, the Treasury in initiating this proposal claimed that it would aim to secure substantial transfer of risk to the private sector. As an example, promoters have to put up at least 5% of equity to satisfy lenders in these road schemes.

Build Lease Transfer (BLT)

The private sector investors finance, design, build and retain legal ownership of a facility for a stipulated period of time, but the host government leases it back for operation. A similar concept has been used successfully in a private sector building project, where the host government was replaced by the Standard Chartered Bank. The bank used this innovative method to procure its new headquarters building in Hong Kong at no cost.

The Standard Chartered Bank has the leasehold of a prime site in the Central Business District of Hong Kong, where its previous headquarters stood. In 1986, the bank awarded a 25-year sub-lease to Nishimatsu Property (Hong Kong) — a subsidiary of the Japanese construction company Nishimatsu. In return, Nishimatsu paid a land premium by tender, and financed the reconstruction costs as well as the professional fees of design consultants retained by the bank itself. Upon completion, Standard Chartered has the exclusive right to lease back 70% of the new floor areas at a fixed rental until expiry of the 25-year sub-lease, when the bank takes back the entire development at no cost. In the meantime, Nishimatsu can let out 30% of the commercial floor space on the open market. The benefit of this scheme to the bank goes mainly to its liquidity position because bank regulators weigh cash capital more favourably than capital tied to a bank building. For Nishimatsu, this deal boosted their turnover figure by nearly HK$1 billion (US$128 million), and improved the status of the company in Japan.

Lease Renovate Operate Transfer (LROT)

This method is best illustrated directly with an actual example. The Venezuelan government owned a disused iron reduction plant called Minorca. A Japanese consortium consisting of Kobe Steel Ltd and some trading companies leased the disused plant from the government for eleven years, renovated and converted it to use a modern production process. The price paid by the Japanese consortium included the improvement cost and a monetary fee per ton of product produced, which varied according to the selling price of the product. The private consortium financed construction from a limited recourse loan from the IFC with co-financing from eleven Japanese banks. The government department supplied the raw materials and assistance in obtaining necessary licenses. With some difficulties, the Japanese consortium overcame the foreign exchange restrictions by operating an offshore escrow account, into which foreign currencies generated by the exports of the products were paid. Added to this income, Kobe Steel Ltd looked to the potential market for the new production process, which this project brought about. At the completion of the lease, the government is supposed to receive the renovated plant in good operating conditions free of charge.

Build Transfer Operate (BTO)

This model (known as Affermage) originated in France and is being spread through Africa, Central and Eastern Europe. Essentially, public facilities such as water and power are financed and built by the public sector, leaving maintenance and operation to the private sector. A power station on the Ivory Coast was developed and owned by the government, which signed a concessionary agreement for a 15-year term with the private sector. The latter is entrusted with the operation, maintenance and repair of all facilities related to power generation, transmission and distribution throughout the Ivory Coast.

Recently, several existing land tunnels in Hong Kong have been awarded by tender to the private sector following the government's decision to privatize their management and operations. The Hong Kong government has also tried to privatize the operational element of some environmental protection projects. For example several refuse transfer stations, which centralize the collection of refuse and ensure its delivery, in bulk, to landfill sites in sealed containers, have been designed and built by private sector companies at their own costs. Following completion of construction, ownership of the stations is vested in the government but the company is given the concession to operate them for 15 years. Government paid a fixed sum on completion of construction and an operating fee based on throughput during the concession period. Another facility, the first chemical waste treatment centre in Hong Kong, has been developed under a similar DBO arrangement. A private consortium obtained a 15-year franchise to operate the facility after its completion. The design and construction costs were initially borne by the consortium with deferred payment from the government within 5 years of completion. The centre is designed to treat 100 000 tonnes of chemical waste per year, and the government intends to partially recover the costs from charging registered waste producers for the treatment.

Evaluation criteria for privatized project proposals

Governments inviting private sector proposals in infrastructure projects usually handle the matter through two consecutive stages — a call for expression of interest, followed by a request for proposals.

The first stage is a preliminary invitation to interested parties for the submission of company information and a brief proposal. In reality, it is the testing ground for the degree of interest expressed by the private sector and hence may influence the final decision to privatize or not. An example is the Lantau Fixed Crossing, a major suspension bridge project in Hong Kong, which was withdrawn from the full privatization programme after the first stage. At the second stage, governments issue more detailed information to the short listed interested parties via a project brief or request for proposal document. This document will indicate the evaluation criteria to be adopted by the government in assessing any proposals. This is an important guideline to the private sector preparing their design, planning and cost estimation.

Examples of criteria for evaluating BOT proposals

Hong Kong Eastern Harbour Crossing (EHC) and Tate's Cairn Tunnel (TCT)

The project brief issued as part of the tender documents for both EHC and TCT outlined the Hong Kong Government's assessment criteria for BOT bids. Broadly speaking, the criteria applicable to both the EHC and TCT were similar and included the following aspects:

(a) the level and stability of the proposed toll regime
(b) the benefits to the community and the government (in the EHC brief, financial return to government was specifically referred to)
(c) the length of the franchise period (a short one being preferred)
(d) the speed of completion
(e) the proposed corporate and financial structure of the concessionaire, favouring a high level of equity contribution by the consortia
(f) the financial strength and support of interested parties
(g) the quality of engineering design, construction methods, programme, maintenance requirements and so on
(g) the management and operation abilities.

Terminal 3 at Lester B. Pearson International Airport (LBPIA) in Toronto, Canada

The criteria for evaluating development proposals for the third terminal at LBPIA are broadly similar but more refined to reflect the multi-faceted commercial activities which are possible in an airport terminal complex (see Fig. 13.1). They are listed below for comparison:

The development concept including:
(a) *Commercial development plan*: compatibility with the planned long-term development of airport and related land uses; possibility of phased expansion.
(b) *Terminal complex design*: meeting the mandatory design and construction, safety and security, and operations and maintenance requirements; providing an acceptable solution to existing capacity constraints at Terminals 1 and 2.
(c) *Delivery plan*: opening date of the third terminal; delivery at minimum disruption to airport operations.

The business relationship including:
(a) *The management plan*: the consortium's corporate structure; extent of government involvment.
(b) *Operations and maintenance plan*: the proposed operating relationship with airport management; impact on operation of two existing terminals.
(c) *Financial plan*: proposed financial return to government over the life of the project, consistent with associated risks; sources of capital financing.
(d) *Retail plan*: reasonableness and likely achievability of proposed retail plan and its impact on any contribution to government.

Figure 13.1 Departure hall of Terminal 3, Toronto International Airport

    (e) *Lease arrangements*: proposed lease arrangements for the construction and operation of the terminal complex and related developments.

Qualifications including:
    (a) *Personnel*: design team, construction management team and operation management team.
    (b) *Development experience*: scale and relevance of previous development projects.
    (c) *Performance experience*: track record of previous performance in major projects.

Table 13.2   Evaluation criteria of a hypothetical tunnel project

	Criteria	Priority rating	Rationalized priority rating
C1	Level of proposed toll	18	0·15
C2	Benefits to community	20	0·16
C3	Financial return to government	10	0·08
C4	Length of franchise periods	15	0·13
C5	Speed of completion	8	0·07
C6	Equity contribution by sponsor	16	0·13
C7	Financial strength of sponsors	8	0·07
C8	Quality of proposed construction	12	0·10
C9	Maintenance and operation	13	0·11
		120	1·00

Upon receipt of the proposals, an evaluation committee is usually convened by the government to analyse the submissions. Each consortium will be provided with the opportunity to address the committee to explain their proposals, respond to questions posed by the committee and ask questions related to the process.

Due to the multipicity of attributes usually found in any set of evalution criteria, it might appear that the selection process would be difficult. Yet it need not be so. There is a technique called Multi-Attribute Utility Analysis (MAUA) that can be used to identify the best proposal in this circumstance. A simulation of the MAUA technique is presented below.

Multi-Attribute Utility Analysis (MAUA)

For the purpose of illustrating the methodology of the MAUA technique in evaluating BOT proposals, the evaluation criteria for a hypothetical tunnel project are assumed. Using fictitious data, the following scenario emerges.

The evaluation criteria as listed in Table 13.2 are each assigned different priority ratings according to a scale of 1 to 20 (1 being of the lowest importance, 20 the most important).

In the above schedule, a rationalized priority rating is calculated for each criterion by dividing the corresponding priority rating by the total of the priority ratings (in this case 120). This is done to obtain smaller

Table 13.3 Multi-attribute utility analysis: proposals rated against each criterion

Evaluation criteria									Utility
C1	C2	C3	C4	C5	C6	C7	C8	C9	
									110
	P1	P1		P2			P4		—
P2			P2		P1			P3	—
P4	P3			P3		P3	P1		—
		P4	P1			P4		P4	—
P3		P3	P4	P4	P4	P2	P3		60
	P2			P1	P3	P1		P1	—
					P2				—
	P4		P3					P2	—
P1		P2					P2		—
									10

Notes:
C1 to C9 = evaluation criteria for BOT proposals
P1 to P4 = alternative proposals
10 to 110 = utility scale

numbers for ease of manipulation.

Assume that there are four proposals submitted, designated as P1, P2, P3 and P4 respectively. Each proposal will be considered and objectively evaluated (as far as possible) against each criterion on a measure of utility. A scale of utility of 10 to 110 has been used for each criterion to avoid the conceptual problem of outcomes with a zero utility against certain criteria which could occur if a scale of, say, 0 to 100 were used (see Table 13.3). When evaluating the proposals against each of the criteria, each criterion must be considered individually and the proposals are assessed relative to each other against each criterion. For each pair of criterion and proposal, the utility factor is multiplied by the corresponding rationalized priority rating and the results are totalled for each proposal to give the total utility of that proposal (see Table 13.4). It is then possible to rank the proposals by their total utility factors. In this example, the preference order of the proposals is P1, P4, P3, P2.

The advantage of this technique is that it is based on a systematic evaluation method which improves the objectivity by looking at the combined effect of criteria, taking into consideration the relative weightings of the criteria and the relative ranking of proposals against each criterion. Nevertheless, there is still room for subjectivity because this technique does require human judgement on utility and relative

Table 13.4   Evaluation of proposals

		P1		P2		P3		P4	
Criteria	RPR*	U*	R*	U	R	U	R	U	R
C1	0·15	20	(3·0)	90	(13·5)	50	(7·5)	80	(12·0)
C2	0·16	100	(16·0)	60	(9·6)	80	(12·8)	30	(4·8)
C3	0·08	100	(8·0)	20	(1·6)	50	(4·0)	70	(5·6)
C4	0·13	70	(9·1)	90	(11·7)	50	(6·5)	70	(9·1)
C5	0·07	50	(3·5)	100	(7·0)	80	(5·6)	60	(4·2)
C6	0·13	90	(11·7)	40	(5·2)	50	(6·5)	60	(7·8)
C7	0·07	50	(3·5)	60	(4·2)	80	(5·6)	70	(4·9)
C8	0·10	80	(8·0)	20	(2·0)	60	(6·0)	100	(10·0)
C9	0·11	40	(4·4)	30	(3·3)	90	(9·9)	70	(7·7)
Totals	1·00	67·2		58·1		64·4		66·1	
Rank order		First		Fourth		Third		Second	

*RPR = Rationalised Priority Rating, U = Utility, R = Result, R = RPR × U

importance of the criteria.

References

1. LIM S.H. Privatization: latent unpopularity. *Financial Times*, 29 Aug., 1991.
2. MA T. *Privatization of infrastructure projects in Hong Kong.* Thames Polytechnic, unpublished BSc dissertation, 1991.

Bibliography

BUKER H.H. Business opportunities in the pipeline transmission system through BOT. *Proc. Asian Conf. on planning, packaging and implementing BOT projects.* Singapore, 1988.

NEW CIVIL ENGINEER. DBFO signals way to mega road contracts. *New Civil Engineer*, 26 May 1994.

MARTINAND C. et al. *Private financing of public infrastructure: the French experience.* DAEI, 1994.

NEGAMI T. *Minorca project in Venezuela.* Paper presented at Int. Bar Assoc. seminar, November 1989.

Project Briefs of Eastern Harbour Crossing and Tate's Cairn Tunnel, Hong Kong.

TO E. Bank benefits from imaginative policy. *South China Morning Post*, 22 March 1989.

Chapter 14

Case studies

Introduction

The aim of this chapter is to present a small number of carefully chosen case studies for selected BOT schemes so as to illustrate how the information and techniques given elsewhere in this book operate in practice. The cases presented cover a wide range of work, an extended time-frame and a wide geographical area. The first two, an underwater tunnel in Hong Kong (one of the first and most successful BOTs ever) and a power station in China, have both almost reached the end of their concession periods, the third is an airport terminal in Canada bogged down in political infighting, while the final two, a Malaysian toll road and a river crossing in the United Kingdom, are both recent schemes where the concession period is still very young.

Information for the case studies has been assembled from a number of sources including publications, interviews with project personnel, and publicity and other material published by project participants. The Hong Kong Cross Harbour Tunnel and the Malaysian North-South Highway studies draw heavily upon unpublished academic work by Walker,[1] while the Shajiao 'B' power station study draws upon similar work by Walker[1] and Li.[2]

The Hong Kong Cross Harbour Tunnel

This project, opened in 1972, was arguably the world's first true BOT project, and shows clearly how such a scheme evolves from conception to a viable entity satisfying the win—win aspirations of all. The following review highlights many of the characteristics of a successful BOT project — a recognizable revenue stream, a financially constricted government, a local champion, a long gestation period, a positive outcome and the continuing evolution of the concept.

Background

In the 1950s the population of the British Colony of Hong Kong doubled, primarily due to legal and illegal immigration from China. An indication of this growth was a 10% increase per annum in bus passengers for the years 1954–59 with the 1960 figure representing an increase of 27% over that for 1959. In the 1950s Hong Kong was basically made up of two population centres, the city of Victoria on Hong Kong Island, and the town of Kowloon on the mainland. The evergrowing traffic between these two centres was carried by numerous ferry services. In 1954 the government commissioned a report on a fixed link across the harbour (a bridge or a tunnel), but after due consideration decided against the scheme. In 1956 government proposed that private commercial interests should be permitted to carry out this work if they so wished.

An early champion of a cross harbour link was a prominent local business man, Lawrence Kadoorie later to be Lord Kadoorie. He wrote, in a paper published in 1956:

> It is almost unbelievable, and indeed unexampled in modern civilized communities for two large towns each of over a million and a quarter inhabitants to face each other and depend for the transport not only of persons but of food, raw material, and goods upon the narrow bottleneck of the lines of sea transport between them, lines that are vulnerable to storms and typhoon.

Joint consulting engineers, Scott Wilson Kirkpatrick and Freeman Fox, also early champions of the concept, reported[3] in April 1961 of the tunnel proposals:

> A tunnel is feasible and would not give rise to significant objections by any interests. Its initial cost would be £13·2 million, interest charges £2·6 million to £4·4 million and the total capital sum to be raised between £15·8 million and £17·7 million. On the same basis, it could be expected to pay off its cost in about 16 years.

The Hong Kong Government continued to take a less optimistic view of the link's potential, concluding that it was not a priority. The government knew that its fiscal resources were being stretched to the limit by the more urgent needs of low cost housing, hospitals and schools to cater fro the rapidly increasing population. There were some highway department officials who perceived a need but who also realized that the government was not in a position to proceed with the scheme, and the eventual outcome was to let the private sector embark on the project. Following considerable discussion and negotiation, in

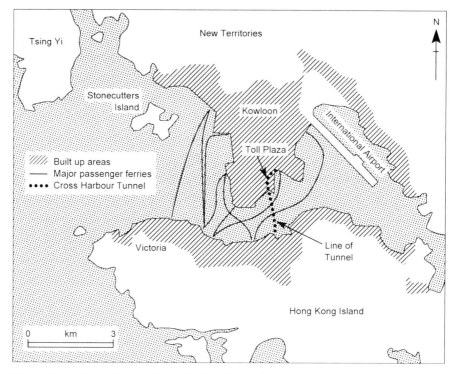

Figure 14.1   Hong Kong's Cross Harbour Tunnel

August 1965 a Hong Kong consortium comprising Wheelock Marden & Co. Ltd, Hutchison International Ltd, Kwong Wan Ltd, and Sir Elly Kadoorie Successors Ltd, operating under the title of 'The Cross Harbour Tunnel Company Limited', was granted the right to promote and operate a toll tunnel between Hong Kong Island and the mainland.

In October 1966 the Cross Harbour Tunnel Company invited qualified contractors with their respective financial consortia to submit tenders for construction of the project. Overspill from China's 'Cultural Revolution' however intervened and the project was put on hold. Hong Kong's lifestyle and confidence returned to normal in 1968 and negotiations with Lloyd's Bank Ltd, of London for a loan of £14·7 million backed by UK export credit guarantees were successfully concluded in 1969. The construction contract was awarded to a consortium led by Costain International Ltd, supported by Raymond International Inc. of New York and Paul Y Construction Co. Ltd of Hong Kong on 26 June 1969. Table 14.1 gives details of the project.

Table 14.1 Details of the Hong Kong Cross Harbour Tunnel project

Main contract	
Total tendered sum	£18 667 000
Contract period	3 years

Principal dates	
Joint consulting engineers' report	April 1961
Granting of franchise by Hong Kong Government to Hong Kong Cross Harbour Tunnel Co. Ltd	August 1965
Project out to tender	October 1966
Tenders returned	February 1967
Contract signed	June 1969
Work began at site	September 1969
Tunnel completed across harbour	February 1972
First traffic through tunnel	August 1972
Tunnel opened formally	October 1972

Principal dimensions	
Tunnel portal to portal length: m	1852
Submerged tube length: m	1604
Number of traffic ducts	2 dual lane
Carriageways (dual lane) width: m	6·7
Maximum gradient out of tunnel	6% (1:16)
Traffic headroom: m	4·88
Minimum water depth over tunnel in main shipping channel: m	12·34
Number of toll lanes	14

Project analysis

The tunnel opened ahead of schedule in August 1972. The tunnel toll was set at HK$5 (there were at that time HK$16 = £1.00), which pundits said was too high and would deter tunnel use. Within one year, the tunnel was approaching design capacity and in 1974, in accordance with its franchise, the Cross Harbour Tunnel Company Limited offered 25% of its equity to the public after first refusal by the ferry companies. This coincided with a local bank rate increase and the offer was undersubscribed, much to the annoyance of the London-based underwriters who accused the Hong Kong Bank of obstructing the issue. Ultimately the bank offered to buy the shares which the brokers duly accepted. Within one year the market price tripled and five years

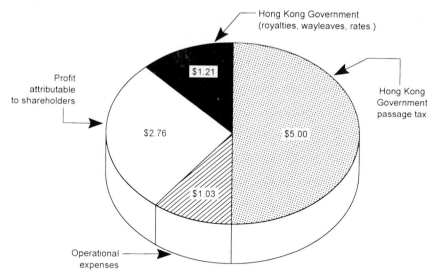

Figure 14.2   Who receives the private motorist's HK$10

after opening all debt was paid off — the lenders were happy; the equity holders are happy; with only one toll increase in the 23 years since opening the users are happy (as evidenced by their continued patronage); government benefits by receiving approximately 61% of toll income via taxes and royalty payments (see Fig. 14.2 for breakdown), and in 1999 will be handed a well maintained piece of infrastructure at no cost, at which time they may choose either to run the operation by themselves or to offer a new concession, perhaps by competitive tender.

The win-win situation for Hong Kong's society has been achieved. To achieve this success, the revenue stream, crucial to all BOTs, must have performed at least as well as expected. How was it calculated, and how well did the predictions match the actual results?

Early stage traffic projections were commissioned by The Tunnel Company, via their consultants, from the highly regarded UK Road Research Laboratory, at that time a branch of the UK's Department of Scientific and Industrial Research. Their report gave three estimates of the expected average daily traffic (ADT) which they termed minimum, probable and possible. The probable estimate was regarded as the most likely, which they stated was based on a conservative assessment. The minimum traffic figure, a worst case scenario, was intended for the purposes of the financial feasibility exercise only, whilst the possible traffic was assessed on a different basis and was not intended to represent an upper limit but rather to indicate the scale of traffic that might exist. The figures are given in Table 14.2.

Table 14.2 Average daily traffic: number of vehicles

	1966	1976
Minimum traffic	16 000	30 000
Probable traffic	17 000	47 000
Possible traffic	23 000	64 000

Based on these figures they recommended a two-lane dual carriageway concept which in turn allowed a construction cost to be identified. Their financial model identified interest rates as the controlling sensitivity factor, and three probability envelopes were developed as detailed in Tables 14.3, 14.4 and 14.5 for prevailing rates of 6, 7 and 8% with all sums in £000s and the Capital Outstanding referred to as the amount at the beginning of the year.

During the period in which the tunnel was built and paid for, the prevailing interest rates were approximately 5%, and the predicted and actual traffic flows are given in Table 14.6.

Seven years after granting the concession, the first toll paying traffic passed through the tunnel. Four years after opening it began to make a profit, by 1977 had repaid all debt and by the early 1980s was frequently being described as a 'cash cow'. A 1986 local newspaper article stated:

> the Cross Harbour Tunnel Company generates the sort of profits many firms only dream of — HK$144 million after taxes on a turnover of HK$269 million.

The Company's report for 1993 gave 44 912 073 vehicle journeys for the year which equates to 85 vehicles/minute going through 14 booths. The same report gives the operating profit after tax as HK$236 362 000 which translates to $450/minute (at HK$11·8 = £1). This early example of a BOT has been, and continues to be, a success for all concerned. The fundamental factors behind its success can be summarized as follows.

(a) Higher than expected traffic flows generated by a vibrant economy. Between 1981 and 1991 the per capita real gross domestic product in Hong Kong grew at an average of 6·8% per annum and reached a level of US$14 545 in 1991.

(b) Lower than expected interest rates during the construction phase of high debt levels.

(c) While construction was underway the British Government was forced to devalue sterling which made the ECGD loan repayments much easier.

Table 14.3   Interest rate for Hong Kong Tunnel: 6%
(a) minimum traffic

Year	ADT*	Net revenue	Interest	Capital outstanding
1966	16 340	1160	949	15 814
1967	17 763	1277	936	15 603
1968	19 186	1389	916	15 262
1969	20 609	1506	887	14 789
1970	22 032	1618	850	14 170
1971	23 455	1735	804	13 402
1972	24 787	1839	748	12 471
1973	26 118	1949	683	11 380
1974	27 450	2054	607	10 114
1975	28 781	2162	520	8667
1976	30 113	2267	422	7025
1977	31 445	2377	341	5680
1978	32 776	2481	219	3644
1979	34 108	2591	83	1382

*Pays off in 14th year, surplus £1 126 000
(b) probable traffic

Year	ADT*	Net revenue	Interest	Capital outstanding
1966	25 573	1773	949	15 814
1967	27 750	1941	899	14 990
1968	29 926	2104	837	13 948
1969	32 103	2272	791	13 181
1970	34 279	2434	702	11 700
1971	36 456	2602	598	9968
1972	38 509	2757	478	7964
1973	40 562	2912	341	5685
1974	42 615	3061	187	3114
1975	44 669	3212	14	240

*Pays off in 10th year, surplus £2 958 000
Source: 1961 Joint Consulting Engineer's Report

(d) Avoidance of cost overruns and construction delays with variations tightly controlled primarily by adoption of tried and tested construction techniques by an experienced team of contractors and consultants.

Table 14.4   Interest rate for Hong Kong Tunnel: 7%
(a) minimum traffic

Year	ADT*	Net revenue	Interest	Capital outstanding
1966	16 340	1160	1168	16 685
1967	17 763	1277	1169	16 693
1968	19 186	1389	1161	16 585
1969	20 609	1506	1145	16 357
1970	22 032	1618	1120	15 996
1971	23 455	1735	1085	15 498
1972	24 787	1839	1039	14 848
1973	26 118	1949	983	14 048
1974	27 450	2054	916	13 082
1975	28 781	2162	836	11 944
1976	30 113	2267	743	10 618
1977	31 445	2377	672	9594
1978	32 776	2481	552	7889
1979	34 108	2591	417	5960
1980	35 439	2695	265	3786
1981	36 771	2804	95	1356

*Pays off in 16th year, surplus £1 353 000
(b) probable traffic

Year	ADT*	Net revenue	Interest	Capital outstanding
1966	25 573	1773	1168	16 685
1967	27 750	1941	1126	16 080
1968	29 926	2104	1069	15 265
1969	32 103	2272	1031	14 730
1970	34 279	2434	944	13 489
1971	36 456	2602	840	11 999
1972	38 509	2757	717	10 237
1973	40 562	2912	574	8197
1974	42 615	3061	410	5859
1975	44 669	3212	225	3208
1976	46 723	3361	15	221

*Pays off in 11th year, surplus £3 125 000
Source: 1961 Joint Consulting Engineer's Report

Table 14.5 Interest rate for Hong Kong Tunnel: 8%
(a) minimum traffic

Year	ADT*	Net revenue	Interest	Capital outstanding
1966	16 340	1160	1414	17 675
1967	17 763	1277	1434	17 929
1968	19 186	1389	1447	18 086
1969	20 609	1506	1451	18 144
1970	22 032	1618	1447	18 089
1971	23 455	1735	1433	17 918
1972	24 787	1839	1409	17 616
1973	26 118	1949	1375	17 186
1974	27 450	2054	1329	16 612
1975	28 781	2162	1271	15 887
1976	30 113	2267	1200	14 996
1977	31 445	2377	1154	14 429
1978	32 776	2481	1056	13 206
1979	34 108	2591	942	11 781
1980	35 439	2695	811	10 132
1981	36 771	2804	660	8248
1982	38 103	2910	488	6104
1983	39 435	3020	295	3682
1984	40 767	3124	77	957

*Pays off in 19th year, surplus £2 090 000

(b) probable traffic

Year	ADT*	Net revenue	Interest	Capital outstanding
1966	25 573	1773	1414	17 675
1967	27 750	1941	1385	17 316
1968	29 926	2104	1341	16 760
1969	32 103	2272	1320	16 497
1970	34 279	2434	1244	15 545
1971	36 456	2602	1148	14 355
1972	38 509	2757	1032	12 901
1973	40 562	2912	894	11 176
1974	42 615	3061	733	9158
1975	44 669	3212	546	6830
1976	46 723	3361	333	4164
1977	48 776	3511	91	1136

*Pays off in 12th year, surplus £2 284 000
Source: 1961 Joint Consulting Engineer's Report

Table 14.6 Predicted and actual traffic flows for Hong Kong Cross Harbour Tunnel

Year	Actual	Predicted	
		Probable	Minimum
1972	26 174	38 509	24 787
1973	34 190	40 562	26 118
1974	38 915	42 615	27 450
1975	41 626	44 669	28 781
1976	49 480	46 723	30 113
1977	59 348	Not given	31 445
1978	74 121	Not given	32 776
1979	87 178	Not given	34 108
1980	95 632	Not given	35 439
1981	104 613	Not given	36 771
1982	108 987	Not given	38 103
1983	108 187	Not given	39 435
1984	100 763	Not given	40 767

(e) Shorter than predicted construction phase — 1961 report and financial model cited 54 months; the actual period was 35 months.

(f) Political championing by Britain's prime minister Harold Wilson in pushing through ECGD loan approval without Hong Kong Government guarantees.

(g) Early local championing by influential local businessmen, Lawrence (later Lord) Kadoorie, Douglas (later Sir Douglas) Clague and John Marden.

(h) A government which acquiesced with the concept.

The story does not end, however, for this charmed BOT when its concession expires in 1999. The holding and operating company, the Cross Harbour Tunnel Co., has arranged to live on, by being a 37% owner of a new consortium to build a third BOT cross harbour tunnel under the name of The Western Harbour Tunnel Co., (WHT Co.). This project is expected to cost HK$7·5 billion when opened in 1997. To fund its share the Cross Harbour Tunnel Co. announced, in August 1993, that a one-for-two rights issue was to raise HK$830·4 million. The issue also came with a warning from the company's directors that the longstanding policy of paying 85% of annual profits as dividends will be lowered until about the turn of the century when tolls from the new tunnel come on stream. The original sponsors and 30-year operator of what could be classed as the world's first BOT now continue via another 30-year franchise.

The 1993 BOT agreement for what is essentially a very similar tunnel has evolved from the model in the 1960s. A significant area of change is how the concession agreement addresses the important issue of toll increase or decrease. The earlier agreement had a clause which simply stated the operation should be neither, 'excessively remunerative nor not reasonably remunerative' and an independent arbitrator would decide should it become an issue. The 1993 concession, is much more specific and ensures the internal rate of return remains within a predetermined range throughout the franchise period.[5] For the first three years of operation this range is set at 15% to 16·5%. Thereafter, the range is set at 15 to 18·5%. This is to be achieved by allowing the WHT Co. to increase tolls in the event that cash flows fall below a minimum threshold due to poorer traffic volumes, higher inflation or higher interest rates than expected.

Shajiao 'B' power station, Peoples' Republic of China

The Shajiao 'B' power station is a conventional 2 × 350 MW coal fired plant situated near Tai Ping on the Pearl River Estuary, about halfway between Hong Kong and Guangzhou in the Guangdong province of the Peoples' Republic of China (PRC). The Guangdong region, adjacent to Hong Kong in South West China, is developing at breakneck speed; in 1993 the Governor of the province was reported as stating that 'our GDP forecast is 12·9% growth every year for 20 years'.[6] This explosive growth has resulted in a flush of new road, rail, port, bridge and other infrastructure works in and around the Pearl River Estuary. Within Guangdong Province is the Shenzhen special economic zone which, because of its common boundary with Hong Kong, is at the leading edge of this spiralling economic growth.

This rate of growth has required considerable expansion of electricity generation facilities. Notwithstanding the fact that China ranks fourth in the world in terms of total annual power generation, there is still a wide gap between supply of and demand for electric power, and the central government has listed, in the eighth Five Year Plan: 1991–95, expansion of the electric power industry as one of the top development priorities. Unfortunately, however, the PRC does not have the necessary resources to finance development at the speed which is necessary to support the economic growth of the region and, therefore, when Gordon Wu, a prominent Hong Kong businessman who had already planned to fund and build a 1200 room hotel in Guangdong, proposed a second power station at Shajiao the idea landed on fertile ground. Once the idea was accepted by the Chinese Government, there then followed a period of negotiation with others such as Bechtel Group and EPDC of Japan with both making proposals directly to the Chinese. Gordon Wu's credibility and persuasion eventually won the day, and a series of agreements was signed in 1984/85 allowing Hopewell Power (China) Limited to proceed with the development of the first power plant in China to be procured on a BOT basis.

The joint venture

Shajiao 'B' is a joint venture between Shenzhen Special Economic Zone Power Development Co. (SPDC, Party A) and Hopewell Power (China) Ltd (HPC, Party B). HPC is 50% owned by Hong Kong's Hopewell Holdings Ltd, 5% by Kamematsu-Gosho (HK) Ltd, a Japanese firm, and the remaining 45% by a cluster of Chinese parties. We have already seen, in Chapter 5, how the 'empty chair' theory of financial engineering was implemented in this project in order to overcome a number of financing problems.

The joint venture period is ten years, that is from 1 April 1988 to 31 March 1998, and at the end of this period Party B will transfer ownership of the Station to Party A at no charge. Under the terms of the agreement Party B was required to put into commercial operation two units each of 350 MW capacity by 1 April 1988. Any profit gained before 1 April 1988 due to early commissioning of the station was to be given to Party B as a bonus. The station was actually completed some 6 months earlier than scheduled, and the bonus paid was of the order of HK$400 million (US$50 million).

The BOT agreements

In principle the joint venture agreement for Shajiao 'B' required Party B to be responsible for the complete design, manufacture, delivery, construction, testing and commissioning of the plant, including the provision of all labour, supervisors, construction equipment and temporary works on a full turnkey basis. In undertaking the project on this basis Hopewell thus took responsibility for delay and cost overrun risks.

Supplementary to the main agreement were a power off-take agreement, under which the Chinese agreed to purchase a minimum of 60% of the plant capacity on a 'take and pay' basis, and to pay Hopewell a fixed price per kilowatt hour for the whole of the ten-year cooperation period, and a coal supply agreement under which the Chinese also

Table 14.7 *Key dates for Shajiao 'B' power station*

Contract schedule	
First unit	'Plant completion' (defined as full load operation, after completion of commissioning) required 30 months after the issue of a Letter of Intent
Second unit	'Plant completion' required 33 months after the issue of a Letter of Intent
Actual progress	
Commencement	Construction began on the 1 July 1985
First unit	Plant completion on the 22 April 1987 (i.e. 22 months)
Second unit	Plant completion on the 22 July 1987 (i.e. 25 months)

agreed to arrange for the supply of coal for the whole of the cooperation period at a fixed price per tonne. Payments for fuel are made from the electricity sales proceeds. Key dates are given in Table 14.7.

Financing

The total declared cost of the Shajiao 'B' station is approximately HK$4 billion (US$512 million). Party B, Hopewell Power (China) Ltd, was responsible for the financing of all the construction costs of the station, and Party A, the SPDC, is committed to purchase a specified minimum amount of electricity from the station and to provide coal both at pre-determined prices throughout the joint venture period.

The Chinese government assisted in the arrangement of an emergency loan facility to the investor group to provide funds in the event of force majeure, and also provided certain guarantees regarding protection against exchange rate fluctuations.

On the basis of the joint venture agreement, Hopewell arranged the project financing from a syndicate of 46 international banks. The banks agreed to look only to the electricity sales proceeds for repayment, but the power offtake and coal supply agreements were taken into consideration by funding institutions.

The project was funded by a combination of shareholder equity, subordinated loans in Renminbi, deferred payments and a variety of debt packages. The bulk of the debt financing took the form of a supplier credit from Japan arranged by Mitsui & Co. This supplier credit was backed by Export Import Bank of Japan and was denominated in Yen. The sponsors were attracted by the ten-year fixed-interest rate on offer and the fact that the Chinese authorities were willing to accept the exchange rate risk.

In reality the Japanese Export Credit involvement was of very questionable benefit in that they would not accept any project risk and were protected by a comprehensive guarantee provided by the banking syndicate arranged by Citicorp. In addition to providing the guarantee the same syndicate of banks provided a Euroyen loan and a HK$ loan in respect of the non Eximbank portion. A Renminbi loan was taken from PRC banking sources on a deferred payment basis i.e. not to be repaid until the supplier credit and other commercial bank Yen and HK$ loans were repaid. The financing package, considered to be highly innovative at the time, was successfully concluded in April 1986.

In 1987, Citicorp identified a major refinancing opportunity, and Japanese supplier credit was replaced by a floating rate Euroyen syndicated loan. The floating rate was subsequently swapped to a fixed rate, thus resulting in substantial interest cost savings during the remaining loan life.

The construction contract

Hopewell subsequently negotiated a 'turnkey contract' (fixed price, fixed completion, agreed quality) for construction of the station with a consortium of equipment suppliers and contractors, thus protecting itself to some extent against penalties for late completion included in its own joint venture agreement. The consortium comprised:

- Mitsui & Co. — commercial leader
- Toshiba Corporation — technical coordinator; turbine and generator islands
- Ishikawajima-Harima Heavy Industries Co. Ltd — boiler island
- Slipform Engineering Ltd (Hopewell's civil construction subsidiary) — civil and architectural work.

Deferred credits were provided by the consortium allowing for repayments over a 7·5-year period.

Others involved included Ove Arup and Partners and James Williamson and Associates (civil engineering design), Hopewell/Costain (project management), Ewbank Preece Engineering Ltd and Guangdong Power Design Institute (electrical and mechanical engineering consultants), and Frank and Vargeson (quantity surveyors).

Li[2] reports that a large local labour force of up to 800 was employed. In addition, assistance was provided by the PRC navy in pulling and laying cables.

Technical aspects of the plant

The Shajiao 'B' station is adjacent to the Shajiao 'A' plant, built earlier by the PRC. Toshiba of Japan was the principal plant supplier and overall technical coordinator.

The station appears to typify control of the technological risk factors through the use of design and construction methods which are both well tried and economic, although without some of the frills which might be expected in stations constructed elsewhere.

The following technical appraisal is adapted and summarized from Li,[2] following his site visit and a presentation by the plant contractor.

The general impression of the plant was that it was relatively simple and old fashioned. The turbine is designed with a relatively low basic level of efficiency and requires more frequent and extensive overhaul maintenance than up-to-date turbine technology. From an operational viewpoint, Shajiao 'B' compares favourably with plants installed currently. A high level of automatic control is provided and labour saving equipment is provided for materials handling.

Construction was aimed at having the first unit synchronized early and so anything which would hinder this was either left out of the design or left in abeyance until a more convenient time. For this reason a properly paved public access road to the station was not completed at the time of first synchronization. The cold water pumps, generator transformers, bunker bay, ancillary water systems and 500 kV switchgear are of outdoor construction, so erection of these plant items could commence as soon as the civil foundations were completed, without waiting for superstructures.

In terms of design, the administration building and the workshop building are on a less grandiose scale and style than their counterparts in Hong Kong and many other countries. There are many features of the layout conducive to fast construction and economy, particularly in the civil engineering works.

(a) The central control room is built between the two boilers. This eliminates the need for cable tunnels, as segregation occurs naturally and cable lengths are also minimized.

(b) The mezzanine floor is raised to the same level as the turbine hall. This complements (a), enabling cabling and other services to be routed above ground, beneath the mezzanine, and eliminates cable and service trenches within the turbine hall. The structures then become simple slabs.

The above combine to make the control block a relatively simple structure. Toshiba indicated that for a four unit station they would probably have two control rooms, one for each pair of units. Whereas the more common practice is to have one control room for a station with four units. The control block is a critical path area, where the structures are very complex, in order to ensure cable and equipment segregation between the four units.

(c) Elimination of switchgear and equipment rooms. Switchgear and equipment rooms introduce requirements for complex air-conditioning systems, cable penetrations and routes, fire detection and protection, etc. In Shajiao 'B' the switchgear are in areas merely fenced off in the turbine hall and its annex and not in separate rooms. All control equipment is located in a single, air-conditioned unit equipment room, adjacent to the control room as opposed to having a number of equipment rooms distributed in the station.

(d) Elimination of cable and pipework trenches in external areas. Site services are routed above ground, rather than in trenches. Again this simplifies and reduces the scope of the civil engineering works.

These layout considerations generally represent good ideas that, it is interesting to note, other electricity undertakers are now generally following in the design of larger stations.

The cold water pumphouse is, in construction terms, a very much simpler structure than in conventional designs. The forebay is of very large proportions, albeit a simple rectangular box. This eliminates the need for careful hydraulic design, including hydraulic modelling. The design could, therefore, be finalized quickly. Band screens, rather than drum screens, are used — again simplifying the structures. The civil engineering and plant designs do not appear to have been optimized — the civil engineering works have been made to fit the plant requirements. However, as a consequence of the design approach, the cold water system appears prone to siltation problems.

Shajiao is, evidently, a virtual repeat of previous stations provided by the same suppliers. As a consequence, little lead time was required in initial engineering before manufacture and procurement could commence. Most importantly, as the mechanical design of plant components and connections are known, final layout and foundation requirement information could be provided for civil engineering design almost immediately. It is understood that final plant data of a high quality was being issued to the civil engineering consultant five weeks after the issue of the letter of intent. As a result of the 'repeat' nature of the design, the contractor had a strong knowledge of his product. In finalizing the engineering, the contractor was not interfered with in respect of client requirements and local statutory regulations. He was, therefore, able to concentrate his efforts on how to manufacture and construct to meet the programme, not what the plant should be. In other words, the contractor was able to make an 'early design freeze'.

The plant and systems appeared to have been extensively value engineered, eliminating frills and margins.

However, having stated that the plant is relatively simple, it should be noted that there are no conspicuous omissions in the scope of supply. Most components, however, looked smaller and more basic than the conventional equivalents. The exception is automatic control where Shajiao 'B' has a sophisticated unit control scheme that serves to reduce the need for operator attendance.

The simplicity of the plant reduced the general scope and extent of plant erection. Components arrived at site in larger assemblies. The condenser, for example, was already tubed in the works and this would save about five weeks in the erection period. Other components arriving in a significantly advanced state of fabrication included air-heaters, mills, ship unloaders and the turbine oil system.

The simple two unit layout, with a central control room, also meant that cable and pipe routes were easier to lay and run. An absence of engineering changes during erection ensured that cable laying could continue without interruption. The boiler house had no roof and much of the boiler ancillary plant was erected from above, using a climbing crane thus simplifying erection.

It would appear likely that corners were cut in commissioning procedures, and there are further indications that technical quality has been subservient to programme.

Conclusions

This project must be classed as successful from the point of view of the sponsor. The project is now well over halfway through its concession period and performing more or less as planned. It is evident that, on this project, programme was always the predominant goal, probably largely driven by the promise of potentially large bonuses for early delivery. The repeat nature of the plant was obviously a most important factor in achieving a quite remarkable programme for a project of this type. The repeat nature of the plant also ensured that cost could be accurately forecast and well controlled, and in addition virtually guaranteed that the plant would perform as required.

The project also illustrates many of the factors required for a successful BOT.

- (*a*) A local and influential champion, Gordon Wu, able and willing to promote the scheme and to lobby effectively for its acceptance.
- (*b*) Demand for the product in the form of a huge demand for electrical power in Guangdong Province. The general consensus of economic opinion is that China's 'market socialist' economy, having multiplied six-fold since 1978, will continue to grow by leaps and bounds well into the next century. Nowhere is this more evident than Guangdong Province, immediately adjacent to Hong Kong. The primary driver of urbanization was therefore well and truly in place.
- (*c*) Government officials willing to cooperate.
- (*d*) Good control of technological risk through the use of tried and tested turbine and construction technology.

Other factors which have contributed to this success are as follows.

- (*a*) Completion six months ahead of schedule. In terms of construction and completion, performance by Hopewell/Slipform and Mitsui was nothing short of phenomenal. Although much of the site formation work had been completed, at Hopewell's risk, in advance of agreement of the financing package, completion of a station of this size six months ahead of the contract was truly remarkable.
- (*b*) The main civil engineering contractor was also a member of the Hopewell Group, and there was therefore considerable incentive to shorten the construction programme to a minimum.
- (*c*) The Chinese party relied absolutely on the technical competence of Party B, and did not interfere in any way with the design and construction process.
- (*d*) Good project management, and the delivery of the plant in large prefabricated assemblies.

From the host government's point of view the project must also be judged to be successful. In general it would appear that the performance of Shajiao 'B' has been satisfactory. The first unit was synchronized on 18 April 1987 and achieved full load for the first time on 14 May 1987. Although there were some early teething troubles, deficiencies were rectified and plant availability has since been high, reportedly achieving 92% availability during the first year.

Although the early completion bonus paid to Hopewell drew initial protest from the Chinese side, it has been reported that the objection was quickly overcome when it was pointed out that the 3·1 billion kWh of electricity generated ahead of scheduled completion date permitted factory production in Guangdong Province amounting to some US$500 million in economic value which would otherwise have been lost due to factory closures through power shortages.

Toronto Airport

In the May 1985 Budget document, the Canadian Government stated that it would consider a new management structure for its federal airport system — one which would 'provide for a self-sustaining system' and would 'allow for the independent operation of local airports'. The transport minister commissioned airport management studies which revealed the following problems of federal ownership and management:

(a) large and growing financial deficits which created a burden on the Canadian taxpayers
(b) limited responsiveness to local and regional needs because of the centralization of the system
(c) inefficiency of the system due to extensive government involvement.

By 1987, a new policy document published by a government department, Transport Canada entitled *A future framework for the management of airports in Canada* explicitly considered, among other alternatives, the option of private sector investment in traditional and non traditional airport services.

Terminal 3: a new private airport development

Largely as a result of the above deliberations, Terminal 3 of Lester B. Pearson International Airport in Toronto became the first privately financed, designed, built and operated airport in Canada. A call for expression of interest was advertised in 1986, to which eight consortia responded. Four were shortlisted and eventually the consortium headed by Canadian developers Huang and Danczkay Properties Inc., Claridge Properties (together owning 73%) and Lockheed Air Terminals of Canada Inc. (owning 23%) obtained a 40-year ground lease from Transport Canada in April 1988 to develop and operate the facilities. The latter federal government agency remains responsible for air-traffic control and airport security.

The development consists of the terminal building with retail shops and restaurants, a 500-room airport hotel and car parks, which all together cost some C$520 million (US$433 million) to build. The consortium formed the Airport Development Corporation, which paid ground rents to Transport Canada in return for the right to develop and reap income in the form of airline fees from six airlines, rentals from the hotel, retail shops and restaurants, and car parking fees.

The development, also known as the Trillium Airport, was planned to handle 14·5 million passengers a year, but by the time it was opened, on 21 February 1991, Canada was experiencing its first drop in international air passengers in a decade. Factors such as the Gulf War and global recession meant that passenger numbers for 1991 were 2·5 million fewer than in 1990. As a result tenants no longer found their businesses to be profitable, with airport rents higher than choice retail space in downtown Toronto, and as a result some demanded renegotiation of their leases with the corporation. Two retailers, including DFS Canada Ltd, a giant US-based operator of duty-free shops, even filed lawsuits against the developers on the ground of inaccurate passenger forecasts. DFS subsequently pulled out of the airport in September 1992.

While the tenants were grumbling about the high rents and poor business at Terminal 3, travellers on the other hand found it an efficient airport terminal and a relief from the then congested Terminals 1 and 2. One airline spokesman was recorded as saying: 'It's a great facility and it really is the crown jewel of all the airports we operate out of'. It was also said that the private sector completed the terminal much faster (34 months from contract signing to completion), and probably at a lower cost, than the federal government could have done, but its tenants had paid a high price for having a private owner. An estimate put Terminal 3's per-passenger costs as three times those in Pearson's other terminals. Travellers also found the cost of goods and services at the new Terminal more expensive.

Another highlight of Terminal 3 occurred in April 1992, when Huang and Danczkay sold its stake to its former partner, the Claridge Group. The developer's decision to pull out of Pearson was said to be due to their pursuit of other large projects such as the proposed new Athens International Airport project in Greece. The sell off required the approval of Transport Canada, which owns the land. Claridge and Lockheed together then owned the terminal building, the gates, the ramp area and the infrastructure under the corporate identity of Terminal Three Limited Partnership.

Terminals 1 and 2: a big controversy over privatization

The eventful privatization of Toronto's Airport did not end with

Terminal 3. In fact, before the completion of Terminal 3, the then transport minister Doug Lewis announced the privatized redevelopment plan for Terminals 1 and 2 in October 1990. The ageing Terminal 1 was originally opened in 1964 with an annual throughput of 4 million passengers. By 1992, it handled 20·5 million passengers and served 28 carriers, and this figure is expected to reach 28 million by 1999. Likewise, Terminal 2 has been the base of Canada's major carrier, Air Canada, and it received a recent C$50 million facelift before the privatization call.

Those who favoured the call for privatization urged the redevelopment or expansion of Terminals 1 and 2 by citing the annual passenger growth rate of 3% and the worry that the terminals would soon be operating at capacity. They also predicted the creation of some 3200 jobs in recession-striken Toronto, as well as the ability to clinch a good price due to the slow economy. Other claimed advantages included minimal risk exposure for the government and a saving of public funds.

A formal Request for Proposals was therefore issued in March 1992 but shortly before this, an opposition leader, Jean Chretien who later became prime minister of Canada in the 1993 election voiced his objection to the arrangement and alleged that 'the deal was aimed at helping the business pals of the government'.[7] At least three consortia submitted proposals, and in December 1992, a firm called Paxport Inc. was announced as the winner with a C$700 million (US$538 million) scheme for the redevelopment and improvement works. This decision generated a political controversy because Paxport's major shareholder is the Matthews Group Ltd, whose founder, Donald Matthews, is a prominent Conservative Party (the then ruling party) backer. Official sources denied that the decision was based on favouritism, but concern against the quickly concluded privatization deal added fuel to the fire. Opposition arguments were that:

(a) given the current recession, Pearson Airport would not reach full capacity until the next century. So why hurry with the expansion?

(b) even if decentralization is beneficial, Terminals 1 and 2 should be divested to a non-profit local airport authority, as had already happened in Vancouver and Montreal. Shortly before this controversy, Calgary International Airport was also handed over to a non-profit local authority under a 60-year lease. The problem in Toronto appeared to be that agreement could not be reached with the government as to the recognition of the proper local airport authority

(c)   the profitability of the three terminals should be used to upgrade air transport facilities on a federal basis and not be handed over into private hands, given the fact that the three terminals together made a profit of C$60 million (US$46 million) in 1992.

Despite all of this opposition, a privatization contract giving the Pearson Development Corporation (Paxport Inc. plus Terminal Three Limited Partnership) a 37-year lease, with a likely 20-year extension, was signed on 7 October 1993, only two weeks before an impending general election. During the election campaign, opposition candidate Jean Chretien again promised to review the deal if he were to be elected. The result of the election overturned the short-lived government led by Kim Campbell, and the new prime minister-elect immediately suspended the imminent transfer of the terminal site, and ordered a review of the privatization deal by Robert Nixon, the former Ontario Treasurer. A damning report was produced after 30 days, which concluded that:

> To leave in place an inadequate contract, arrived at with such a flawed process and under the shadow of possible political manipulation, is unacceptable.

The recommendation was that the privatization contract should be scrapped, as it was against public interest. The advice was taken by the prime minister, and the contract was cancelled on the 3 December 1993.

As might be expected, Pearson Development Corporation pursued a claim against the federal government for monies already expended on the scheme of some C$30 million (US$23 million), and foregone profit of a further C$145 million (US$112 million). At the time of writing, no settlement has yet been reached, but there has been clear indication from the new Liberal Government that compensation, if any, would not include lobbying fees and loss of profit. A government bill is also being considered in Parliament House which would have the effect of removing the claimant's right to sue for any compensation if no settlement is possible under the above-indicated conditions. Government sources said that the new law was justified because the developers, and the previous government, went ahead with the contract signing just weeks before the federal vote, despite clear opposition from the would-be winner. It was also reported that the rationale behind this bill is to avoid any further delay which would hamper the government's attempts to wind up the issue and get airport development moving again. In the meantime, a government negotiator has been appointed to try to reach agreement with the developers on a compensation package.

Figure 14.3   An aerial view of the whole Toronto Airport area

Conclusion

The Toronto Airport saga illustrates some of the risk factors which can be associated with BOT projects, and shows that these risks are not restricted to the countries of the developing world.

The risk posed by inaccurate or inadequate traffic forecasts is clear from the opening scene of Terminal 3. Unexpected events such as the Gulf War and recession sent world air travel into a tailspin and rendered the original cash flow forecast inaccurate. In this particular case, a portion of this risk was transferred to the tenants of the terminal's retail facilities through their tenancy agreements. Many of them claimed loss in the beginning, but fortunately there are recent signs that business is improving.

The political risk which eventually resulted in cancellation of the contract, as happened in the Terminal 1 and Terminal 2 redevelopment, is a restricting factor for future BOT projects, as lawyers acting for the consortium argued that the situation would be tantamount to expropriation. Critics against this view justified the government's action saying that the contract could easily have been held over until after the election for consideration by the new government. Whatever the rights and wrongs of the situation, Toronto is a valuable reminder to BOT promoters that political risks are not restricted to the developing world

(Fig. 14.3). The Toronto experience points clearly to the necessity for very careful consideration of all likely scenarios by BOT project promoters and governments.

The Malaysian North – South Highway

Malaysia is a fast developing country experiencing rapid urbanization. It has recently been described as:

> ... the Asian tiger with the biggest bite. Exciting and volatile at the same time, it has kept a constant GDP growth of 8% for six years and the construction rate for 1994 is predicted at 11·7%.[5]

During the early 1980s the government embarked upon a drive for economic diversification, and recognized the need for rapid development of the primary infrastructure. By 1985 it had begun to implement a concerted privatization strategy backed by substantial financial incentives to make the policy work. The Malaysian government has implemented a number of BOT schemes including roads, and water and electricity supply facilities, and at the time of writing (early 1995) it continues to actively encourage private sector involvement in infrastructure development.

Malaysia is regarded as politically stable, and as having a generally liberal exchange control policy. The Ringgit is classed as a stable currency, and although the economy slumped due to the global recession in the mid 1980s, it has, in more recent years, enjoyed comparatively high levels growth in gross domestic product with relatively low levels of inflation. The development of the Malaysian economy coupled with the growing commercial wealth of the country and government encouragement has attracted foreign investors interested in infrastructure development, but has also generated a class of local entrepreneurs who are increasingly willing to invest their own money in projects of this type.

The North – South Highway project

The North – South Highway is a key feature in the development of the Malaysian road transport system. The completed highway runs down the western side of the Malay peninsula from the Thai border in the north to Singapore in the south, a total distance of almost 900 km, and links many of the country's newly industrialized areas. The route also provides an alternative to short-haul air travel, and will compete with sea and rail for goods traffic along the western coast. Prior to development of the route, travel from the north of the country to the south was often measured in days, due to poor roads and heavy traffic congestion. The primary drivers of an apparently viable revenue stream coupled with a government committed to privatization thus encouraged development of the route as a BOT project.

Approximately 350 km of highway had already been constructed by government using traditional procurement methods, but the project was brought to standstill by the economic slump of the mid-1980s with some 55 km still under construction.

Development of the BOT project began in August 1985, when United Engineers Malaysian Bhd (UEM) prepared and submitted a preliminary concept for the complete scheme to the Malaysian authorities. UEM then formed a multinational consortium, comprising Mitsui, Taylor Woodrow International, Dragage et Travaux and three Malaysian companies to prepare a pre-emptive bid for the project in January 1986.

The Malaysian Government subsequently invited competitive bids for the scheme. Five bids were submitted and at the end of December 1986 United Engineers received a letter of intent to proceed with the scheme. Considerable negotiation followed, complicated by internal political wrangling, the result of which was that the concession agreement was not signed until mid-1988, by which time the United Engineers consortium had formed a separate project company, Projek Lebuhraya Utara Selatan (PLUS) to carry out the work.

The concession agreement

The concession agreement was eventually assigned to PLUS in July 1988, and the first of some 42 work package contracts was let in November 1988, with completion of the whole project programmed for March 1995. The concession period is 30 years from the date of the agreement, expiring in 2018.

Predicted construction cost at the outset was M$3.44 billion (US$1.28 billion), and this was financed through a conventional debt—equity structure with an equity—debt ratio of about 10:90. Local inflation and the Gulf War are reported to have increased the costs by a further M$976 million (US$363 million). The debt comprises a Malaysian Government Support Loan coupled with a combination of onshore and offshore loans, export credits and revenue bonds. In addition the project sponsors arranged the work package contracts such that the majority of the equity would be funded by the work package contractors. Tiong[8] describes the financial engineering:

> This project received a M\$650 million support loan from the government. To ease its cash flow, the sponsor promised to pay its subcontractors, be they local or foreign, 87% of the contract values in cash and 13% in equity shares in the project company which will be listed on the local stock exchange. The shares can only be sold at the end of the construction period. This effectively passed the bulk of the equity risk to the subcontractors.

This approach ensures that sub-contractors not only have a stake in the success of the project but also a powerful incentive to complete the work on time and within budget.

In addition to the support loan, the project also received other government benefits, including a degree of protection in the event that traffic flow predictions were not achieved through a traffic volume supplement agreement, and some protection against external risks through an external risks supplements agreement.

Vellu[9] reports that the concession agreement also provided for the consortium to take over the operation of the existing 377 km of tolled Federal Highways 1 and 2 in order that they could receive early income and so smooth their cash flow.

Conclusions

Although this a very new scheme which has barely yet reached the end of its construction phase all of the indicators are good. The road has now been opened to traffic ahead of schedule, and the journey time from north to south has been cut from days to hours. The road represents the only major high speed route from north to south, and so should enjoy strong and consistent traffic flows. In addition the substantial government support provided, together with the strategy of placing the majority of the equity risk with the subcontractors considerably reduced the risks to the project sponsors. All of the indications are that the project should be successful.

The Dartford Bridge

The need for an additional crossing on the River Thames at Dartford in Kent has been apparent for many years. In 1987−88 crossings through the existing Dartford tunnels were reported to be in excess of 90 000 vehicles per day against a design capacity of 65 000, while by 1991, just before the new bridge was opened, traffic flows were reported to have reached a record 102 000 vehicles per day with queues of up to 5.5 km.

The need was in fact recognized by government as early as the beginning of the 1980s, but is was not until the autumn of 1986 that a deal to build a bridge on a BOT basis was signed between the Department of Transport and a consortium led by Trafalgar House. The agreement followed a long period of discussion and indecision, followed by a competitive tendering process which initially began with 8 contenders. Three consortia were eventually shortlisted, led respectively by Trafalgar House, Mowlem and Balfour Beatty. All three consortia initially proposed tunnel solutions, but Trafalgar House also proposed an alternative cable stayed bridge option, and it was this option which eventually won the day. This despite allegations by one of the unsuccessful bidders that the Department of Transport changed the rules of the competition in the last week of the assessment so as to make the bridge option more feasible, and that the winner of the competition exerted 'political pressure' in the wake of its failure to win the contract to build the Bosphorus bridge 'partly because of the government's failure to match Japanese soft loan terms offered to Turkey'.[10] The Department of Transport however defended its decision on the basis that the winning proposal offered the best value for money both for the government and for the motorist.

The new bridge will double the capacity of the existing crossing to 130 000 vehicles per day. This project is particularly important because it set the scene for other major British private sector infrastructure projects including the second Severn crossing and the Birmingham North Relief Road.[4]

The Dartford Bridge, designed by Trafalgar House Technology Limited and DrIng Helmut Homberg and Partner, is impressive by any standards. It is 812 m long with a central clear span of 450 m and rises to provide a vertical navigational clearance of 57·5 m. The bridge therefore allows uninterupted road and river traffic at all times.

Construction began in August 1988, and the bridge was formally opened to traffic in October 1991, on time and within budget. The bridge was built by the Cementation Cleveland Dartford Consortium, consisting of Trafalgar House subsidiaries, with Cementation Construction responsible for the substructure and Cleveland Bridge responsible for the superstructure work.

The concession agreement

The concession agreement is notable in a number of respects. Firstly, the agreement makes provision for the project sponsors to acquire the lease to operate the existing tunnels for the period of the concession, and also requires them to clear off the existing £55 million debt on the existing road tunnels presently carried by Kent and Essex County Councils. Both the existing tunnels and the new bridge are now operated by a new company, the Dartford River Crossing Company.

The agreement also makes provision for a variable concession period. The maximum period is set at 20 years, but the bridge and tunnels will be handed back to Government as soon as the debt charges and costs have been recovered. Present predictions indicate that the concession period could in fact be as short as 14 years. Rises in toll charges are permitted no more than once a year, and are pegged to the rate of inflation.

Financing for the project as a whole was planned and organized by Kleinwort Benson with virtually the entire cost, some £184 million, being debt financed with a neglible and nominal equity contribution. The majority of the funds were raised from institutional investors led by the Prudential Assurance Company and a syndicated bank loan developed by the Bank of America.

Conclusions

The Dartford Bridge must represent one of the best potential BOT opportunities ever, and is surely cast in the same mould as the original Hong Kong Cross Harbour Tunnel (see first case study). Even taking account of the in-fighting which took place in the early stages, all of the factors for a successful BOT were in place from the very beginning. Reliable traffic flow figures clearly pointed to a cast iron revenue stream, thus encouraging institutional investors and permitting the financial advisors to raise the entire cost through debt financing. In addition the scheme was promoted by a strong and, no doubt, politically aware sponsor, and construction costs and time-frame were carefully calculated and controlled. As in the case of the Malaysian North–South Highway and the Bangkok Second Stage Expressway transfer of an existing asset, in this case the existing tunnels, to the project company provided much needed early cash flow. Assuming that running costs remain under control it is difficult to see any way in which this project could fail to provide the sought for win-win solution for all concerned.

References

1. WALKER C.T. *BOT infrastructure: anatomy of success*. City Polytechnic of Hong Kong, Unpublished MSc dissertation, 1993.

2. LI W.Y. *Construction management strategies for capital investment projects with special reference to China.* City Polytechnic of Hong Kong, Unpublished MSc dissertation, 1993.
3. SCOTT, WILSON KIRKPATRICK and PARTNERS/FREEMAN, FOX and PARTNERS. *Hong Kong Harbour Crossing investigation.* Joint Report, Vol. I and II, unpublished, 1961.
4. RUFFORD N. Projects galore could follow Dartford deal. *New Civil Engineer*, 2 Oct. 1986, 4.
5. LANE E. The party goes on. *Int. Construction*, 1994, Sept.
6. *Asia Magazine*, 2 Feb. 1993.
7. *Calgary Herald*, 13 Mar. 1992.
8. TIONG R. *The Structuring of BOT.* Technological monograph, Nanyang Technological University, Singapore, 1992.
9. VELLU S.S. BOT opportunities in Malaysia. *Proc. Conf. on BOT opportunities in Malaysia.* Singapore, 1988.
10. MONTAGUE S. Rule change swings Dartford Bridge. *New Civil Engineer*, 21/28 Aug. 1986, 5.

Chapter 15

Infrastructure economics and the role of government

Introduction

The origins of the BOT approach lay in the need to find access to private sector finance for the provision of basic infrastructure (power, water, transport, communications) which was currently being provided by the public sector in both developed and underdeveloped countries. It is an approach to privatization in which specific facilities are funded, built and operated by the private sector for a defined period.

The historical reasons for the heavy involvement of the public sector in the provision of infrastructure even within non communist countries are varied. Some are political and are linked to the strong attraction of socialism in decolonized countries and to the socialist contribution to the political development of the mixed economies in post-war Europe. But there are important economic reasons why governments have always had (and will continue to have) an important role in the provision of infrastructure services, particularly those requiring the construction of major facilities serving a wide range of users.

The main topic covered by this book is the role of BOT in the construction of major projects. This chapter concentrates on operational issues and in particular the way in which these affect the relationship between the sponsor and government. It deals with a number of issues including:

- major projects as a component of service provision
- economic reasons for the continuing involvement of government
- the changing role of government as privatization takes place.

This analysis leads to a simple classification of BOT projects, which will be used in Chapter 17 as a means of examining the problems facing governments and BOT sponsors in a variety of situations.

Throughout this chapter, the emphasis will be on the provision of services — the operational 'O' of BOT. Projects outside socialist countries are almost always constructed by privately owned and competitive contractors. The distinguishing element of BOT is the private sector operation of a facility providing services needed by individuals, companies or the community as a whole in a profitable manner. Nevertheless, there are several important politico-economic reasons why the public sector has been (and will continue to be) involved in such projects.

(a) Provision of benefits to those who are not direct users of the service (government as customer).

(b) The likelihood of monopoly (government as regulator).

(c) Long-term risk (government as guarantor).

(d) National security (government as defender).

Government as customer

Taking the first of these, the value arising from a major project results from the benefits it provides to two groups of users:

- those who actually make use of the service and can be charged for its use
- those who do not use the service as individuals, but benefit from it indirectly or jointly as members of society in a way which does not allow them to be charged.

Similarly, the costs of a service can be divided into those for which suppliers can be paid directly and those which are paid by society as a whole, such as pollution and environmental degradation.

A simple example would be a bypass round a town which lies on a pre-existing trunk road. Its provision will benefit the through travellers who use it by reducing their travel time and hence cost. They can be charged for its use through a toll system. But it also benefits the residents of the town, reducing through goods traffic and traffic congestion, thereby enhancing the quality of life. It is much more difficult to estimate the value of these benefits, which are often referred to as 'social benefits' to distinguish them from the 'user benefits' which accrue to the direct users of a new service or facility. But to ignore these benefits is likely to lead to the underprovision of basic infrastructure services. The provision by private operators of additional roads in a developed country exemplifies many of those problems and will be discussed in more detail in later chapters. If the bypass in this simple example was to be built and operated by a private sector company under an agreement with government which ignored social benefits, one of several situations could arise.

(*a*)   The private sector operation of the bypass (however worthwhile in terms of its total benefits) might not be feasible, since whatever the toll, the income from direct users alone might not be sufficient to make it profitable.

(*b*)   The private sector operator might set a toll which maximized its profit but which was so high that many potential users continued to drive through the bypassed town on the 'free' pre-existing roads and congestion was not relieved.

Similar difficulties to those affecting benefits also apply to costs, particularly those associated with major projects. The costs of major projects fall into two groups — direct costs (land, plant, machinery fuel, labour, finance) for which the providers can be compensated and indirect (or social) costs associated with construction or operation. These include factors such as visual intrusion, atmospheric pollution and noise. The strength of the NIMBY (not in my backyard) response from local residents to many large projects attests to the reality of these indirect costs.

Over the last 30 years economists have developed a sound analytical framework for handling problems of this nature, namely cost-benefit analysis. This technique seeks to identify all the costs and benefits of improved service provision, including both direct and social costs and benefits. It then seeks to identify the optimal course of action for society as a whole. In recent years, greater attention has been paid to equity issues, namely, the degree to which the costs and benefits fall on different groups within society, and to finding the best way of ensuring that those who gain pay whereas those who lose are properly compensated. The methods used have been extended to cover very 'soft' costs and benefits such as those arising from environmental effects.

The technique has been criticized as a basis for decision making on two broad grounds. The first is that it attempts to place financial values on matters such as the value of human life and environmental quality which its critics believe cannot be measured by such materialistic standards. This argument fails to recognize that every decision to proceed with (or indeed, axe) a major project includes implicit valuations of such factors. Cost-benefit analyses can help to make these assumptions more explicit.

A more important criticism (and one which is important to the provision of private sector infrastructure) is that the valuation of social costs and benefits is imprecise and can include a very subjective component. This is not so much a criticism of the analytic framework but a recognition of the problems of valuation and the difficulties of ensuring that those who gain indirectly make a fair contribution for their benefits and that those who lose are compensated.

The proper valuation of social costs and benefits is particularly important when government has to act as agent for the public. When the public sector owns and operates facilities such as a road system, it can use rough assessments of the social costs and benefits of a range of projects as one element in a process of public expenditure prioritization. But when a private sector operator offers to build a road, the government has to consider carefully what its own role should be as a customer, acting as the agent of the community in purchasing the social benefits from the private sector operator. This issue will be discussed in more detail in Chapter 17.

Government as regulator

A second fundamental problem which has resulted in the continuing ownership and operating of infrastructure services by the public sector in non-socialist countries is that of monopoly. This issue is likely to be of particular importance in the provision of services which require major projects.

Roughly speaking, a natural monopoly arises when the long-run marginal cost of a service (i.e. the cost of supplying one extra customer) falls steadily as the number of customers rises. This situation is known as an economy of scale. In such a situation, the largest supplier can undercut the price of smaller suppliers and squeeze them out. Once a single supplier has achieved dominance, this supplier can charge a monopoly rent. This means the service supplier can charge a higher price than would be charged if competition existed and make a superprofit since users have no other source to turn to.

Not surprisingly, major projects are often associated with monopolies or partial monopolies. Really large projects often arise when major benefits of scale exist or when the minimum, threshold, size of the project is large and the capacity of the first supplier is likely to be sufficient for several years. This latter effect often occurs in the case of major transport crossings, such as the Channel Tunnel.

The early post-war approach to such monopolies in European mixed economies was that they were best owned by the public sector, since this ensures that economies of scale can be achieved without placing power in the hands of private sector monopolists. More recently, it has been recognized that public sector monopolies can prove to be inefficient and lacking in customer focus. It has also been realized that true natural monopolies are rarer than was previously believed and that changes in technology can radically alter the economies of scale in particular industries. Rather than owning monopolies (or potential monopolies) the government's role is now seen to be one of regulation, ensuring that where competition is feasible it is encouraged and that where monopolies exist (as for example in the provision of water and sewerage supplies in the United Kingdom) private sector suppliers operate efficiently, provide acceptable levels of customer service and receive a fair return on the capital employed.

The regulation of service monopolies has received a great deal of attention from economists in recent years, but is very imperfectly understood by the public and by many governments. Some privatizations (such is the UK gas industry privatization) created large, vertically integrated private sector companies which are particularly difficult to regulate. Many commentators believe that Britain has been extremely fortunate that individuals with courage and ability have been willing to undertake the regulatory role. Private sector companies operating in competitive markets have a strong incentive towards providing the levels and variety of service their customers require at a competitive price. But the traditional ills of public sector monopolies (doctrinaire attitudes to customer needs, inefficient use of capital, overmanning) can occur in private sector monopolies if they are not subjected to appropriate means of regulation and to public comparison with similar businesses operating in other locations or markets. If the benefits of private sector participation in the provision of utility services (access to private capital markets, improved efficiency, better customer service) are to be achieved in areas where monopolies or potential monopolies exist, intelligent regulatory action by government is needed.

Government as guarantor

A third reason for the ongoing involvement of government in the provision of infrastructure services, particularly those requiring major projects, is risk. Many large projects (such as the Channel Tunnel) involve uncertain costs and long payback periods. They may also involve commercial and competitive uncertainties. For example, the Channel Tunnel is dependent on the provision of road and rail links and through rail services by the British and French governments.

Contractors have to contend with major issues of risk when carrying out construction contracts, but operations lasting 20–30 years carry with them much longer-term risks, particularly for international companies whose financial base may lie outside a particular country of operation.

In the past, these risks have often been accepted openly or tacitly by government, but with the advent of privatized operation they have to be assessed and (if transferred to a private operator) taken into account in assessing the costs of project finance and operation.

The basic principles of risk management are relatively simple. Where possible, risks should be allocated to the party best able to assess and control each risk. This party then seeks to both minimize and 'average' the risk across a number of projects, charging a price which compensates for the average level of risk. If averaging in this way is not possible, the risk bearing party seeks to spread its risk even wider, through insurance or other means. Considered in the context of a BOT project as a whole, the overall level of risk can (at least in theory) be expressed as a probability that the project will fail to reach its projected level of profitability and hence its return on capital employed. This can be offset by an increase in the required rate of return, the increase being referred to as the risk premium.

The difficulty in the BOT field is that the risks involved in the long-term operation of infrastructure facilities can be very difficult to assess and control. They include risks such as the long-term expropriation of assets under changed governments, long-term changes in currency valuations, and changes in the competitive situation (such as the construction of a new road parallel to an existing BOT tolled highway). Governments with little experience of private sector finance may not appreciate that there are some risks which public companies simply cannot accept and others for which the risk premium is very high. Similarly, a specialist company in a field such as power generation may not be able to balance foreign exchange risks internally, since it does not have export interests to offset the foreign exchange risks associated with importing specialist machinery.

The uncertainty of the level of risk can give rise to a serious long-term problem referred to as 'the winners' curse' in project development. Competitive negotiations for BOT projects (either through competitive tendering for a single project or cross-project comparisons of returns by governments negotiating separate BOT contracts) can lead to a situation in which the contract winners are those who underestimate the risks. If problems do occur, the operators may not have the financial strength to continue. Governments need to think hard before attempting to transfer risks which cannot be readily evaluated, managed and priced across to the private sector. Governments must recognize that they have a much greater ability than many private companies to absorb risks, and should in some cases and for certain defined risks adopt the role of guarantor.

Government as defender

A fourth reason for the control of many large infrastructure operations remaining in the public sector is national security. This has become an important issue in the financing of telecommunications networks and the electricity grid in the People's Republic of China, but it also influences the provision of air services. National security arguments are given as being a prime reason for the restrictions on majority foreign ownership of US airline operators and have also influenced the progress of proposed BOT airport projects.

Governments are right to take national security issues seriously, but if they wish to take advantage of the potential benefits of access to private sector capital and management skills they must seek to preserve the necessary rights through contractual terms ensuring access to the facilities on reasonable terms when necessary rather than outright ownership.

Defining the roles of operator and government

Most Western countries have a long tradition of the separation of government and justice, and well-formed principles of commercial law. In many countries requiring major improvements in infrastructure this is not the case. Commercial law is uncertain and subject to change; commerce between the public and private sectors is as much dependent on personal relationships as legal agreements.

In principle, the roles of the two parties can, in a Western environment, be defined in legally enforceable contracts with proper specification of roles, responsibilities and rewards. This must be the aim in developing the final agreement. In reality, the frequent lack of understanding on the part of Western governments as to their separate roles as customer, regulator, guarantor and protector, coupled with post-election changes in governments which bring different political objectives to the fore means that promoters must be acutely aware of what the relationship ought to be when developing their proposals. In developing countries, it is even more important that potential infrastructure operators come to an understanding with government as

Table 15.1 BOT project classification

Complexity of product	Complexity of markets	
	Low	High
High	Defence facilities Maintenance facilities Public waste management Computer facilities	Airports Telecoms networks Channel Tunnel Private railways
Low	Power stations Water supplies Sewage treatment Incinerators Telecoms links Imputed toll roads	Toll crossings Toll roads Container ports Light rail links

to the nature of their relationship, since it may be difficult to enshrine this relationship completely in a legal document.

The relationship will be dependent on the fundamental politico-economic issues discussed earlier in this chapter. Based on those factors, BOT opportunities can be broadly defined into groups which have rather distinct operating problems requiring solution and embodiment into the agreements between the parties. One simple way of classifying projects is to divide than in two dimensions:

- complexity of the output (i.e. services and/or products)
- complexity of the markets.

Table 15.1 shows a division of types of project on this basis. Note that the technical complexity of the project itself is not included. This may of course increase project risk significantly, and needs to be taken into account in the manner discussed earlier in this book. The purpose of this classification is to explore problems of private sector operation — rather than construction — on the nature of the BOT agreement.

BOT project classification

The most straightforward group is the simple output/simple market category. This includes standalone facilities such as power stations, water and sewage treatment facilities, waste volume reduction stations (such as incinerators) and telecommunication links which are rented from the operators by network operators. In each of these cases, the operator provides a facility for a single customer, which is usually a government agency.

The low output complexity/high market complexity group includes the more complex transport facilities providing services direct to the public and commercial businesses. The complexity of their markets arises in two ways — the range of customers (both private and public) and possible competition from other facilities (parallel roads, second crossings, new ports).

BOT projects falling into the high output complexity but simple market category are those where a wide range of services are provided for a single customer. These types of service may be described as facilities provision and management and could also be regarded as a form of outsourcing. Provision of buildings, maintenance services and computer facilities fall into this category.

The final group contains the facilities most difficult to develop and operate. These are projects which create complex businesses, with a variety of customers, which must compete for different groups customers in a variety of markets. Airports are a prime example of this type of project.

In Chapter 16 we will discuss some of the operational factors which must be addressed in each of these groups and their impact on project development.

Chapter 16

Key success factors for BOT projects

Introduction

In Chapter 15 a classification of BOT projects was proposed based on the degree of complexity of the markets they served and the complexity of the outputs they produced. In this chapter, the impact of each of these variables on the likely success or failure of a BOT project is discussed, using typical types of project as examples.

Simple markets/simple outputs

The majority of BOT projects belong to this first group, in which the market is normally a single buyer and the product is of a simple, generic nature. A typical example would be a BOT power station, providing electricity on the basis of an agreed tariff to a single purchasing body, either a local industrial complex owner or a grid distributor. Other projects of this type include telecommunications links (where the link is rented to a national body for an agreed rent) waste reduction facilities such as incinerators which process waste at an agreed tariff based on waste composition and primary sewage plants which process waste water on behalf of local government for an agreed tariff. In each case, the BOT facility is essentially a factory on a defined site providing a simple output product for an agreed price.

The earlier chapters of this book have dealt in detail with the issues to be addressed in developing basic BOT projects of this nature. But it is worth illustrating the key operational factors which determine success or failure through an example from the independent power industry — that of the People's Republic of China (PRC) in 1994.

At that time, some 30 independent or joint venture private power projects were under negotiation. Some had been under discussion for three to four years following signing of memorandums of understanding. Promoters were however very pessimistic about the likelihood of early finalization of these BOT deals.

In the majority of cases, the basic planning permissions had been obtained without difficulty. The key logistical, engineering and supply issues (nature and size of plant, source and transport of fuel, transmission, offtake) had been agreed with local electric power bureaux and fuel suppliers relatively easily; sufficiently accurate construction cost estimates to allow contract finalization had been developed. Secondary contractual matters (e.g. rights of local PRC contractors to bid for construction work, competitive tendering for imported components such as turbines and generators) had also been resolved relatively easily. Similarly, obtaining provincial and national planning approval had been time consuming but not a cause of great difficulty, and there was a surfeit of overseas capital (exceeding US$1 billion) available to fund power generation. Why in a country desperate for additional electricity was so little progress being made?

The three key issues which were delaying finalization were all financial — tax, foreign exchange and electricity off-take tariffs.

Tax was generally the easiest to resolve, the major difficulty here being the developments in tax regulation which occurred while negotiations were taking place and which sometimes conflicted with earlier agreements.

Foreign exchange presented two serious risks for overseas investors. First, no guarantees that foreign exchange would be made available were permitted by the People's Bank of China, although most contracts included 'best endeavours' clauses. Furthermore, the state and provincial authorities required all tariff payments to be made in local currency giving rise to an exchange rate risk on the foreign capital contribution. Since inflation in the PRC was running at between 15% and 20% p.a., a significantly higher figure than in lending countries, the combination created serious problems for overseas investors.

The greatest difficulty, however, was the agreement of the tariff. For large power plants (project cost in excess of $30 million) the tariff had to be negotiated first with the Provincial Electric Power Bureau. It was then subject to further approval by the Ministry of Electric Power (the state authority) to ensure that it satisfied national guidelines for the rate of return on capital employed. Finally, the tariff was subject to review by the Provincial Price Control Bureau to ensure that it was affordable. This review was required annually, effectively disallowing long-term agreements.

The political reasons for this regulatory regime were straightforward. First, there was concern at Provincial level about the rapid rise in the price of electricity, which had been held at uneconomic levels in the past. Modern plants required tariff increases of three or four times the old regulated price to provide a reasonable return on capital employed. The state authorities were concerned that the agreement reached on the Shajiao 'B' plant in Guangdong had been far too generous, and were trying to fix the return on capital employed at a level broadly comparable with utilities in the US, UK and Hong Kong of approximately 15% of capital employed. Given the risk premium for China (generally considered to be in the region of 3%) this was clearly going to create difficulties.

In the light of what they saw as the high costs of international capital for BOT projects, the power bureaux and the state authorities were in parallel examining alternative means of attracting overseas investment. The power bureaux with extensive experience in power plant construction and operation sought to raise capital directly through public flotations on the New York Stock Exchange; the state authorities were keen to see whether this approach would provide a cheaper source of these capital. To date (November 1994) the performance of these shares has been uninspiring, suggesting that flotations of this nature do not provide a significantly cheaper source of finance.

Interestingly, a number of smaller projects did go through during the period when larger projects were subject to delays. They were small enough to be approved solely by the provincial authorities, thereby avoiding the need for state approval. They included small hydro-electric schemes and small (10−20 MW) diesel power generation facilities. Another group of projects also went ahead — small or medium-sized power plants which had been commenced by provincial bodies but which had run into financial difficulties due to shortage of funds or cost overruns. Perceptive international entrepreneurs were quick to note that creating joint ventures and injecting the necessary capital could bring these projects to early completion and achieve a satisfactory return on the additional funds employed even if the overall project rate of return failed to achieve market requirements.

Currently the larger power projects in China are still proceeding to final agreement rather slowly. The most likely way forward seems to be for the authorities to allow a fair proportion of the tariff to be paid in hard currency, thereby reducing currency risk for the developer, and to adopt a more realistic approach to rates of return on capital employed which accepts the reality of a country risk premium. An approach similar to this is currently being negotiated by IPP developers in the Philippines. Counter guarantees from the central government similar to those which have been extended to power developers in India are another possibility. But these are unlikely to be offered (and may not be needed) in China. The changes will take time and BOT will, in the longer run, probably be only one of a number of means of financing and constructing power plants in China.

There are a number of general points which apply to a broad range of BOT projects (particularly in under-developed countries) which are exemplified by the Chinese power industry experience. These may be summarized as follows.

(a) Large projects tend to be subject to control by a wide range of authorities. Hence even if there is only one 'purchaser' of the output, negotiations will have to take place with a variety of authorities at different levels. Sometimes, smaller projects lying just below an administrative cut-off level may be easier to implement. But sponsors must recognize that there is a trade-off; contract negotiation costs do not fall in proportion to project size.

(b) BOT developers should not overlook the possibility of completing existing projects on a joint venture basis; thereby funding only the marginal capital requirements at realistic rates of return. Careful 'due diligence' appraisal of the existing designs, pricing agreements and project cost estimates is however essential.

(c) Tax and foreign exchange are key issues in the evaluation and negotiation of projects in underdeveloped countries. It is important to take maximum advantage of existing regulations intended to encourage investment and then to evaluate what further concessions may be needed to achieve a viable project.

(d) It is vital to know who has authority on matters where concessions are needed. A local purchaser may be happy to accept conditions which are subsequently found (for wider political or economic reasons) to be unacceptable to higher level state or national authorities.

(e) The risk premium for capital employed is a critical issue and is affected by foreign exchange risks as well as country risk.

(f) The technical problems associated with projects in this class are almost always generally less of an issue than the planning, negotiation and finance factors. The key technical factor is generally the minimization of technical risk so as to ensure timely completion and avoid cost overruns.

Complex markets/simple outputs

The second most common class of BOT projects is those which have relatively simple outputs but rather more complex markets since they depend for their income on a less easily defined customer base. Of these, the most common are private transport facilities such as toll crossings and toll roads, but public transport systems may also be implemented this way. These BOT projects have been encouraged by governments both as a means of raising income for the provision of new infrastructure and as a means of achieving private sector efficiencies in its provision and maintenance.

The additional market risks which sponsors of such projects must face are of two types — those associated with the willingness of travellers to pay a toll or fare and those associated with the availability of alternative routes with lower costs at the time of initial operation or in the future. In combination, these factors determine the maximum level of current and future revenue which can be achieved.

The risks are lowest for crossings in developed countries which link existing toll-free road networks and have little competition. The Dartford Crossing over and under the River Thames which links the north and south sections of the London M25 orbital road falls into this category. Similarly, toll roads opening up important development areas in less developed countries provide a relatively low risk that traffic volumes will not build up since existing parallel routes are likely to be of low quality and congested by local traffic.

Projects with low risks must inevitably face regulation of some form, since they usually represent at the very least a partial monopoly. When offering projects of this nature to the private sector, government bodies may have to specify what alternative routes they are prepared to allow, thereby clarifying the level of competitive risk, or absorb existing competing routes into the BOT franchise. This latter course of action was adopted in the case of the Dartford Crossing, where the existing tunnel and the new bridge were both incorporated into the new franchise. It has also been adopted for the second River Severn Crossing.

Governments must also take a view on how they wish to regulate the return to a crossing company which has a partial monopoly. The appropriate means depends on a balance between the early risks faced by the sponsor and the likelihood that in the longer term the monopoly might allow super profits to be made. Where there is uncertainty in both respects, a rate of return criterion can be adopted under which either the tolls are controlled to achieve a predetermined rate of return or alternatively a variable franchise period can be used to achieve the same end. This approach has the disadvantage that it does little to ensure control over capital costs.

When the risks can be reasonably assessed by the private sector and government can control long-term monopoly power through the provision of additional capacity (prior to the end of the franchise period if necessary), simpler competitive tendering approaches are feasible.

New toll roads present much greater problems than crossings, particularly in developed countries with a high density of development and a dense road network. In underdeveloped countries, the lack of a competing 'free' road network, the lower level of development and the likelihood of major land redevelopment being accelerated by improved communications all reduce risk. The first reduces the likelihood that traffic will remain on the existing system if tolls are imposed on the new road. The second and third (coupled with a government drive to develop more remote areas and a recognition among local people that the road will be beneficial) reduce the planning problems and timescales inherent in a road project as well as the market risk.

There may, however, be a lower willingness to pay tolls and governments may wish to limit tolls to avoid discouraging development. As Scurfield[1] has pointed out, World Bank surveys have shown that few toll road projects get off the ground in underdeveloped countries without significant government guarantees to provide additional finance in the event of a drop in traffic volume (e.g. the Malaysia North—South Highway) or a regulatory structure which by one means or another guarantees a viable rate of return.

In developed countries, the problems of obtaining private sector finance for road improvements are considerable. Farrell[2] has identified some key issues in the United Kingdom which include

(a) the combination of an existing high-density road network and a low perceived value of driver time means that there is an unwillingness to pay tolls except at key crossings where little alternative is available

(b) the very high early costs associated with tendering for a concession deter potential sponsors, since the sponsor is expected to assume all construction cost risks, including ground conditions

(c) the enormously long planning periods required by British planning regulations magnify the problems of high early tendering costs since there is a delay of up to five years in obtaining revenue even if the sponsor is successful

(d) the lack of government recognition of intellectual property rights

in private sector proposals (which are always opened to competitive tender) inhibits sponsors from coming forward with innovative ideas
(e) the unwillingness of the government to provide financial support in recognition of the wider social benefits which cannot be captured by simple tolls reduces the likelihood.

Some of Farrell's proposals will be discussed in Chapter 17, since they extend beyond the confines of current BOT projects. One possibility which may prove valuable in the UK is the use of shadow tolls, an approach which the UK is considering under the Design Build Finance Operate initiative (November 1994). Under this arrangement, the government pays the sponsor a fee dependent on the amount of traffic using the road. This arrangement allows the government to achieve the advantages of private sector efficiency, reduces the capital and operating costs of the road (through the elimination of toll booths) and gives greater relief of congestion elsewhere. In effect, the toll road becomes a simple 'single purchaser' project of the type discussed earlier in this chapter. Such an arrangement does of course fail to provide access to an alternative source of income from users for road construction, although it does give access to private sector capital finance.

Other forms of transport infrastructure may also fall into this group of projects, including urban rail and light rail facilities. Urban and light rail schemes present particular problems, since they are unlikely to be able to finance their capital costs from fare box revenue. One method of overcoming this problem is for government to finance the construction of facilities through competitive tender after which operation can be managed under a private sector operating franchise intended to cover operation, maintenance and infrastructure renewal from fare box revenue. BOT packages including an element of cross-subsidy can also be used. In these, profitable land development rights are included in the BOT package. An alternative arrangement is similar to that proposed for franchising loss-making bus services. Sponsors compete for the BOT franchise under an arrangement whereby the quality of service and the fare levels permitted are specified and the franchise is given to the potential sponsor requiring the lowest annual level of public sector support.

Such projects raise a further point — if private sector operation of such facilities is beneficial, why transfer the facility to government at the end of the franchise period? In the case of bridge and tunnel crossings, there is an argument that once the capital costs have been covered, the facility could revert to the public sector and access be offered free, maintenance costs being met through the public purse. However, for facilities requiring high levels of maintenance or entailing significant operating costs, the appropriate solution would in many cases appear to be a build operate and franchise arrangement, in which a further private sector franchise would be granted covering ongoing maintenance and operating costs through a reduced charge or toll. Issues of this nature will be covered in the following chapter.

Some key factors affecting success and failure in these projects with less well defined customer bases are clear.

(a) Successful projects require an understanding by the government of the nature of the risks facing the private sector and a willingness on the part of government to give appropriate guarantees and/or ensure through appropriate regulation that private sector rates of return can be achieved and debts repaid.

(b) The most successful projects are those that combine low income risk with limited requirements for planning consent and well-defined costs. Key crossing points fed by public sector infrastructure have proved particularly successful. The most difficult to develop are the 'improvement' projects, such as additional toll roads in densely developed countries, where the private sector is called upon to provide incremental capacity on a toll basis in areas where pre-existing congested (but 'free') facilities are available.

(c) BOT can be used for projects where toll or fare box revenue cannot cover the capital costs. Government needs to understand what social benefits are being obtained and to be willing to subsidize capital costs, couple the project with profitable private development or (if it wishes private sector finance to be used) to pay an annual fee which, together with fare box revenue, can ensure project viability.

(d) If government believes in the benefits of private sector managerial efficiency, it should consider ongoing operating franchising or facilities management after the termination of the initial build and operate franchise.

Simple markets/complex outputs

There are a number of circumstances in which facilities providing relatively complex product mixes can be provided to single customer bodies through an arrangement similar to BOT. Examples include the provision of maintenance facilities (e.g. for defence equipment) and the provision of information systems facilities to support public sector activities such as licensing or income tax processing.

Arrangements such as this are generally regarded as 'facilities management' or 'outsourcing'. They differ from the normal BOT arrangements in two respects.

(*a*) Implementation of the facility forms only the first step in what is a complex outsourcing operation.

(*b*) The cost is very dependent on the nature and extent of the outputs required rather than the capital cost of providing the basic facility. The annualized capital cost of the facility may form only a small part of the total annual cost. Correctly specifying the nature of the outputs and quantifying them in a manner which allows competitive tendering and transparent pricing is the key factor in ensuring success.

Since the main focus of this book is directed towards the provision of facilities rather than their ongoing management, this class of projects will not be discussed in detail. It is worth setting out the most important elements as a preliminary to discussing large complex BOT projects (such as airports) in the next section.

The key factor is the specification of the services required and the quality of the outputs. These need to be specified in a manner which allows flexibility in the volumes of individual outputs over time while ensuring that the service provider is fairly remunerated for fixed and variable costs of operation. Some early outsourcing contracts suffered from overspecification of inputs, leading to high delivery costs and a lack of incentive to the service deliverer to improve efficiency. Current contracts place much more emphasis on the outputs needed, specifying quality, quantity and variable price. Where (as in the case of new information systems) there is a definite requirement for 'build' and 'operate' phases, those may well be the subject of separate contracts, even if the same firm is expected to be responsible for the management of both phases.

In summary, complex operations carried out on behalf of a single buyer can be undertaken using BOT techniques, but the much greater emphasis on the outsourcing of complex operations often leads to a rather different type of approach. BOT as discussed in the main part of this book relates mainly to those types of business where the provision and financing of the facility itself is the major business issue. As the complexity of the output increases, the specification and pricing of the output services becomes a more important issue relative to that of the provision of the necessary infrastructure and the benefits of combining build and operate responsibilities into a single contract are likely to diminish.

Complex markets/complex outputs

At the extreme point of this classification lie the projects which provide a complex set of services to a complicated set of markets and which require the construction and operation of major facilities. Airports, in particular, have attracted a great deal of interest because of the very high capital costs and the complexity of their construction, but they are also very complex businesses, operating within a set of complicated markets and subject to both local and international competition. Governments have looked towards BOT as a means of achieving private sector efficiencies and (probably more importantly) as a means of accessing private sector finance for the heavy costs of construction. This has to be balanced against the sense of a loss of national sovereignty if a major airport (particularly one serving the capital city) is placed in private hands. A change of political climate can (as in the case of Athens Airport) delay or curtail a BOT airport project at a late stage of negotiations.

The complexity of the services provided by a modern airport to airlines, their suppliers (fuel, catering, maintenance) their customers (passengers, freight forwarders) and government agencies (immigration, police, customs, health and so on) are self evident. The complexity of the systems required to support even the most basic facilities have been highlighted by the delay in opening the new Denver Airport resulting from the failure of the baggage handling system.

However, it is the complexity of the various markets which gives rise to the greatest uncertainties and risks in airport development and finance. The most important competitive issue is the ongoing role of existing airports. Most major cities have had international air links for a decade or so and possess a smaller airport closer to the centre of population than the proposed new airport. The justification for the continued existence of the old airport and its role relative to the new airport must be assessed and agreed.

The second key issue is that of pricing. The new airport will have a measure of monopoly power and the government will inevitably wish to have power to regulate landing fees and may also wish to regulate other charges for the use of facilities. The basis on which these are to be calculated and the guarantees which the government is prepared to give if income falls below the level required to repay loans are critical factors in ensuring the financial viability of a BOT airport project. It is worth noting that long-term bonds have for many years been used to finance municipal airport construction in the United States but municipal and state guarantees have normally been required.

A third key factor (which may well interact with the first) is the relationship between the airport sponsor and any national or regional airline which may wish to use the airport as a hub for its operations. The network choices made by international freight operators, as well as passenger airlines, can also have a significant effect on airport traffic volumes.

Potential airport sponsors must also consider the quality of the infrastructure which will feed the airport. Modern airports require as a minimum a connection to the regional freeway system and a convenient road link to the conurbation they feed and its business centre. For European style cities with a dense central business core, an off-road public transport system linking the airport to the central public transport system is also desirable.

Further issues which must be resolved may include the relationship with the defence forces/military, particularly if the airport also provides landing and takeoff off facilities for an adjacent military establishment.

These wide ranging business issues have limited the adoption of BOT as a means of overall finance and construction for large international airports. Governments may prefer the alternatives of a fully privatized airport authority (such as the BAA in the UK) or a government-owned corporation which is charged with operating in a commercial manner (such as the new airport authority in Hong Kong). This does not eliminate the opportunities for the private sector. The many sub-businesses within an airport (freight handling, catering, retailing, commercial development and office space) can all be carried out by private enterprise. A particular case is the construction and operation of additional passenger terminal facilities, either through conventional BOT or joint venture arrangements with airport operators.

In summary, the difficulty with these large, supported multifaceted business projects is that they are likely to prove too complex to be accomplished through single BOT contracts, particularly in countries which are sensitive to private ownership of such key elements of national infrastructure. In many cases, the most appropriate course of action may be for governments to set up private or government owned corporations charged with providing and operating the overall facility in a commercial manner while subcontracting or franchising the provision of specific facilities or services. Large projects can then offer a wide range of opportunities for private sector involvement in the finance, construction and operation of component businesses. Subsidiary projects (which may themselves be substantial in size) may offer greater chances of early success and reduced long-term risk for sponsors and financiers.

References

1. SCURFIELD R.G. *The private provision of transport infrastructure*. World Bank, 1992.
2. FARRELL S. *Private finance for new roads*. Private communication, 1993.

Chapter 17

Future developments in the private financing of infrastructure

Introduction

In the previous chapter, the factors which underlie successful BOT project implementation and operation were discussed within a matrix classification which differentiated projects according to the complexity of their products and markets. Table 17.1 shows this matrix once more, indicating the critical factors which govern success or failure within each quadrant.

Access to private sector finance for infrastructure projects previously financed by government was the underlying reason for the original introduction of BOT. The availability of finance, the financial return required and the degree of risk remain the most important factors

Table 17.1 BOT project classification

Complexity of product	Complexity of markets	
	Low	High
High	Financial return Product specification	Financial return Market risk Guarantees Product specification Regulation
Low	Financial return	Financial return Market risk Guarantees Regulation

underlying the success of all BOT projects. Access to finance requires the control of risk and pricing structures which will give a return on capital employed which is acceptable to the private sector.

The need for additional infrastructure finance (particularly in expanding economies) is well illustrated by current Asian Development Bank estimates. These indicate that developing countries in Asia alone will need to spend in aggregate approximately US$50 billion per year on infrastructure in the period 1994–2000. By comparison, total private sector lending for infrastructure project finance (excluding oil and gas) in Asia was probably only between US$7 billion and US$5 billion in 1994.

The gap is not primarily a result of the absence of funds; it is a result of the inability of sponsors to locate and develop projects which satisfy local infrastructure needs and meet private sector levels of return in a manner which is politically acceptable. Unless this mismatch can be addressed, the major part of infrastructure investment funding over the coming decade must continue to be provided by governments themselves. In this chapter some of the developments in project structuring which may help to close the gap will be discussed.

Current areas of change

Change is already taking place as a result of the experience gained in the first wave of BOT projects. One such area is a reassessment of the importance of transferring ownership of BOT projects to the public sector at the end of the franchise period.

The transfer of a physical asset to the public sector is not necessarily an unalloyed blessing. A power station may be a fully depreciated asset but it may also be technically life expired, offering lower efficiency than more modern designs and possibly lower environmental acceptability. It may also entail decommissioning costs — atomic power stations are an extreme example where decommissioning costs are so high that they can affect the ability of a government to privatize facilities, as in the case of the UK power industry privatization programme.

Facilities such as toll roads where the costs of operation and maintenance are low relative to initial construction costs can be operated free of charge on an ongoing basis as part of the government provided road network once construction costs have been recouped. There may be a justification for transfer to the public sector in such cases. Facilities which are not life-expired and which involve significant operational management and expense are probably best held within the private sector through an ongoing operation and maintenance franchise negotiated with the original company or let through competitive tender.

The second change which is taking place is the loosening of the link between project sponsorship and construction. One of the secondary reasons for the development of BOT was the perceived failure of public sector competitive procurement of construction. Contractors were dissatisfied by the high costs of competitive tendering, and government sponsors by delays, cost overruns and litigation. BOT was seen as a means of overcoming some of these problems through the internalization of construction contract matters and the incentivization of contractors who, through their equity investment in the project, had an incentive to ensure successful completion and hence early operational profitability.

There are signs that contractors may, over the next decade, review their role as project sponsors and may tend to separate project sponsorship activities from those more directly related to construction within their business portfolios. There are a number of reasons, of which the most important are the differing finance and management issues posed by project construction and long-term facilities operation.

Contractors' profitability depends in the main on their ability to manage complex projects in which much of the actual work is sub-contracted out to more specialized companies. While they are prepared to pump a share of equity into a project in order to guarantee a share of the construction, they will probably wish to sell their holding within a few years of project completion in order to finance other ventures. This contrasts with the normal role of private utility companies, which normally work within longer terms investment horizons and are prepared to accept lower rates of return, subject to an appropriately low level of risk or a guaranteed financial return.

The separation of these functions is also being brought about by other factors, for example

(a) the insistence on competition for infrastructure construction contracts in Europe, which involves a loss of intellectual property rights for contractor/sponsors who come forward with innovative ideas for project packaging and finance

(b) the long periods required for public enquiries into major infrastructure projects in many developed countries, including the UK

(c) the recognition that while the integration of design and construction can confer significant benefits in reducing contract litigation, modern methods of project management can permit competitive bidding for construction without necessarily leading to damaging adversarial conflicts.

Potential future developments/simple projects

The difficulties currently experienced by some projects within the 'simple market simple product' class should in principle be much easier to resolve than those presented by more complex projects in other groups. Moreover, once there is a full understanding on the part of government of the degree of risk which the private sector can accept and the price which must be paid solutions can be found through an evolution and streamlining of current BOT procedures and a more revolutionary approach may not be needed.

For straightforward projects such as power stations, water treatment facilities, and so on. Governments or government instrumentalities should be able to proceed via a multistage selection process. Following an initial pre-qualification stage, competitive proposals can be obtained from a short list of pre-qualified promoters. Final detailed negotiations over terms of contract can then be held with one or two leading promoters after which the most suitable promoter can be selected. The promoters would be responsible for obtaining finance and seeking construction bids, which could be from in-house construction units or sub-contractors. Provided the government agency responsible for seeking private sector project sponsorship specifies its needs clearly, the facilities needed are of a standard nature, and the risks are sensibly allocated between the parties, the selection process need not be excessively expensive for either party. The price can, to a large extent, be set by the market, although governments must continue to be aware of the need to balance their short- and long-term objectives and to avoid being exposed to the risks of the winners curse.

Potential future developments/complex projects

For more complex projects, simple arrangements of this nature are likely to prove prohibitively expensive for potential bidders. The approach is also likely to fail to achieve simultaneously both the public policy objectives of government and the business and financial objectives of the private sector. Studies of alternative means of achieving these combined objectives in complex infrastructure projects suggest that there probably is no one simple, straightforward answer. But they do suggest a way forward which could lead to tailor-made project frameworks applicable to specific types of project in particular countries.

Two possible approaches to the development of better frameworks for handling couples projects are possible. The first is 'bottom up' and seeks to extend and expand existing more general BOT frameworks yet further to tackle the weaknesses which have been exposed in a particular area of infrastructure finance and development. The second is to start from the top with a clean sheet of paper and try to develop a policy for the development of a specific type of utility or infrastructure in a particular country which can achieve both public and private sector objectives. These two approaches are typified by the ideas of Farrell[1] and Newbery[2] who have separately examined the problems of maintaining and developing the UK trunk road system.

As a means of overcoming the current weaknesses of the UK road privatization proposals referred to in Chapter 16, Farrell has suggested that the tendering process for road concessions be broken up into two or more stages. The first stage would be project specification, and the piloting of a scheme through a streamlined public consultation process. This stage would overlap with the second, the development of bidding documents and the invitation of tenders for the design and construction of the road. The second stage would overlap with a third, the invitation of tenders for the sponsorship of construction and operation of the privatized facility. The chosen operator would then take over, let a design and construction tender, supervise construction and subsequently operate the toll road.

An arrangement of this type has the advantage that appropriately skilled groups can be invited to compete for the work required at each stage and that the project can be fast tracked by overlapping the three phases. It would require a radical restructuring of UK public consultation and would require strong overall project management by government. One weakness is that it fails to allow potential operators to incorporate the results of their experience in the design, since this will have been established prior to the selection of the operators. But it does tackle the problem head-on, recognizing the very real problems which exist, and seeks to find a solution meeting public and private needs.

Newbery, on the other hand, tackles the problem root and branch and after considering the alternative of road privatization puts forward the case for a public road authority. Essentially, he suggests that the UK trunk road system is commercialized, (or corporatized), the existing assets being taken over by a regulated Government owned authority able to raise private finance for road system expansion. Road taxes would become road charges, payable to the authority, thereby bypassing any debate about hypothecation of tax revenue.

Such a revolutionary proposal would change completely the ground rules for the private sector provision of trunk roads. However, as Newbery notes, substantial opportunities would exist for private sector road constructors, maintainers and operators if they can demonstrate the increased efficiency of private sector management. There is in fact no real conflict between the approach proposed by Newbery and the ideas put forward by Farrell. Newbery deals with the national issues of institutional framework, ownership and project selection; Farrell with the more specific problems of implementation. It is becoming steadily more apparent that both require better resolution if progress is to be made.

At a rather less heroic level, a number of studies have been undertaken of alternative institutional and financial frameworks for large projects incorporating both public and private finance. For example, unpublished studies were undertaken by Coopers and Lybrand on behalf of the Hong Kong Government of alternative institutional frameworks for the management and financing of port construction in Hong Kong. Cochrane and Farrell examined alternative combinations of public and private sector finance and management covering the range from full public sector ownership and operation to a fully privatized port. The various alternatives were examined to determine the degree to which they achieved public and private policy and financial objectives.

The study concluded that some facilities which had been proposed were too expensive to achieve even reasonable public sector rates of return after considering the financial and social benefits they provided. Others were in principle desirable but could not achieve private sector rates of return either because the financial return was too low or because of the difficulty of setting charges which ensured profitability without incurring a deadweight loss (i.e. a reduction in the total benefits to society). Only a narrow range of the alternatives examined were found likely to achieve both private and public sector goals. Moreover, the choice between the two most attractive institutional structures (both of which required a combination of public and private sector sponsorship, finance and management) depended critically on the weightings given to the various public sector objectives.

Broadly similar studies are currently being carried out (November 1994) of the alternative approaches possible for the development of a major international airport in South East Asia. Studies such as these further confirm that there is a need for case specific analysis of complex projects to determine the appropriate institutional and financial structure which can address public needs and make best use of private sector capabilities.

Conclusion

In conclusion, the number of relatively straightforward BOT projects which are yet to be finalized in various parts of the world illustrates the current lack of understanding between governments and private sector developers of the nature of project risk and its influence on the return which the private sector can accept. Over the next decade, the present somewhat experimental negotiations in which many governments are involved should be replaced by a full understanding of the best way to progress these relatively simple projects.

The BOT approach has much to offer, although transferring the assets to government at the close of the franchise is likely to prove to be an over-simple approach for the reasons mentioned earlier. Replacing the acronyms BOT and BOO with FBOF (finance, build, operate, franchise) and FBOO (finance, build, operate, own) might draw greater attention to the importance of finance and the long term operational issues in developing workable proposals for private sector participation.

More complex projects raise more fundamental issues. Studies to date suggest that there are no simple, universal answers to the question of how to combine public and private sector objectives. Complex projects such as toll roads, seas ports and airports require individual analysis to assess the public sector goals, the private sector objectives and risks and institutional alternatives available. The appropriate solution may well vary from country to country and project to project. Concepts very similar to BOT are likely to prove appropriate for some components of larger projects; similarly, concepts such as facilities management may be appropriate for others. What is clear is that there is a growing need for careful analysis of infrastructure management and finance on a project by project basis in order to utilize private sector skills more effectively and meet private sector financial objectives. Without proper appraisal and appropriate project architecture, only a minor part of the finance needed for infrastructure development is likely to be forthcoming from the private sector.

References

1. FARRELL S. *Private finance for new roads*. Private communication, 1993.
2. NEWBERY D. The case for a public road authority. *J. Trans. Economics and Policy*, 1994, **28**, No. 3, Sept.